recd aubetro 4930

Property and
Industrial Development

The Built Environment Series

Series Editors

Michael J. Bruton, *Registrar, the University of Wales Institute of Science and Technology*
John Ratcliffe, *Head of Department of Estate Management, South Bank Polytechnic, London*

Introduction to Transportation Planning, 3rd edition *Michael J. Bruton*
The Spirit and Purpose of Planning, 2nd edition *Edited by Michael J. Bruton*
Theories of Planning and Spatial Development *Philip Cooke*
An Introduction to Regional Planning *John Glasson*
Politics, Planning and the City *Michael Goldsmith*
The Development of Planning Thought *Cliff Hague*
An Introduction to Town and Country Planning, 2nd edition *John Ratcliffe*
An Introduction to Town Planning Techniques *Margaret Roberts*
The Dynamics of Urbanism *Peter F. Smith*
Public Transport: its planning, management and operation (2nd edition)
Peter White
Local Planning in Practice *Michael J. Bruton and David J. Nicholson*
Landscape Planning *Tom Turner*

In association with the Open University Press

Man-Made Futures *Edited by Nigel Cross, David Elliot and Robin Roy*

Property and Industrial Development

Stephen Fothergill
Faculty of Urban and Regional Studies
University of Reading

Sarah Monk
Department of Land Economy
University of Cambridge

Martin Perry
Department of Geography
University of Auckland

Hutchinson

London   Melbourne   Sydney   Auckland   Johannesburg

Hutchinson Education

An imprint of Century Hutchinson Ltd
62–65 Chandos Place, London WC2N 4NW

Longwood Publishing Group
27 South Main Street, Wolfeboro, New Hampshire 03894–2069

Century Hutchinson Australia Pty Ltd
PO Box 496, 16–22 Church Street, Hawthorn,
Victoria 3122, Australia

Century Hutchinson New Zealand Ltd
PO Box 40–086, Glenfield, Auckland 10, New Zealand

Century Hutchinson South Africa (Pty) Ltd
PO Box 337, Bergvlei 2012, South Africa

First published 1987

Typeset in VIP Times by
D. P. Media Limited, Hitchin, Hertfordshire

Printed and bound in Great Britain by
Anchor Brendon Ltd, Tiptree, Essex

British Library Cataloguing in Publication Data

Fothergill, Stephen
  Property and industrial development.
  1. Industrial buildings — Economic aspects — Great Britain
  I. Title II. Monk, Sarah III. Perry, Martin
  339.4'869054'0941   HD598
ISBN 0 09 170741 2

Library of Congress Cataloging in Publication Data
Fothergill, Steve.
  Property and industrial development.
  (Built environment series)
  Bibliography: P.
  Includes index.
    1. Industrial Sites—Great Britain
    2. Great Britain—Industries—
    Location. 3. Real estate development—
    Great Britain. . . Land use—Great Britain.
      i. Monk, Sarah.
      ii. Perry, Martin, 1956-
      iii. Title. iv. Series.
HD598.F68   1987
333.3'8' 0941   87-2627
ISBN 0 09 170741 2

Contents

Acknowledgements   7

1   Introduction   9

2   Britain's industrial buildings   15
Investment in property — The factory stock — Vacant factories
— Long-term trends — The property cycle — Britain's factories:
some conclusions

3   The development process   39
Types of development — Market influences — Institutional
investment — Types of developer — The construction phase —
Concluding remarks

4   Property, efficiency and growth   56
Firms' property requirements — The origins of mismatch — The
problems created by mismatch — The capacity to respond to
mismatch — Some conclusions

5   Property's role in location   86
The role of property in the location of manufacturing — Regional
growth and decline — The urban–rural contrast — On-site
expansion — New factories — Property and industrial location:
some conclusions

6   Public sector intervention   111
The benefits of public provision — The public developers — Case
study: English Estates — Case study: local authorities — The
evaluation of public factory building — Impact on the private
sector

7   Small firms   139
The property needs of small firms — The supply of small premises
— Property management and allocation — Case study: the supply
of small industrial units in Cornwall — Small factories and
economic development

8   A strategy for industrial buildings   159
The problem — Reindustrialization and the role of property —
Floorspace requirements — Land for new factories — The role of
the public sector — Planning for expansion — Reducing
mismatch — The importance of property

References   177

Index   181

Acknowledgements

This book is mostly a product of the time we spent at the Department of Land Economy, University of Cambridge. Two of us have now moved on, but we are grateful for the stimulation provided by colleagues in the department and for the practical help and finance to complete this work.

In particular, the book has its origins in a research project funded by the Economic and Social Research Council, but it also draws on our earlier work for the Department of Industry and the Department of the Environment, and on Martin Perry's Ph.D. research. The views expressed, however, are our own and do not necessarily reflect those of our sponsors.

Several individuals deserve our thanks. Michael Kitson made a major contribution to the research reported in chapter 5, and Peter Mottershead also helped in this work. Graham Gudgin, as always, has been an invaluable sounding-board. Thanks, too, to Gordon Cameron, Alex Catalano and Graham Crampton for their comments on drafts of the book. Roger Butcher assisted with computing.

Thanks are also due to Coopers & Lybrand and to Cambridge Economic Consultants for kindly allowing us to use the findings of unpublished reports, and to the numerous friends, academics, and public and private organizations who responded to our requests for data.

Last but not least, thanks to Sue Clark for secretarial support in the first part of the research project, and to Liisa Cleary for seeing the project through to completion and for the considerable task of typing this book.

1   Introduction

The purpose of this book is to examine the role of industrial property in national and local economic development. It takes as its starting point the need to revitalize the economy, to nurture what is left of British industry, and to steer the jobs that are created to the places that need them.

None of these concerns is new. However, it is becoming clear that the old ways of achieving growth and employment are not as effective as they used to be.

Until the mid 1970s, governments sought full employment by controlling the amount of spending in the economy — by Keynesian 'demand management'. They did this mainly by adjusting their own spending and the amount collected in taxes: when unemployment began to appear, spending was increased or taxes cut. By today's standards this worked very well: unemployment did not rise above 1m until 1972. These policies have fallen out of favour with many economists and politicians but still have a great deal to commend them. If more spending power were to be put into the economy, through public spending or tax cuts, more goods would be bought, more would be produced, and more people would be employed to produce them.

Many of those who now reject reflation of this sort believe it merely fuels inflation, though Keynesian economists dispute this. The real Achilles' heel of reflation, however, is the growing integration of Britain with the rest of the world economy. An increase in spending in this country would go not just on UK produced goods and services but also on imports. In practice, unless several other industrial countries joined in a reflationary strategy (and thus increased our exports) the growth in imports could not be financed indefinitely and would limit the extent of British reflation. Unemployment might be brought down by half a million or possibly a million, but no more. To reflate further would require a fundamental change in Britain's trading and financial relationships with the rest of the world, to curb the flow of spending on imports. 'Free trade' would have to be suspended, and politically that might prove extremely difficult.

The limitations to purely Keynesian policies have turned attention to 'supply-side' economic policies, designed to improve the competitiveness of British industry. It is argued that less spending will leak into imports if British goods of the right design can be produced at the right price at the right time.

Supply-side policies mean different things to different people. To Conservative politicians they usually mean the withdrawal of the public sector from as many markets as possible, and the removal of obstacles to the operation of market forces and the accumulation of wealth. In this view, exposure to market forces and the freedom to earn profits impose rigorous disciplines. They weed out the inefficient, and reward the hard working, creative and productive. The economy prospers as a result. If there is still unemployment, this is because market adjustments are slow to operate or because the unemployed are given insufficient incentive to find work.

This book is also about supply-side economics, but it does not start with the presumption that market forces are always the answer. Rather, it takes the view that it is important to understand how market forces operate — and how sometimes they fail. It also takes the view that what happens in the private sector of the economy is a legitimate concern of public policy, because a marriage of private capital and market forces cannot necessarily be expected to achieve social objectives like a reduction in unemployment.

The supply of industrial property is just one aspect of the supply side of the British economy. It is not necessarily the most important. However, there is considerable ignorance about the role that land and property plays in the overall production process, and how they affect the scale and location of firms' activities. Manufacturing industry requires land and premises, just as it requires labour, machinery and financial capital. But does it get the buildings it needs in the locations where it needs them? Land and property are not mobile in the same way as workers or machines; they are also very expensive and durable; and there are financial and institutional constraints on their supply. It is therefore quite possible that firms do not always get what they need. Depending on the extent of the shortcomings in supply, not only the performance of manufacturing industry but also the growth of the economy as a whole is likely to be adversely affected.

It will be clear by now that this book approaches industrial property with a different perspective from that of surveyors, financial analysts, property developers and the other professionals involved with land. Their concerns are primarily the marketability and profitability of potential developments. Their attention is consequently focused on a narrow band of the industrial property market, mostly the provision of new factory units on a speculative basis, to the neglect of the much larger stock of older, owner occupied property. The studies and reports on industrial property that emanate from leading estate agents, for example, reflect this preoccupation with new development. For purely commercial reasons, the property world needs to know about 'yields' and rates of return, capital appreciation and rental growth. Our concern, in contrast, is with industrial buildings as an input to production and a tool of economic development. So although the reader from the property world will find what we have to say informative and useful, he or she will not find a sort of 'developer's guide' to industrial property.

There are two main themes running through the book. The first is the influence of property on economic growth and efficiency. The second is its effect on the location of firms and jobs.

There has been relatively little theoretical or empirical analysis of these questions. This may be because the property world sits at the fringes of both economics and geography. It belongs to economics because property is an integral part of the process of wealth creation and distribution; it belongs to geography because all property has a unique location within urban and regional systems. But it has been inadequately incorporated into both subjects. Indeed, in many theories the supply of land and property is ignored entirely, the implicit assumption being that there is a smooth and automatic adjustment of supply to meet demand.

There is, of course, a substantial body of industrial location theory. Early geographers such as Weber, whose ideas continue to be widely taught, focus on transport and distribution costs. According to Weber's theories, production will be located at the places where these costs are minimized, but no account is taken of potential constraints, such as competition for land and buildings, or absolute shortages. Especially in urban areas, the cost minimizing locations may already be in use. More recent industrial location theory seeks explanations for the geography of industrial change through ever more elaborate studies of firms' investment strategies, and the locational implications of organizational structures. The focus is on individual decision making units — firms — and not the physical and environmental context in which decisions are made. Again, property is neglected.

One reason why industrial geography so often ignores the role of property may be that many studies see industry as rich and powerful, therefore immune to potential constraints. Certainly, there are plenty of studies looking at large companies, including multinationals, and these very large enterprises sometimes have the political muscle to influence planning and land-use controls as well as the financial wealth to acquire the property they need. But if it were true that very large companies are immune to difficulties with industrial property, it should be shown how and why this is the case, rather than merely assumed or asserted. It should also be shown to what extent their property needs and opportunities differ from those of smaller firms.

Economics has also failed to incorporate land and property satisfactorily. In neo-classical theory, price adjustments — in this case rents and land values — regulate the demand for and supply of physical space. For example, Alonso's intra-urban location theory suggests that urban land is allocated between competing uses (residential, commercial, industrial) on the basis of the value to the user of the accessibility of each plot. The more valuable the plot to the user, the more that user will be willing to pay. Thus industry will outbid housing if it can make more profitable use of a piece of land, but in turn shops and offices will outbid industry for the city centre sites they value so highly.

However, this is a very stylized view of how the world works. As a leading property analyst has commented:

In a mixed economy . . . the workings of the price mechanism are conditioned and controlled by public policy to such an extent that the forces of the free market and intervention become interdependent, and at times indistinguishable. The level and pattern of urban land values, for instance, is as much an expression of prevailing planning policy as it is of open-market demand for and supply of space. Moreover, the majority of textbooks of urban land economics have neglected the strength of social, political and behavioural constraints on the property market. (Ratcliffe, 1978 p. 7)

A major real-world complication that neo-classical theory does not accommodate is the distinctive nature of factory buildings. Once a factory has been built it cannot be moved, but over time its location may become 'sub-optimal' in neo-classical terms. The firm occupying the factory can move, but the building may remain a feature of the urban landscape — and the property market — long after the original reasons for its construction have disappeared. Nor is industrial floorspace a standard, homogeneous commodity, of the sort that fits so neatly into neo-classical theory. Factories vary in age, layout, size and design, so that individual units are only occasionally acceptable substitutes for each other. Also, investments in new factory space tend to be individually large, and only some buildings are suitable for subdivision and subletting, so marginal adjustments in the amount of space a firm uses are normally not possible. Once more, this limits the applicability of neo-classical theory.

It is revealing to contrast the way in which the housing market is commonly thought to work with the way the industrial property market is usually assumed to operate. As we have seen, either industrial companies are viewed as all-powerful agents who obtain whatever accommodation they need as they require it, or the supply of industrial property is ignored entirely. But in the housing market, households are certainly not seen in this way, and the importance of the social, economic and institutional context within which individual housing choices are made is widely emphasized. Research on the allocation of council housing and building society mortgages, for example, illustrates the importance of questions of availability and eligibility. Moreover, the supply of housing is rarely seen as a perfect response to the pattern of demand. It is clear, for instance, that in Britain the decline in the supply of privately rented accommodation has little to do with the underlying need for this sort of housing. More generally, it is recognized that the various institutional groups in the housing market — developers, building societies, banks, estate agents and local authorities — often pursue policies that serve their own interests rather than the needs of households looking for somewhere to live.

Although the link is rarely made, there are in fact a great many parallels between the markets for housing and factory space. The market for factories functions much more like the housing market than is generally appreciated. In both markets there are time lags, not least because a house or factory cannot be built overnight. The amount of new building coming onto the market each year is very small in relation to the total stock, so the inherited stock of old accommodation is the dominant influence on the market as a whole. Land-use controls, financial and institutional constraints, and the continual evolution of firms' needs, all make it inevitable that supply and demand are far from perfectly matched.

In making location decisions, most firms, like most households, are tightly constrained by the availability of only a limited number of buildings or plots of land that are broadly acceptable. Indeed, given that the number of vacant industrial premises is so small compared to the number of houses for sale, the industrialist's range of choice is usually more limited than that of the household. For large firms seeking large sites, which are fewer still in number, the locational options may be even more circumscribed.

For small firms, the parallels with the housing market are especially strong. Most of these firms lack the resources to build their own factories and are therefore forced to look for space to rent. In the industrial property market there is no direct equivalent of the council housing waiting list, but the policies and practices of property managers in effect establish admission rules to allocate rented factory space. To secure a good quality modern unit on a private trading estate, a firm must demonstrate that it is financially sound and has a good track record. It must be willing to take on a long lease with full responsibility for upkeep of the building, and it should not be engaged in a noxious or unsightly branch of manufacturing. Many small firms, especially those that have been established for only a short while, cannot meet these stringent criteria. They must look elsewhere to fulfil their property needs.

None of this is intended to suggest that in Britain there is a general shortage of accommodation for all kinds of industrial enterprises. Especially during a recession, shortages are likely to be confined to limited geographical areas and certain types or sizes of factory building. The point is simply that the assumption that the supply of industrial property adjusts quickly and smoothly to meet firms' needs is unrealistic. Once the possibility of 'market failure' of this sort has been conceded, we must expect the supply of industrial property to exert an influence on firms' performance and hence on the national economy. We must also expect it to influence where firms locate.

We start in chapter 2 by looking at the relationships between Britain's factory stock and the rest of the economy. The focus at this stage is strictly national. We explore how broad aggregates in the property market, such as new investment and vacant space, respond to trends in manufacturing output, investment and employment.

Chapter 3 outlines the way in which the development industry works and how new factory space is created. It pays particular attention to private speculative development, including the growing role of financial institutions.

Chapter 4 moves to a different scale and looks at the relationship between factory space and growth and efficiency of individual firms. This issue has been neglected until now, and the information we present here is entirely new. The concept of 'mismatch' — the disparity between a firm's property needs and the buildings it occupies — is central to this chapter. We explain how mismatch arises, the forms it takes, the problems it creates, and the factors that constrain firms and sometimes prevent them from finding satisfactory solutions.

Chapter 5 introduces locational issues. Having examined how factory space is created, we now look at where the increases in floorspace go, and why. We show how the shift in employment away from cities towards small towns and rural areas has been matched by what is happening in the industrial property market. More specifically, we explore the role that property plays in causing these shifts in employment.

The public sector's involvement in the industrial property market is examined in chapter 6. Several central and local government agencies build factories on a speculative basis in the hope of promoting economic development, especially in depressed areas. This activity was established in an *ad hoc* way in response to specific problems, and has subsequently been expanded in an essentially uncoordinated fashion. This chapter explains the potential benefits of public sector factory building, and presents estimates of the overall scale of public sector involvement and the contribution of the different agencies. It also considers evidence about the impact of factory programmes, including the extent to which public sector factory building displaces private sector activity.

Chapter 7 investigates the distinctive property needs of small firms and the ways in which they are met. After years of official indifference, small firms have emerged as a major focus of public policy, and this is reflected in a new concern for their accommodation. The public sector therefore figures prominently in this chapter.

Finally, chapter 8 looks at what might be an appropriate strategy for industrial property. It starts from the urgent need to reindustrialize the British economy and considers what response from the industrial property market would be necessary to enable this to occur. We identify obstacles that would need to be overcome, and the last part of the chapter puts forward specific proposals that would improve the supply of land and buildings for industry.

2 Britain's industrial buildings

One of the striking features of Britain's factory stock is its diversity. A few of the oldest buildings still in use date from the late eighteenth century, and successive waves of investment have each left their own legacy of factories. Superficially at least, a Victorian multistorey textile mill has little in common with a glass-and-steel high technology unit or a heavy engineering fabrication shed — except that they are all designed for 'industrial' uses.

The diversity in firms' requirements complements the diversity in the factory stock. Just as in the housing market different households have differing needs and differing abilities to pay, the building that ideally suits one firm may be entirely unsatisfactory to another. A large old building is rarely an adequate substitute for a small modern one; nor is a multistorey building an adequate substitute for a single storey layout. The demand for industrial buildings is segmented — by size, design, location and tenure.

But this diversity should not obscure the fact that as a whole the industrial property market displays coherent and sometimes persistent trends. Not least, this is because the industrial property market does not exist in isolation from wider economic trends. The demand for and supply of factory buildings is an integral part of the national economy.

This chapter looks at the broad trends in industrial property and their relationship to the rest of the economy. It begins by looking at the scale of industry's financial investment in property, and then outlines the main characteristics of Britain's factory stock, including a close look at empty factory space. This is followed by a description of long-term trends in the industrial property market, including the links between manufacturing output, employment and the demand for floorspace. Finally the chapter examines the short-term fluctuations that affect industrial property.

Investment in property

It is common to think of industrial investment as consisting of items such as robots and other machinery, since these are the tools with which goods are actually made. But the vast majority of production takes place in buildings of one kind or another, and the sheer scale of industry's consequent investment in property should not be overlooked.

Table 2.1 shows the financial value of industry's investment in buildings. The figures come from the *United Kingdom National Accounts*, compiled by the Central Statistical Office. They classify investments on the basis of ownership, so the figures include the property actually owned by manufacturing firms, which comprises perhaps three-quarters of the total stock, but exclude the rented factories owned by property companies, financial institutions and the public sector. Factory buildings together with plant and machinery make up manufacturing's overall investment in 'fixed' assets.

	Value of industrial buildings and works in 1984 (at replacement cost)		Average annual investment in new buildings and works, 1974–84	
	£m (1980 prices)	as % of all fixed assets	£m (1980 prices)	as % of all fixed investment
Metal manufacture	6,900	30.9	76	12.4
Chemicals	8,300	25.9	135	13.4
Engineering: mechanical, etc.	11,500	40.1	148	16.1
electrical, etc.	5,100	35.4	80	13.7
vehicles, etc.	9,800	43.7	108	15.8
Food and drink	11,300	41.8	190	19.5
Textiles and clothing	5,200	37.0	43	14.0
Other manufacturing	12,800	33.4	176	13.2
ALL MANUFACTURING	71,000	34.4	956	14.7

Table 2.1   *UK manufacturing industry's investment in buildings*

Source: United Kingdom National Accounts

The figures demonstrate the enormity of industry's financial involvement in property. The first half of the table deals with the total value of its building assets. In 1984 this was £71bn (at 1980 prices) — just over a third of the value of all the fixed assets of the manufacturing sector. This proportion was consistently high across all industries, and even in chemicals, which employs a great deal of process plant and machinery, buildings accounted for a quarter of all fixed assets.

The second half of the table deals with new investment in property. Between 1974 and 1984 this averaged just under £1bn a year (at 1980 prices) or between 12 and 20 per cent of all new fixed investment, depending on the industry.

Clearly, factory buildings are far from being a marginal concern to industry. Quite apart from the day-to-day need to house production, they represent a major entry in firms' balance sheets and a substantial claim on the funds available for new investment.

A comparison between the two halves of the table — between new investment and the value of building assets — is also revealing. For example, in all industries and in the manufacturing sector as a whole, buildings account for a higher proportion of assets than new investment. This reflects the long life of buildings compared to plant and machinery, which often wears out quickly or needs to be replaced because it has become outdated. The machines bought 50 years ago have mostly long since been scrapped; the buildings put up to house them are mostly still in use.

More importantly, a comparison between the two halves of the table reveals just how low new investment in factory buildings has slipped. Dividing the value of building assets by the annual rate of investment between 1974 and 1984 suggests that it would take nearly 75 years to renew the stock of factory buildings, and this makes no allowance for any additional factory space that may be needed to accommodate increases in industrial production. The same calculation using the average annual investment between 1981 and 1984 (£650m at 1980 prices) indicates that it would take as many as 110 years to renew the existing factory stock.

There is a potential problem here. Because of the long life of factory buildings, many are likely to have been designed for products and processes that have been superseded. At the same time new investment in factory buildings is so low that the replacement of obsolete or obsolescent premises is proceeding very slowly indeed. If many firms therefore continue to operate in outmoded or inappropriate buildings, this will almost certainly have a detrimental effect on their efficiency and possibly their growth.

The factory stock

The buildings comprising manufacturing's investment in property are very diverse, as we noted. Indeed, at the margin it is difficult to define exactly what is 'industrial' and what is not. This poses a problem because many modern units on trading estates can be used for either light manufacturing or warehousing. The distinction between 'factories' and 'warehouses' is thus blurred, though it would be wrong to assume that the two uses are interchangeable in all cases. Planning controls, for example, ensure that some buildings can be used for only one purpose or the other.

The government's own figures, published in *Commercial and Industrial Floorspace Statistics*, get round this definitional problem by classifying buildings according to their use rather than their design. These figures are based upon data collected by the Inland Revenue in assessing the rateable value of properties. Coverage is unfortunately limited to England and Wales, though it is likely that many of the same trends are also to be found in Scotland and Northern Ireland. 'Industrial' and 'warehousing' properties are treated as two separate categories in the figures, and for the most part we follow this convention, focusing on industrial property in which production actually takes place.

On this definition, in April 1985 there were 113,800 industrial properties in England and Wales, providing 232.2m m² of floorspace. These buildings comprise the vast majority of the space used by manufacturing industry, including office and storage space within factories, though the figures exclude some buildings, such as chemical works and shipyards, where the floorspace is difficult to define and measure. Buildings used solely as warehouses provided another 137.3m m². These figures compare with a total stock of floorspace in commercial (i.e. private sector) offices of 50.8m m² and 81.3m m² in shops of all kinds.

As is to be expected, the distribution of industrial floorspace across the country, shown in Figure 2.1, broadly reflects the distribution of industrial employment. The West Midlands county, Britain's traditional manufacturing heartland, has the largest stock of floorspace (22.6m m² in 1985) followed by London and Greater Manchester (each with 20.3m m²) and West Yorkshire (14.9m m²). Away from these major urban areas the stock of industrial floorspace has often been growing quite quickly, as chapter 5 explains, but the amounts of floorspace in any one county generally remain much smaller.

Most industrial properties are very small. Table 2.2 shows that in 1985

	No. of units	Floorspace (millions m²)
Less than 500 m²	63,400	13.5
500–2,499 m²	34,100	38.6
2,500–9,999 m²	12,000	57.7
10,000 m² or more	4,300	122.3
TOTAL STOCK	113,800	232.2

Table 2.2   *Size of industrial units, England and Wales, 1985*

Source: Commercial and Industrial Floorspace Statistics

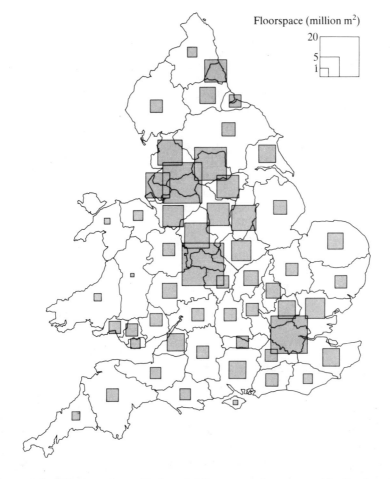

Floorspace (million m²)

Figure 2.1   *The location of industrial floorspace by county, England and Wales, 1985*

Source: Commercial and Industrial Floorspace Statistics

more than 63,000 units — over half the total — were of less than 500 m², a size which at average densities of occupation could be expected to accommodate firms with up to only 10 or 15 employees. The majority of floorspace, on the other hand, is in large factories: the largest 4,300 units accounted for 122.3m m², or just over half the total.

From the point of view of economic efficiency, the quality of the industrial building stock is likely to be as important as the overall quantity. Poor quality buildings — buildings that are badly suited to modern production methods — may impede productivity, investment and expansion. As we explained, old buildings may be unsuitable because they were designed to house products and production processes that have long been superseded. Old buildings are also likely to have been extended and altered over time, which may result in a poor layout on a cramped site, and they may pose problems of high maintenance and heating costs, or provide a depressing environment for employees.

There are no comprehensive statistics on the age of Britain's industrial buildings, but Table 2.3 presents figures derived from two surveys. One of these covers the inner area of Birmingham (JURUE, 1980) and the other the cities, towns and rural areas of the East Midlands (Fothergill, Kitson and Monk, 1985). Together they provide details of nearly 4,000 factories, spread across most parts of the manufacturing sector. There is an important urban–rural contrast in the age of industrial buildings (described in chapter 5) so to derive estimates for the age of buildings in the country as a whole it has been assumed that the age of buildings in the survey areas is broadly the same in similar urban or rural areas in the rest of the country. For example, it has been assumed that the age of industrial buildings in inner Birmingham is typical of inner areas in the other conurbations. A small revision based on national trends in new building and demolition has also been made to bring the survey data up to date.

Date of construction	% of stock
Pre 1919	18
1919–45	22
1946–65	23
1966–75	20
Post 1975	17
TOTAL STOCK	100

Table 2.3   *Estimated age of industrial floorspace, Great Britain, mid 1980s*

Source: Authors' estimates

Though the resulting figures inevitably provide only an estimate of the age of Britain's factory buildings the picture that emerges is disturbing. Some 18 per cent of the stock of floorspace (equivalent to between 40m and 50m m²) dates from before the end of the First World War. As much as 40 per cent (around 100m m²) dates from before the end of the Second World War.

It would be surprising if any other industrial country had such an old factory stock. One reason is that Britain was the first to industrialize, so that there is a substantial legacy of Victorian factory buildings. Architecturally and historically some of these are priceless national assets; industrially and economically they are probably a millstone. A second reason is the relatively slow rate of growth (by international standards) of the British economy, especially during the postwar period. This has meant less new factory building and less renewal of the inherited stock. Third, the extensive destruction in Europe during the Second World War cleared away many older buildings and rebuilding was required on a much larger scale than in Britain.

Further qualitative aspects of Britain's factory stock can be estimated from the same survey data. These are shown in Table 2.4 and relate just to manufacturing firms with 25 or more employees, which account for roughly 90 per cent of manufacturing jobs.

	% of factories	% of jobs
Production on more than one floor	44	48
At least half the site covered by buildings	77	75
Vacant land adjacent to site	33	41
Rented property	25	16

Table 2.4 *Characteristics of the industrial building stock, Great Britain, early 1980s*

Note: Figures exclude firms with fewer than 25 employees

Source: Authors' estimates

The first line of this table shows the proportion of factories that have production on more than one floor. A common design consists of a multi-storey office with a single storey production floor behind, and generally multistorey offices are unlikely to cause difficulties. Multistorey production space is more problematic because it can introduce discontinuities in production flows and bottlenecks as work-in-progress waits to be moved from floor to floor. As the table shows, more than 40 per cent of factories, accounting for nearly half of all manufacturing jobs, are estimated to have multistorey production. This is a high proportion, though it does overstate the problem because some larger factories with multistorey production include single storey premises on the same site. Also, not all manufacturing production is necessarily handicapped by this sort of layout, and in some firms a multistorey layout may be advantageous. In some food and drink processing, for example, it facilitates gravity feed of ingredients.

The second and third lines of the table deal with room for expansion. This is potentially important because the extension of an existing factory to accommodate growth usually has advantages over complete relocation or the diversion of production to a new branch plant. Sometimes there are technical obstacles to splitting production between two sites; sometimes there are managerial obstacles; and on-site expansion can often be achieved more quickly than the development of an entirely new site. These issues are examined in detail in chapter 4. However, the table shows that three-quarters of Britain's manufacturing industry operates on sites where at least half the area is already built upon. Given that there are usually claims on the remaining space — for car parking, circulation and outdoor storage, for instance — many of these sites are unlikely to permit further extension of the factory buildings.

An alternative to expanding within the present site is expansion onto immediately adjacent land. Only a third of Britain's factories, accounting for 40 per cent of jobs, are estimated to have vacant land (including agricultural land) nextdoor to their site. The East Midlands survey asked whether firms thought this land could be made available to them: only two-thirds thought it could, so these figures overestimate the real opportunities for expansion.

The final line of Table 2.4 shows the tenure of industrial buildings, estimated from the East Midlands survey data. As a general rule, the larger the factory the more likely it is to be owner occupied. Hence in this survey, which excluded very small firms, only a quarter of the firms were in rented premises.

Vacant factories

Not all factory space is in use, of course. During the recession of the early 1980s, the empty shell where once hundreds were employed and the newly, completed unit unable to find a tenant became widespread and highly visible symbols of Britain's industrial decline. But just how much of the factory stock stands vacant?

Many firms have contracted to the extent that parts of their buildings have become surplus to their requirements. Entire floors in multistorey buildings may be vacated, and individual buildings forming parts of larger complexes may be left empty. Partial vacancies of this sort are difficult to monitor because the empty space rarely comes onto the market. The survey reported in chapter 4, however, suggests that comparatively little space is actually allowed to fall vacant in this way. A more common response is for firms to use space inefficiently — in other words to allow their activities to expand to fill the available space.

Statistics on complete vacancies, where the whole factory stands empty, are compiled by King & Co., a leading firm of industrial estate agents. Their figures, which cover England and Wales, are derived from several sources — their own records, the records of other estate agents, government bodies (e.g. English Estates) and the trade press — and in recognition of the growing interchangeability of industrial and warehousing uses they no longer distinguish between the two. Though affected by certain exclusions, the figures probably provide a reliable guide to the extent of vacant floor-space, an impression confirmed by a comparison we made between the King & Co. figures for Leicestershire and the detailed records compiled by the county council.

According to King & Co., in England and Wales in December 1985 a total of 11.4m m² of floorspace was vacant and on the market, either for sale or rent. This represented 3.1 per cent of the combined stock of industrial and warehousing floorspace. As a proportion of the total stock, empty factory space therefore appears quite modest, especially bearing in mind that by 1985 there had been only a weak recovery from the deep recession of the early 1980s. The prominence of empty factories in certain areas should therefore not obscure the fact that the vast majority of the factory stock remains occupied and in use.

Vacant space is unevenly spread across the country, as Table 2.5 shows.

	Vacant industrial and warehousing space (m²)	*as % of total stock*
North	1,109,000	5.1
South East	3,588,000	3.8
West Midlands	1,870,000	3.6
North West	2,074,000	3.3
Yorkshire and Humberside	1,296,000	3.0
Wales	400,000	2.6
East Midlands	907,000	2.6
South West	378,000	1.4
East Anglia	145,000	0.9
ENGLAND AND WALES	11,767,000	3.1

Table 2.5 *Vacant floorspace by region, England and Wales, December 1985*

Note: The following are excluded:
— premises of less than 5,000 ft² (465 m²)
— premises that are unofficially on the market but still occupied
— multistorey mills that are unsuitable for re-use or refurbishment
— semi-derelict premises where it would be difficult to justify refurbishment
— vacant premises held off the market

Source: King & Co.

There is a large contrast between East Anglia, at the foot of the table, where less than 1 per cent of the stock of floorspace was vacant in 1985, and the Northern region at the top, where the proportion was more than 5 per cent. Some aspects of this regional pattern can be readily understood. For example, the proportion of vacant space was high in the regions hit hardest by the recession of the early 1980s, and in regions like the North where government factory building maintains a plentiful stock of available floor-space. The South East is an anomaly, however: despite ostensibly being the most prosperous region of all, with the greatest pressure on the stock of space of all kinds, the King & Co. figures indicate that it had the second highest proportion of vacant space. It is difficult to provide a satisfactory explanation, but two influences may be at work in this region. One is the high level of private, speculative development activity, which may inflate the number of new buildings awaiting a first tenant — a factor noted by King & Co. The other is the preponderance of old and unsuitable premises in London, where a survey by Bernard Thorpe & Partners (1982) had previously noted a high proportion of vacant space.

The King & Co. figures show that 14 per cent of the vacant space was in 'new' buildings — that is, buildings that had not been occupied since completion and buildings that had yet to be occupied following extensive refurbishment. Just over 18 per cent of the vacant space was in 123 units of over 100,000 ft^2 (9,300 m^2) concentrated mainly in the North, North West, West Midlands and South East. The majority of these large buildings are more than 10 years old, and King & Co. argue that they are often in locations and of a design that makes then unsuitable for modern industrial needs. 'The only foreseeable future for some of these buildings lies in demolition and the redevelopment of the site, not necessarily for industrial use' (King & Co., 1986).

An alternative estimate of vacant property is provided by the estate agents Hillier Parker in their annual *Survey of Industrial Voids*. This is confined to rented industrial and warehousing space, and is based on a survey of 48 financial institutions, pension funds and property companies which have investments in this segment of the market. The survey indicates that the extent of vacancies depends in part on how a 'void' is defined. In 1985, for example, only 2 per cent by value of these institutions' industrial investments were not producing income. However, 5.2 per cent by value were unoccupied — the difference between the two figures mainly being premises that had been vacated but where the lease had not expired. Unoccupied floorspace as a proportion of all the institutions' floorspace was 8 per cent — a higher figure presumably because much of the empty space was in low value buildings. Voids were more likely for factories than warehouses, and more likely outside of Southern England. They were also highest for buildings less than 5 years old and in new developments, where delays in securing a first occupant inflate the figures (Hillier Parker, 1986).

Some more detailed figures on the sort of factory space that is vacant and on the market are shown in Table 2.6. These are for Leicestershire, in the Midlands, which is probably typical of a shire county with an important industrial base. Here in June 1982, in the depths of recession, 479 factory units comprising 282,000 m² of floorspace were vacant and on the market. This excludes buildings specifically reserved for warehousing, but includes buildings suitable for either industrial or warehousing use. The majority of vacant units were new, small, single storey and available for rent (or sometimes sale or rent). The majority of vacant space, however, was in larger, older units, mainly for sale. Just 23 factories of more than 20,000 ft² (1,860 m²) accounted for over 40 per cent of the stock of vacant space.

	% *of units vacant*	% *of floorspace vacant*
LAYOUT		
Single storey	78	72
Multistorey	22	28
	100	100
AGE		
'Old'	29	41
'Modern'	19	35
'New'	52	24
	100	100
TENURE		
For rent	61	42
For sale	23	48
Sale or rent	16	10
	100	100
SIZE (ft²)		
Up to 5,000	50	18
5,000–20,000	18	28
More than 20,000	5	41
Flexible	27	13
	100	100

Table 2.6 *Characteristics of vacant industrial property in a shire county: Leicestershire, June 1982*

Source: Leicestershire County Council

Figures on the quality of vacant factories in a conurbation are provided by a survey carried out in the Black Country area of the West Midlands. In 1984 this identified 705 vacant industrial premises (West Midlands County Council, 1984). Roughly half were of post-1960 construction, but these accounted for only a quarter of the site area of all the vacant property, indicating that the older vacant units were on average much larger. Less than 4 per cent of this older, pre-1960 property was assessed as being in good condition. Of the total vacant stock, 14 per cent (by floor area) was judged to be obsolete, in that it was unsuitable for reoccupation and appropriate only for redevelopment. A further 40 per cent was old but re-usable, assuming some refurbishment. The remaining 46 per cent was modern and, according to the county council, could expect to be reoccupied if the market picked up. Comparable information for neighbouring Birmingham suggested that nearly a quarter of its vacant industrial floorspace fell into the obsolete category.

What all these figures reveal is the polarized nature of the stock of vacant factory space. On the one hand there is a great deal of empty modern property. Most of these units are small, and many of them brand new. Because new small units are generally built on a speculative basis it is inevitable that some of them are vacant, awaiting their first occupant, especially during a recession. The other empty modern units can also expect to find occupants eventually.

On the other hand, there is a stock of empty space in hard-to-let categories: large, old buildings, often multistorey, for sale rather than rent. These are the buildings made available by the closure or relocation of businesses, and potential occupants will generally prefer newer, single-storey property where a choice is available. Also, because the buildings are larger there are fewer potential occupants. Some of this hard-to-let space may never again find an industrial occupant. After a while on the market it may be demolished, so that the value of the land can be realized, or it may be subdivided to provide smaller units that are individually more lettable, or it may be converted for completely different uses.

Long-term trends

Having described the broad characteristics of Britain's factory stock we can now turn to the changes that are taking place. It is appropriate to start with the relationship between production and factory floorspace because the demand for industrial buildings is what economists call a 'derived demand'. This means that buildings are not wanted as an end in themselves but as an input to the production process. The volume of production is therefore a crucial influence on the demand for them.

Exactly how much factory floorspace is needed to produce a given amount of output is ultimately a technical question. It depends on the size of machines, the speed of production flows, the need for circulation and storage space and so on. However, it is possible that over time the amount of space required for a given amount of output may change. There are two main reasons why this might occur.

The first is that there may be a shift in the composition of output, e.g. away from industries that use large quantities of space towards those that produce the same value of output from smaller amounts of floorspace. The composition of manufacturing output is changing all the time, as industries rise and fall, so this could be expected to influence the demand for factory space.

The second reason is technical change within each industry. For example, new machines might operate more quickly so that more output is obtained from the same space. Or a new product might be smaller and require less storage space. Again, technical change in products and production methods is a continuous process.

On the basis of theory alone it is impossible to predict the scale and direction of any resulting changes in the ratio between output and floorspace, so it is necessary to look at what has actually been happening.

The trend in manufacturing output per unit of floorspace is shown in Figure 2.2. The floorspace figures used here include both occupied and vacant space, and the aggregate trend is likely to hide disparate trends in individual industries. The overall pattern is clear, however. Until the severe recession at the start of the 1980s the ratio between output and floorspace showed no trend in either direction but merely fluctuated a little from year to year. Between 1980 and 1982 output per unit of floorspace fell by some 15 per cent, mainly as a result of the unusually large and sudden contraction in output. Thereafter it began to rise to nearer the 'normal' level of earlier

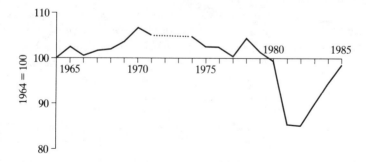

Figure 2.2 *Manufacturing output per unit of floorspace, England and Wales, 1964–85*

Sources: United Kingdom National Accounts
     Statistics for Town and Country Planning
     Commercial and Industrial Floorspace Statistics

years. The recession apart, the output/floorspace ratio therefore appears to be fairly stable. The implication is that in the manufacturing sector as a whole, technical and compositional changes have been broadly neutral in their effect on the amount of output per unit of floorspace.

Since many new machines are more compact and faster than the ones they replace, the long-run stability of the output/floorspace ratio is perhaps surprising. What may be happening is that newer, more productive machines are being introduced, so that less space is required for the actual machining, processing or assembly, but at the same time because each machine is more productive it may require more stocks of materials or components to be held at the start of the production line (to ensure a minimum number of days' supply) and more storage space at the end to cope with the increased volume of output. Automation may thus lead to a shift in the use of factory space, from production to storage, without changing the total amount needed.

Looking to the future, the stability of the output/floorspace ratio need not necessarily be maintained. It might be argued that the advent of microelectronics has brought a qualitative change: that in future machinery will be so much more efficient that large quantities of factory space will never again be required, and that the industries of the future will manufacture high value products which need little room for production. Against this view, however, it is important to note that only parts of the manufacturing processes are amenable to microelectronic technology. Also, where microelectronics is introduced it may cut costs by replacing workers, but the new machines may need just as much space as the old.

Whatever its causes and the prognosis for the future, the long-run stability of the ratio between output and floorspace has two consequences. One concerns 'employment density' — the number of workers per unit of floorspace — and the other the stock of floorspace itself. Both are sufficiently important to consider in detail.

Let us take employment density first. The amount of output per unit of floorspace has changed little, as we showed. However, the number of workers needed to produce each unit of output has fallen substantially in the past and continues to fall. This is the rise in 'labour productivity'. The inevitable consequence is therefore a reduction in the number of workers per unit of floorspace.

This large fall in employment density is shown in Figure 2.3. Between 1964 and 1985 the average density fell from 36 to 21 workers per 1,000 m², a trend decline of nearly 3 per cent a year. During upturns in the economy the decline eased and during recessions it accelerated, presumably a reflection of fluctuations in capacity utilization and vacant floorspace. But the long-term trend was unmistakably downwards.

The decline in employment density fits with what can be observed in shopfloor layouts. The typical layout of 20 years ago — row upon row of workers at benches or machines — is disappearing. Machines are becoming

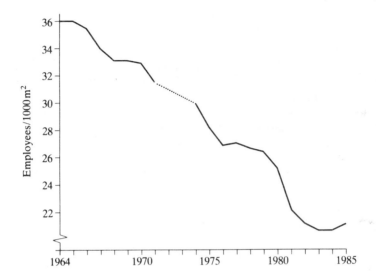

Figure 2.3 *Manufacturing employees per 1,000 m² of industrial floorspace: England and Wales, 1964–85*

Sources: Department of Employment
  Statistics for Town and Country Planning
  Commercial and Industrial Floorspace Statistics

more productive, automated and require less manual control. The production line, too, is changing. Robots and 'pick and place' machines are replacing workers, so that the human role is becoming one of supervising and maintaining machines rather than the actual performance of production tasks. The modern shopfloor has more sophisticated equipment, but fewer people.

Indeed, the decline in employment density shown in Figure 2.3 may understate the scale of change on the shopfloor because there is a long established tendency for the proportion of shopfloor employees in the manufacturing workforce to fall, and correspondingly for the proportion of workers in office based jobs like administration, marketing and product development to rise (Crum and Gudgin, 1978). Figure 2.3 is based on all manufacturing employees, including white-collar workers; because of the shift in the structure of the workforce the fall in density on the shopfloor itself has almost certainly been steeper.

It should be stressed that the reduction in employment density is not something that firms actively plan to achieve. It is a by-product of their attempts to maximize the productivity of their workforce in the face of competitive pressures. It does, however, have major implications for the location of employment because it means that over time a factory of a given physical size tends to employ fewer and fewer workers. It also means that in a town where the overall stock of factory floorspace is static (say because of restrictive planning controls) a gradual reduction in manufacturing employment can be expected. These locational effects are explored at length in chapter 5.

The second major consequence of the long-run stability of the output/ floorspace ratio is that a sustained increase in manufacturing output requires an increase in industrial floorspace. Conversely, a sustained fall in output renders large quantities of floorspace redundant.

Trends in the stock of industrial floorspace in England and Wales are shown in Figure 2.4 for the period since 1964, the earliest year for which statistics are available. During the long postwar boom, which finally petered out in the 1970s, manufacturing output rose substantially. Consequently a large increase in floorspace was required, and this is manifest in the sustained growth of the stock during the 1960s and to a lesser extent the 1970s. During the second half of the 1960s, the stock rose by around 3m m² a year. Manufacturing output peaked in 1973, but then fell back before climbing to another peak in 1979. This faltering economic growth in the 1970s was reflected in a slow-down in the growth of the stock of industrial floorspace. After 1979 the economy as a whole and the manufacturing sector in particular suffered the worst recession for half a century, and by the mid 1980s manufacturing output was still below its earlier levels, even though there had

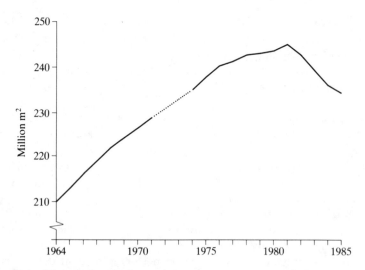

Figure 2.4   *The stock of industrial floorspace, England and Wales, 1964–85*

Sources: Statistics for Town and Country Planning
     Commercial and Industrial Floorspace Statistics

been a modest recovery from the depths of recession. After a lag, the stock of floorspace, too, began to fall in response to the reduced demand for factory space, so that by 1985 the stock had returned to the level of the early 1970s.

The fall in the stock of factory space during the first half of the 1980s should not be regarded as the start of an inexorable downward trend. As we explained, the crucial factor is what happens to manufacturing output. By 1985 the recovery in output and the shedding of redundant floorspace had brought the output/floorspace ratio back close to its historical trend. Assuming no change in that trend and no further reduction in manufacturing output, the decline in the stock of floorspace can therefore be expected to tail off. If growth in output is sustained, even at a slower rate than in the past, a small increase in the stock is again likely.

It is worth noting at this point that trends in warehousing floorspace have been very different from those in the industrial sector. The stock of warehousing space rose every year between 1974 and 1985, a cumulative increase of over 40m m² or nearly 45 per cent. The divergence is a reflection of the quite different influences on the demand for warehousing space. Whereas the demand for factory space depends on the volume of industrial production, which has more often than not been stagnant or falling, the demand for warehousing space depends much more on the volume of retail sales, which has been increasing. This has boosted the demand for national, regional and local distribution depots, many of them to handle the greatly increased volume of imported goods that now take a large slice of many markets.

The modest net changes in the stock of industrial floorspace do, however, hide larger additions and reductions. Additions to the stock are the result of the construction of new factories, the extension of existing factories, and changes from other uses (from warehousing, for example). Reductions in the stock occur through demolitions and changes to other uses.

These 'components of change' are shown in Table 2.7 for England and Wales between 1974 and 1985. Caution is required in interpreting the figures: they are calculated by summing the statistics for each year during the period, and there is likely to be some double counting. For example, a new unit completed in one year may be affected by a change of use in the next. Also, the figures for demolitions include only the demolition of whole factories; floorspace lost through partial demolitions is included with 'other reductions', along with changes to other uses. But bearing these points in mind, the figures provide a reasonable guide to the main flows of property in and out of industrial use.

Let us consider additions first. A widespread assumption about new industrial floorspace is that it takes the form of entirely new factory buildings, either for a specific firm or built on a speculative basis by the public or private sector. Most literature on industrial property fosters this preoccupation with new units. In fact, the largest addition to the stock of industrial

	Millions m²	*as % of stock in 1974*
ADDITIONS		
New units	+23.9	+10.2
Extensions	+29.3	+12.5
Changes of use	+13.5	+5.8
REDUCTIONS		
Complete demolitions	−14.2	−6.1
Other	−55.0	−23.5
NET CHANGE	−2.5	−1.1

Table 2.7   *Components of change in the stock of industrial floorspace, England and Wales, 1974–85*

Source: Commercial and Industrial Floorspace Statistics

floorspace is the extension of existing factories. Between 1974 and 1985, extensions contributed 29m m², compared with only 24m m² in entirely new units. Changes from other uses to industrial, at 13m m², were a lesser source of new floorspace. The additions to the stock of floorspace were nevertheless quite small — just under 1 per cent a year from new units, and just over 1 per cent a year from extensions.

Over this period, losses from the stock of industrial floorspace, at just over 2.5 per cent a year, more or less balanced the gains. Demolitions of whole factories accounted for a fifth of these losses, or about 0.5 per cent a year. 'Other reductions' were by far the biggest source of loss from the factory stock.

A comparison with changes in the stock of warehousing space sheds some light on the nature of these 'other reductions'. As we noted, this category includes changes to other uses, and on the whole, given the nature of industrial buildings, the only alternative use will be warehousing. We would therefore expect losses of industrial space through change of use to be balanced by equivalent gains in the stock of warehousing space. In fact, between 1974 and 1985 only 31m m² of space changed to warehousing from other uses, whereas 'other reductions' in industrial space accounted for 55m m². The implication is that of this 55m m², perhaps only 30m represent changes of use and the remaining 25m must have been lost in partial demolitions. Adding this to complete demolitions, the total loss of industrial floorspace through demolition was probably nearly 40m m², much more than first appears from the statistics. This compares with a gain of 53m m² in all newly built industrial space.

New industrial units are on average smaller than the factories that are demolished. Between 1974 and 1985, for example, almost half the space built in new units was in premises of less than 2,500 m², and in this size band new building exceeded complete demolition by three to one. Demolitions were much more important in the larger size bands.

One reason for this difference is the 'life cycle' through which many industrial buildings pass. When they are first built they may be small, but where circumstances permit they may be extended over the years, either by the original occupant or by successive occupants. Eventually they become larger factories, possibly even complexes of several buildings of varying ages on the same site. However, if they then fall vacant it is difficult to find new occupants: many of the buildings will be old, they will often have been designed or adapted to meet previous occupants' specific needs, and in any case there are fewer potential occupants for large factories than for smaller units. Demolition becomes the appropriate option. A building which started its life as a modestly sized new unit thus ends it as a much larger demolition.

But quite apart from this life cycle there has been a genuine shift in the structure of demand for factory space. In England and Wales between 1974 and 1985 the number of units of less than 500 m² rose by nearly 11,000, and the total floorspace in these units increased by over 2m m²; meanwhile the amount of floorspace in units of more than 10,000 m² fell by over 5m m². The rise of small factory provision is examined in detail in chapter 7.

Size is only one of the characteristics that differentiates the new factories that are being built from those that are being demolished. Equally, if not more striking, is the difference in the intensity to which sites are being developed.

Over time, factory buildings have on average come to occupy less of their total site and single storey layouts have become the norm in most industries. The ratio between floorspace and site area has thus fallen considerably. One of the reasons is technological: in the nineteenth century the multistorey factory facilitated the vertical transmission of power from a central point, usually a steam engine. Now, individual machines have their own electric motors. Another reason is economic: in the nineteenth century, poor urban transport meant that centrally located land was at a premium, and industrialists built upwards to minimize land costs. The attraction of central urban sites for manufacturing industry has diminished since that era, and car parking, room to manoeuvre heavy lorries and in some cases landscaping are new claims on the use of industrial land. If a site is developed with an eye to the future it may also include land held in reserve for expansion.

The impact of these changes is worth illustrating because their scale is not widely appreciated. Take the example of the replacement of an old multistorey mill by a modern single storey unit on the same site. Let us assume the total floorspace of the mill is 10,000 m², on four floors on a site which is entirely covered by the building. There are plenty of old mills that fit this description. In this example the site area will be 2,500 m². If the new building covers 40 per cent of the site — a typical proportion for a modern development — it will have a floor area of 1,000 m². This is a 90 per cent reduction compared with the old mill. In addition, let us assume that the employment density in the new building is only half what it was 25 years ago in the old mill — an assumption in line with the broad trend we described. In these circumstances the reduction in employment would be 95 per cent. The magnitude of this job loss, arising from changes in the way land is used, emphasizes the enormity of the problem which redevelopment poses for older industrial areas, especially in inner cities where land is in short supply.

The property cycle

Superimposed on these long-term trends in the industrial property market there are shorter-term fluctuations, again related to what is happening in the national economy.

Because the demand for factory space depends a great deal on the volume of production there is a close link between fluctuations in manufacturing output and fluctuations in vacant floorspace. Figure 2.5 illustrates this. In this diagram the scale for vacant floorspace has been inverted so that a fall in the line represents an increase in vacant space, and the relationship to output is thus clearer. As can be seen, the trend in vacant space follows manufacturing output, with a lag of roughly a year. For example, output began to rise during 1976 and 1983 after periods of decline and stagnation; a turn-around in vacant floorspace in each case occurred a year later.

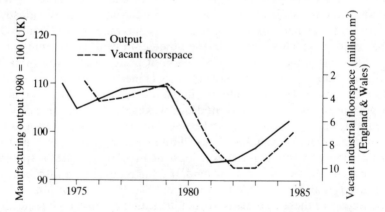

Figure 2.5   *Manufacturing output and vacant industrial floorspace, 1975–85*

Sources: United Kingdom National Accounts
         King & Co.

A lag of this sort is to be expected. Coming out of a recession, firms are normally able to increase output without taking on more space because they have been operating at less than full capacity. Only after growth has been maintained for several months are many likely to require additional space, though even then it will be only a minority that need more (perhaps the firms that had little spare capacity to begin with). The need for additional space becomes widespread only if the growth in output is sustained, say for 3 or 4 years. Going into a recession firms are equally slow to adjust their use of space. Initially, a reduction in output will lead to a reduction in capacity utilization, and many firms may see this as a temporary phenomenon requiring no special response. The fall in production needs to be either very large or sustained before firms look closely at their use of property and consider closing factories and disposing of buildings. Even then, they may opt to retain factory space so that they have the capacity to meet an economic upturn.

Firms' conservatism in the management of their property is emphasized by the modest size of the fluctuations in vacant floorspace. The severe recession between 1979 and 1983 was associated with a 15 per cent reduction in manufacturing output. During the same period the increase in vacant factory space was equal to only 3 per cent of the total stock of industrial floorspace. So although the recession did increase the number of empty factories, its main effect appears to have been to reduce the intensity with which the remaining occupied stock was used. The sharp fall in the ratio of output to floorspace during this period has already been noted.

Some of the reasons why firms are slow to adjust their use of property to changes in output levels are explored in chapter 4. In many instances, the reason is simply that factories are indivisible inputs to the production process — fixed overheads rather than variable factors of production. The quantity of labour employed can be adjusted in small amounts: a few extra workers can be taken on when order books are full, and workers who leave need not be replaced if business is slack. Even more marginal adjustments to the input of labour can be made by varying the amount of overtime. But adjustments of this sort are not possible with factory space. A factory unit is usually either occupied in its entirety or it is vacated. New investments in factory space, too, are generally individually large. These sorts of decisions about factory buildings are not to be taken lightly or on the basis of short-term market trends because they can have repercussions for a firm's finances and efficiency long into the future.

In theory the delay between the decision to build new factory space and its eventual completion ought to counteract these lags. During the early stages of an economic upturn these delays mean that demands for additional space can only be met from the stock of vacant factory buildings, and the amount of vacant space might therefore be expected to fall quickly. Conversely, during the early stages of a recession the amount of vacant space might be expected to rise steeply as firms cut back their requirements at the same time as large quantities of new space, ordered during the boom, are finally completed. In fact, as we have seen, the trend in vacant space lags behind the trend in manufacturing output. The implication is that firms' conservatism in taking on or shedding space is a more powerful influence on the stock of vacant floorspace than any cycle resulting from the lag between ordering and completing new buildings.

Industry's investment in new buildings fluctuates with the trade cycle, as Figure 2.6 demonstrates. The bottom part shows manufacturing output, the middle investment in buildings (at constant prices) and the top investment in

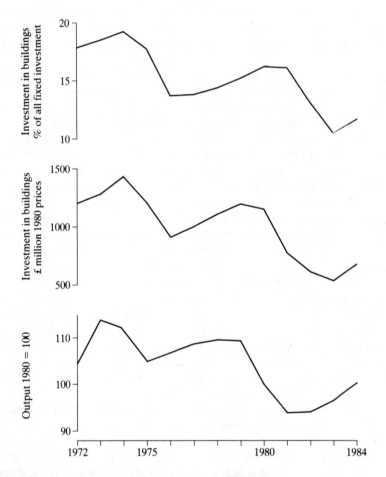

Figure 2.6   *Output and investment in buildings and works in UK manufacturing, 1972–84*

Source: *United Kingdom National Accounts*

buildings as a share of all new fixed investment. Broadly, the three time series move together. When output is high and rising, new investment is high and investment in buildings accounts for a high proportion of all fixed investment. It is not difficult to see why this arises. Investment in new buildings is required most when expansion needs to be accommodated, whilst investment in new plant and machinery within existing factory buildings is something which goes on all the time and is not as dependent on increases in production to justify it. Hence building investment accounts for a higher proportion of the total during a boom than during a slump.

Again there are time lags. The severe recession between 1979 and 1983 provides the clearest example. Manufacturing output began to fall steeply during 1980; investment in new buildings did not fall steeply until 1981; and building investment as a proportion of all fixed investment did not fall steeply until 1982. These lags result from the time taken to complete building projects — an issue examined in the next chapter. Buildings started near the top of an economic boom, for example, will still be under construction as output begins to turn down, and once a building has been started it is usually not a practical option to suspend its construction until the economic climate improves. Most investment in plant and machinery does not suffer from the same delays: once the decision to buy a piece of machinery has been taken it can usually be delivered quickly, and the order can sometimes be cancelled if the firm subsequently encounters difficulties. During the early stages of a recession, firms thus find it easier to make swifter reductions in investment in new machines than in new buildings. As a proportion of all fixed investment, spending on new buildings therefore remains high even though the buildings may no longer be justified by the growth in production.

Britain's factories: some conclusions

In summary, the dominant picture that emerges is of a factory stock that is only partially suited to the needs of modern industry. A disturbingly large share of Britain's factory buildings fall into problem categories: old, multistorey and lacking in room for expansion. Added to this, investment in new factory space has fallen to such low levels that the existing stock is barely being renewed. As a result, the problems are probably getting worse rather than better.

The close links between the demand for factory space and new investment, on the one hand, and broader trends in the national economy on the other, mean that the blame for the diminished supply of new industrial property cannot be attributed simply to the failings of the property industry. On the contrary, the cutback in investment in industrial property by manufacturing firms and speculative developers alike has been a logical response to the problems of the national economy and the fall in industrial production. However, it must now be likely that the cumulative under-investment in industrial property, and the consequent ageing and deterioration of the stock, are to some extent reinforcing the difficulties that face British industry.

In chapter 4 we look in depth at the effects of shortcomings in industrial buildings on the growth and efficiency of the firms that use them. Chapter 5 then traces some of the locational consequences. Before that, however, it is appropriate to look more closely at the process by which factories actually get built — the 'development process'.

3 The development process

The previous chapter showed that the amount of new factory space built each year is small in relation to the total stock, and how as a result the supply of industrial buildings consists largely of older properties. But this does not diminish the importance of new building. It is the key mechanism through which the stock of factory space adjusts — albeit slowly — to changes in demand. The process by which new factory space is developed is therefore crucial in determining what becomes available and where.

This chapter deals mainly with the provision of speculatively built factory units by the private sector. This segment of the market has been the traditional focus of attention for academics and the property industry, but in mirroring their concerns we do not intend to suggest that private speculative development is the main source of new factory space. Indeed, purpose built developments by manufacturing firms are undoubtedly the largest single source of new industrial floorspace, and the public sector, too, is an active developer of factory space.

However, private speculative development is particularly worthy of attention. One reason is simply that this sort of development in the industrial, commercial and retail sectors makes up a property 'industry' employing several thousand people and involving many millions of pounds. A second reason is that private speculative development probably provides more new industrial units in total (though not more floorspace, as we noted) than any other type of development. Third, the economic and institutional influences on the provision of speculative space are complex and deserve explanation. Finally, because of the potential importance of private speculative development to local economies, a great deal of energy is devoted by local authorities to create the conditions that facilitate this sort of development.

Types of development

It is appropriate to begin by outlining the three routes through which new factories are built. Speculative development is just one of these.

The first route is the development of premises by a firm for its own use. Most new large factories are purpose built for an owner occupier. The firm usually buys the land, engages architects to produce a design to meet its specification, and has the factory built by a contractor or development company. Land acquisition costs and construction costs are met out of the firm's financial reserves, with the aid of government grants in Development Areas, or raised in loans. The length of loans typically varies between 7 and 21 years, and banks are the main source. A firm's eligibility for a loan is assessed primarily against its trading record and expected profits, with the location and design of the factory being of secondary significance (Hardy, 1979). A recent innovation, popular amongst small and medium sized companies, is to use the firm's own pension fund to purchase the factory.

The second route through which new factories are built is less common. This is where a firm agrees to lease the premises before construction starts, and the premises are built to its specifications by a developer who retains ownership of the completed development. The degree of tailoring to the firm's requirements varies: the greater the modification to meet its needs, the less marketable the premises if a new tenant has to be found and hence the less attractive the scheme to the developer. From the occupant's point of view, this sort of arrangement avoids tying up capital in land and buildings that might be more profitably deployed in other ways. From the developer's point of view, a long lease is essential.

The third route is the speculative construction of new factories. Since these factories are not built with a specific occupant in mind, the buildings tend to be fairly standardized to maximize the number of possible occupants. Many are designed for a dual function as either production or warehousing units. Most are built for rent, though according to NEDO (1983) the few developers offering completed units for sale generally find a high demand. The size of speculative factories built by the private sector is usually between 500 and 2,500 m^2; smaller units have traditionally been considered to be too risky and a management problem, while the market for larger premises is too limited. Private speculative developments are predominantly funded, directly or indirectly, by pension funds, banks and insurance companies.

Which of these routes a manufacturing firm takes in order to meet its property needs depends on its particular circumstances, such as its size, the nature of its activities, and the urgency of its need for additional space. A large firm will invariably opt for purpose built, owner occupied property, partly because its needs are often specialized and partly because of the scarcity of large, new premises for rent. A very small firm, on the other hand, will usually lack the finance and expertise to build its own factory. Many firms avoid new premises altogether, of course, preferring instead to rent or buy second-hand property.

Market influences

The speculative development of industrial premises by the private sector follows a process similar to that in other sectors of the property market. Land passes through a series of stages. Each stage involves professionals and institutions with their own aims and objectives but each is dependent on what went before and what is intended to come after. The development process has been described as a 'pipeline' in which there are 'barriers' (such as planning approvals) and 'pumps' (priming actions such as investment decisions) between each stage (Barrett, Stewart, and Underwood, 1978).

The Pilcher Report on commercial property development (Department of the Environment, 1975) described six typical stages in the development process. The details depend on the funding arrangements, the location and the point in time. But in broad terms the stages are:

1   the assessment of demand for new buildings;
2   the identification of suitable sites;
3   the design of appropriate accommodation;
4   the arrangement of finance for site acquisition and construction;
5   the management of design and construction;
6   the letting and management of the completed buildings.

The crucial consideration at the first of these stages, and to a lesser extent at the second, third and fourth, is the state of the market. The market is critical because private sector institutions like banks and pension funds do not have a fixed sum that they allocate each year to industrial property development. To the private sector investor, property must compete with other potential investments and investment in industrial buildings must in turn compete with investment in other property such as shops and offices. Moreover, the funds for industrial property are distributed between competing locations of varying profitability.

Coopers & Lybrand Associates (1984) stressed that in order for the private sector to become involved in the provision of speculative industrial space, two preconditions have to be fulfilled.

First, the private sector requires evidence of scarcity in order to be confident that the development will be marketable. Information on local property markets is notoriously fragmented, so developers are rarely able to gauge the rate of take-up of property in an area. What they are usually able to assess, however, is the amount of vacant space at any one point in time, and a large quantity will normally deter potential new development. The private sector prefers pre-let schemes, or ones in which the local authority takes a 'headlease' and thus guarantees the rent. Otherwise, it aims to let a completed development within 6 months, and certainly within a year. Hillier Parker in their *Survey of Industrial Voids* (1986) reported that in 1985 the average time between a new industrial property becoming available for occupation and actually producing an income was 10 months.

Second, the private sector must be able to secure an adequate return in its investment. The crucial influences here are the level of rents and the anticipated growth in rents. These are relevant not only to the developer who intends to hold on to a completed scheme but also to the developer intending to sell (to a financial institution, for example) because they determine the capital value of the development. The higher the rent, or the greater the anticipated growth in rent, the higher the capital value.

The market for industrial property is a competitive one in which no one supplier or user of factory space is sufficiently dominant to control rent levels. Central and local government intervene as suppliers of speculative factory space, through planning controls and occasionally through subsidies, but they do not directly regulate rents in the industrial sector — in contrast to their regulatory influence in the rented housing market. The level of industrial rents in different areas and their movement through time therefore reflect the balance between demand and supply and the myriad influences on these market forces — e.g. firms' locational preferences, the supply of land, planning controls and fluctuations in the national economy.

In Britain the level of industrial rents displays a distinctive pattern, shown in Figure 3.1. Rents are highest in and around London, especially to the west and south west of the capital. Outside the South East of England, rents fall away significantly, and in much of northern and eastern England, Scotland

	1975	1980	1985
Rent index (1975 = 100)			
London	100	184	233
Rest of South East	100	183	239
Midlands, South West, Wales	100	196	217
Northern England	100	188	188
Scotland	100	173	173
ALL INDUSTRIAL	100	186	216
Rent index adjusted for inflation (1975 = 100)			
London	100	92	84
Rest of South East	100	92	86
Midlands, South West, Wales	100	98	78
Northern England	100	94	68
Scotland	100	87	62
ALL INDUSTRIAL	100	93	78

Table 3.1   *The growth in industrial rents, 1975–85*

Source: Investors Chronicle/Hillier Parker

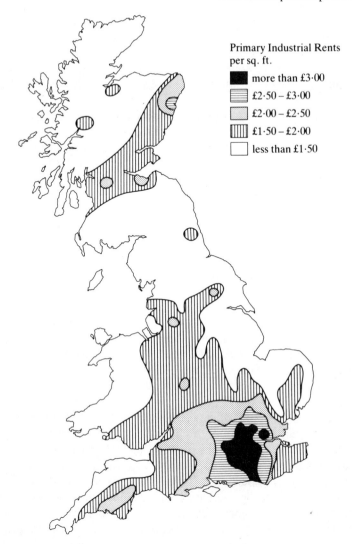

Figure 3.1   *Industrial rents, 1982*

Source: Hillier Parker (1982)

and Wales they are less than half the level prevailing around London. Rents in several provincial cities — Birmingham, Manchester, Newcastle and Edinburgh, for example — are, however, a little higher than in surrounding areas and, reflecting its role in the development of North Sea oil, Aberdeen has the highest rents outside the South East.

Industrial rents have generally risen, as Table 3.1 shows. On average, between the mid 1970s and the mid 1980s they more than doubled, though the rate of increase slowed in the 1980s. Allowing for inflation, however, the picture is very different. In real terms, average rents actually fell by some 20 per cent between 1975 and 1985. The fall reflects the severe recession in the manufacturing sector, and the consequent depressed demand for factory space.

The trend in rents also displays a distinct geographical pattern. The increase has been greatest in South East England, though even here a fall occurred in real terms. The increase was smallest in Northern England and Scotland, where no rental growth at all occurred between 1980 and 1985. So up to 1985 at least, the North–South gap in rent levels was actually widening.

The greater resilience of industrial rents in southern England is something that private sector investors are acutely aware of. They are also well aware that developments in the South are usually more easily let and thus more secure. They have consequently bid up the value of developments in the South, in anticipation of secure and rising rents, and in doing so have lowered the 'yields' obtained in this part of the country.

Yield is the annual rent expressed as a percentage of the capital value of a development. On the whole, the greater the expectation of rental growth, the greater the capital value and thus the lower the initial yield. Or to put it another way, where industrial rents are low and falling, the capital value of industrial developments is even lower. The geographical distribution of yields, shown in Figure 3.2, therefore reveals a pattern similar to that of rents, with, in this instance, the lowest yields (and highest capital values) in and around London and west along the 'M4 corridor' towards Bristol.

From the investor's point of view, an important distinction where yields are concerned is between 'primary' and 'secondary' property. Prime properties are those in the best locations, built to high specifications and in good condition, and let on long leases with frequent upward-only rent reviews (usually every 5 years). Secondary property does not meet these stringent criteria and is at the border of what a financial institution would normally buy, and beyond this category there is a great deal of property that institutions would never consider buying. The greater security of prime property and the prospect of rental growth means that the capital value of prime property is higher and the yield lower: in 1986 the yield on prime industrial property was 8.0 per cent, compared with an average yield of 10.6 per cent (*Investors Chronicle*/Hillier Parker, 1986). In practice, the definition of prime property used by major private sector investors excludes nearly all industrial property outside southern England.

However, it would be wrong to see the private investor's choice as simply being between primary and secondary industrial property. For the majority of investors, industrial property is only one among several options.

On the whole, industrial property is regarded as a risky investment. Shops and offices have almost always been regarded as a better bet for rental

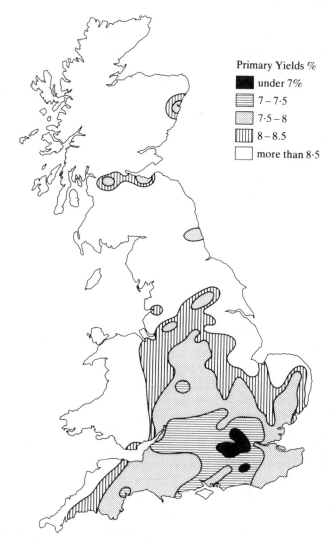

Primary Yields %

■ under 7%

≡ 7 – 7·5

▧ 7·5 – 8

▥ 8 – 8.5

□ more than 8·5

Figure 3.2   *Industrial yields, 1982*

Source: Hillier Parker (1982)

growth, so investors have been willing to accept lower initial yields. Industrial property has required high yields in order to entice investors. Thus in 1986, yields on prime property were only 4.00 per cent for shops and 4.75 per cent for offices, compared with the 8.00 per cent obtained on industrial property (*Investors Chronicle*/Hillier Parker, 1986). The gap also widened during the first half of the 1980s as the recession shook investors' confidence in industrial property. Beyond the property market, investment in industrial buildings must also compete with other financial investments, notably government bonds and company shares. Bonds are very secure, but offer only fixed interest. Company shares, like property, are an uncertain investment but offer the possibility of significant growth in income and capital value.

Institutional investment

It has been argued that 'in order to understand the characteristics of post-war property markets it is necessary to consider the overall growth of institutional investment in the period' (Cadman, 1984). But this was not always the case. In pre-war Britain property investment markets hardly existed at all. Not only was there less speculative commercial and industrial development, but more companies owned and occupied their own buildings. Virtually the only major investors in property for rent were the Church and the Oxbridge colleges.

In postwar Britain this traditional pattern changed radically. The need to rebuild many city centres created lucrative investment possibilities for the purchasers of bombed-out sites when wartime restrictions on new building were eventually lifted. At the same time rented property was becoming more attractive to firms. Under the 1954 Landlord and Tenant Act, for example, the tenant obtained safeguards against repossession by the landlord in exchange for leases with agreed provisions for rent reviews. Scarrett (1983) suggests that without this statutory framework many firms would have avoided their insecure position as tenants in favour of acquiring their own premises. A large market for rented property would not have emerged, and there would have been fewer opportunities for financial investors.

In the 1950s and 1960s the first postwar property boom therefore got underway. Men such as Jack Cotton, Charles Clore, Harry Hyams and Joe Levy, whose colourful biographies have been documented by Marriott (1967), rose to great personal wealth and influence through property speculation. This was a time when development land tax had yet to be introduced and when financial institutions' involvement in property was limited to the provision of mortgages for developers and a small amount of investment in completed schemes.

The period of indirect involvement in property by financial institutions, based around mortgage finance, eventually gave way to active participation. The increase in regular personal saving through private pension schemes, life assurance policies and unit trusts had a great deal to do with this because it placed vast sums in the hands of financial institutions in search of profitable outlets. Property has inherent attractions for many of these institutions. The usual practice of insurance companies and pension funds is to match their liabilities with investments of similar term. The average term of life assurance liabilities is long, and for pension funds it is even longer. An attractive asset is therefore one which is long term, provides a stream of income which rises with inflation, and offers the prospect of a substantial capital gain. Property fits these requirements ideally, even though the short-term stability of property markets is a cause of concern.

Thus when a Conservative Government came to power in 1970, its relaxed financial and taxation policies sparked off an unprecedented flow of institutional investment into property. Banks, pension funds, insurance companies and developers promoted schemes based on the assumption that rents and capital values would continue to escalate. But when the first oil price 'shock' of 1973/4 undermined confidence and led to higher interest rates, the economy moved quickly from boom to recession. The property sector was caught off balance. Projects that had looked feasible when interest rates were 5 per cent and rents were rising rapidly turned into a burden when interest rates rose to over 10 per cent and rents declined. Four large property companies and many smaller developers went into liquidation. Even some banks ran into difficulty because of overinvestment in property and had to be 'rescued' by the Bank of England.

Nevertheless, even during the property boom of the early 1970s financial investors still tended to view industrial property as an unsatisfactory asset. The specialist nature of much industrial building made it difficult and costly to re-let, and compared with offices and shops there is often greater wear and tear on factory buildings. Also for factories on cheap surburban sites the value of the land usually represents a smaller proportion of the investment, so that the value of the investment as a whole depreciates more rapidly than for city centre commercial developments.

But long-term trends were beginning to make industrial property a more attractive asset. The increased importance of light manufacturing and the expansion of warehousing generated a demand for standardized premises with a wider range of potential tenants, making letting easier. The lower capital cost of modern industrial buildings, compared to offices, allowed financial institutions to spread their investments across a range of developments, thus minimizing risk. This attracted smaller institutional investors in particular. Also, as standard designs and terraced layouts were popularized, construction times fell so that the supply of industrial buildings could be adjusted more quickly to demand. And the sheer scale of funds at the disposal of the institutions, in search of profitable outlets, cannot be discounted as a factor behind the move into industrial property.

For a while, institutional investors therefore increased their holdings of industrial property and newer pension funds, for example, generally invested a higher proportion of their assets in industrial buildings. Even so, holdings of industrial property generally remained smaller than those of office and retail property.

Then, at the start of the 1980s the severe economic recession, which impinged particularly on manufacturing industry, dealt a major blow to the institutions' confidence in industrial property. Many opted to decrease their industrial holdings. Taking a long view, too, it is questionable whether large-scale investment in industrial property can be sustained. Much of the increase in capital values since the end of the 1960s has been dependent on a fall in investment yields, itself resulting from the growth of the pension fund movement and the volume of institutional money in the market. As we have seen, after allowing for inflation there has been no real growth in industrial rents to sustain real capital growth. Cadman (1984) argues that in future the institutions will require more convincing evidence of the relative advantages of investments before committing themselves to major property develop-ment projects. Indeed, the financial institutions' investment in industrial property can be justly described as hesitant, and dependent on favourable conditions for letting factory buildings.

Such investment is also geographically limited. Debenham, Tewson and Chinnocks (1983) found that, in 1983, two-thirds of pension funds' property holdings were in the South East, and over 40 per cent in London itself. In contrast the whole of the North of England (the North West, Yorkshire and Humberside and Northern region) accounted for only 7 per cent. The funds have equally restrictive criteria concerning the type of property and tenant. Their evidence to the Wilson Committee (1980), for example, indicates that they are interested only in modern properties, built to high standards, and let on long leases, to tenants of unquestionable financial standing who take full responsibility for repairs and insurance. They also prefer to fund or acquire general purpose buildings in preference to units designed especially for manufacturing.

The involvement of financial institutions in the supply of industrial prop-erty is therefore something of a mixed blessing. By deploying a part of their massive resources they have facilitated the development of new premises for rent to meet a demand that had previously been poorly supplied. But they do not appear to have done a great deal for areas away from the South of England, or for firms whose property requirements do not fit into neat, standard categories. Indeed, the involvement of the financial institutions may have worsened the situation for disadvantaged areas and firms because the scale of the institutional funds that could potentially be ploughed into industrial property has probably obscured the narrow terms on which those funds are made available.

Types of developer

In terms of organization and financing, property development takes no single form. In a study of the provision of speculative factory units by the private sector, CALUS (1979) distinguished four types of developer:

1 The developer-seller, whose prime concern is the organization and management of property development. These companies do not retain the buildings or estates they develop but sell them to occupants or more commonly to financial investors. The developer-seller finances a scheme from internal reserves or by short-term loans from banks and other financial institutions. Profit is made in the form of a capital gain on the sale of the completed development.
2 The builder-developer, which is usually the offshoot of a construction company. The subsidiary development company channels the majority of the building work back to the parent company. The completed development may be retained or sold.
3 The developer-investor, whose prime interest is in the development and subsequent management of industrial estates. The actual building work may be undertaken by a subsidiary of the main company, or may be subcontracted to an independent builder. Income is derived not from selling the estates or individual buildings, but from retaining the premises and letting them to tenants.
4 The investor-developer, often a financial institution whose concern is the generation of income from investment in long-term assets. Some of these companies do not have the necessary expertise to undertake developments themselves and therefore either buy completed developments, usually from a developer-seller, or finance a scheme which they buy back from the developer. Alternatively, they may employ a team of professionals to undertake schemes on their behalf.

The contrasts between some of these agents in the industrial property market can be illustrated by a comparison of Slough Estates, Fleming Property Unit Trust, and the Legal & General Group. All these organizations hold large industrial portfolios, but they have become involved in this market from different directions.

Slough Estates is a developer-investor, and the longest established private company in the industrial property market. The company's interest in industrial estate development dates back to the 1920s when it started building factories on the site of an abandoned army depot at Slough. By 1984 the value of its property assets in the UK had grown to £530m. The largest investment remained the Slough estate, which accommodated 360 tenants in 680,000 m^2 of manufacturing and warehousing floorspace, making it one of the most extensive areas of mixed industrial activity in the country. The company's total property portfolio amounted to 1.7m m^2; this compares with the 2.2m m^2 of floorspace owned by English Estates, the Department of Trade and Industry's factory building agency. Unlike most development companies, Slough Estates has continued to specialize in one sector: in 1984, 72 per cent of its floorspace was in industrial premises and 24 per cent in warehousing, with the balance in offices and retail premises. A more

significant diversification has been the acquisition of overseas assets, totalling a further £200m, principally in Australia and North America.

Slough Estates is involved in all aspects of the development process, from
planning and design to the management of completed schemes. New factories are provided on a speculative basis and as purpose designed units for
lease to specific tenants. The company also purchases schemes completed by
other developers, although the main focus is on building their own estates.
The combined rent roll of its UK property was over £46.5m in 1984, a figure
well in excess of the £15.6m collected by English Estates from its more
extensive holdings in the assisted areas. The high income yielded by Slough
Estates' portfolio is a reflection of its geographical concentration in the
South East of England: only 10 per cent of the company's floorspace was
outside this region.

In contrast, Fleming Property Unit Trust, established in 1970, is solely an
investor in property and does not initiate development itself. In 1985, the
company had total assets of £288m, making it the UK's largest property
unit trust. This represented an eight-fold growth in the value of its assets
since 1976. Ownership of the trust was divided between 519 unit holders, of
which 415 were pension funds, 57 charities and 47 local authority super-
annuation funds, all eligible for the tax exempt status of the trust. Offices and
shops made up 72 per cent of the portfolio in 1985, while industrial and
warehousing property made up only 18 per cent — a reduction from a peak
of 27 per cent in 1982.

Fleming usually purchases industrial buildings from development companies when they have been completed and let. As a purely financial investor, the company's risks are thus minimized, and the future level of rental
growth is the only important uncertainty. The terms of the leases help
determine the attraction of a potential investment, and most occupants of
the company's factories are branches of national and international firms
(known in the property world as 'bluechip' tenants). In 1985, the industrial
holdings were divided between 22 separate schemes, each representing an
investment of over £500,000. Smaller schemes are avoided because of their
proportionally greater management costs. Three-quarters of the industrial
buildings (by value) were in the South East, with a marked concentration in
London itself. Only the South West and Wales accounted for further
significant amounts of industrial property. Further north, Fleming's industrial investments were limited to just two schemes: a large purpose designed
factory in Peterlee, and five units in Aberdeen.

The Legal & General Group is one of the City's largest financial institutions. It was originally involved in the provision of life assurance, but now
also undertakes investment on behalf of over 600 pension funds. Like other
similar financial institutions, it therefore handles large sums in search of
profitable and secure outlets. Investment in property is just one of these; the
others include UK company shares, overseas equities, index linked bonds

and gilt edged bonds. Also, because property competes with these other investments, the share of Legal & General's assets held as property tends to be volatile and responsive to changes in rates of return and expectations.

Within the property market, Legal & General is an investor-developer, initiating some developments itself but also purchasing completed developments. In December 1985, over 40 per cent of the £2.1bn of pension funds managed by Legal & General was invested in land and property, but overall only 17.5 per cent of the company's assets were held as property. This proportion had fallen over the previous 2 years. Only 8 per cent of the property portfolio managed for the pension funds consisted of industrial buildings. In contrast, offices accounted for 46 per cent, and shops another 41 per cent.

The construction phase

Towards the end of the development process, after the assessment of market demand and the arrangement of finance, comes the actual design and construction of the project. So before moving on in the next chapter to look at the efficiency of buildings in use it is worth looking at how this stage in the development process is organized, and in particular whether the construction industry is sufficiently quick and efficient. The issues are, of course, relevant to both purpose built developments and the provision of speculative factory space.

The traditional arrangement by which factories are built involves the firm or developer in separate relationships with consultants preparing the design and a contractor carrying out the construction work. A study by NEDO (1983) of industrial building in the early 1980s found that over half the customers used this approach. It offers the advantage of independent professional advice on the building process, and also facilitates the introduction of variations as the work proceeds.

The alternative arrangements are diverse. One is for the customer to act as their own design and building contractor, directly employing subcontractors for their specialist skills. This greatly increases the customer's responsibility and internal costs but reduces payments to outside firms. To be successful, this approach requires considerable managerial input and experience of building projects, and in practice the requisite skills tend to be found only in larger companies with their own building and works departments. At the other extreme are design-and-build arrangements under which most of the customer's responsibilities and control are transferred to the contractor. This approach is attractive to the customer because negotiations are with a single organization, but it deprives them of an independent check on the progress and quality of the work. Along this spectrum many different arrangements are possible. For example, customers sometimes appoint various specialist consultants to manage the project on their behalf and relieve them of some tasks and responsibilities.

NEDO concluded that non-traditional methods of organizing factory building are more likely to achieve fast project times. In their study, all but one of the projects that had development times a half or a quarter less than average were organized in non-traditional ways. A non-traditional arrangement is, however, no guarantee of a fast completion, and much depends on the competence of the firm offering the management, design or construction service.

NEDO also concluded that construction times for industrial buildings in Britain are nearer those achieved in the United States (the only country for which an international comparison was available) than for any other building type. Nevertheless they did identify 'substantial scope' for improving the general pace of construction without sacrificing quality or increasing costs. They argued, for example, that since similar projects often have widely varying times, many of the slower projects could probably be accelerated to match the best times already achieved.

The average time from 'decision to build' to 'start on site' was about 11 months. Advance factory schemes were typically shorter with an average of 10 months, compared with 12 months for purpose built property. Individual projects examined by NEDO had preconstruction times ranging from 6 months or less to over 2 years. Short or long periods were not solely the result of 'good' or 'bad' practice, and they had little to do with the size of the project. Sometimes they reflected real practical difficulties, but invariably short times were achieved only if the parties to the development were prepared to overlap the various preconstruction activities rather than proceed sequentially.

Contrary to much popular opinion, planning approvals were not a cause of delay, decisions being obtained generally within 2 or 3 months. Several local authorities, anxious to increase employment in their areas, make special efforts to speed up their development control procedures, though speculative developments generally encounter more difficulties and delays than bespoke factory schemes. Individual authorities tend to have different preferences about site coverage, density and landscaping which developers complained were rarely explicitly stated or published.

Building regulations and fire regulations are a more notable cause of delay during the preconstruction period. The problem noted here was the tendency for each authority to interpret the regulations in its own way, leading to differences in the standards expected between areas. For example, some fire officers do not allow windows between offices and warehouses, while others refuse to allow reception desks in entrance halls on the grounds that they cause obstruction. According to NEDO, insurance companies often made even more stringent demands.

The time taken between the customer identifying his requirements and construction commencing is normally longer than the time spent on site preparation and building work. The preconstruction phase is crucial to ensure good planning and clear identification of the customer's needs, though NEDO found that the projects which move quickly in their early stages tend to be constructed quickly as well. Average construction times for industrial building projects ranged from 5 months for projects costing up to £100,000 to 12 months for projects costing £1.5m, and 15 months for schemes of the order of £3m.

The length of the construction period not surprisingly varied with the complexity of the building. Standard advance units were quicker to erect than purpose designed factories, but whatever the type of project there are faster and slower ways of proceeding. The 'buildability' of schemes was one key variant. A detailed examination revealed that building designs in slow projects were not as a rule so simple and straightforward in their shape, layout, foundations, mixes of materials and components and positioning of services. Projects with a high emphasis on 'buildability' enabled, amongst other things, work to be subdivided into self-contained packages, services to be concentrated in particular parts of the building, and the use of pre-finished components and types of finish that reduced the congestion of building trades on-site. Successful projects also tended to have good supervision over the building work, which often depended on having a single project manager, and the minimal use of subcontractors, who add to the problems of coordination.

Reducing the development period can bring penalties in terms of the flexibility to modify the design. But industrial companies usually opt for brisk construction if they are offered it, and NEDO suggested that more would be prepared to embark on new building if they could be assured that it would be a speedy process. Moreover, faster building is generally associated with cheaper development costs.

The residual difficulty, not easily overcome, is the inexperience of many manufacturing companies in the organization of building work. Their expertise lies in the design and production of the goods they sell, not in property development, and only the largest firms have the necessary in-house skills. Few have the know-how to demand 'fast' times, to make informed choices about the organization of their project and to commission it in a way that assures them all of their requirements. Moreover, since in all but the largest firms major building projects are undertaken infrequently, there is little or no possibility of a manufacturer accumulating experience or learning from past mistakes. As things are, inexperienced customers are at a disadvantage because they have no certainty of getting maximum service from the building industry.

As an illustration of how badly building projects can proceed, NEDO described the case of a firm in South East England that wanted a new production unit and office building. The company had been hoping to expand for about 2 years and had inquired about a site when suddenly it was offered the land by an owner anxious to sell. Within a month the land had been purchased and within a further 4 months an architect had been appointed and a planning application made. Discussions were held with 15 nominated subcontractors and after 7 months the scheme was put out to tender to eight local and national contractors. The contract was won by a large regional contractor short of work with an agreed contract period of 10 months for the factory and 12 months for the office block at a total project cost of £2.2m.

In addition to the 15 contractors nominated in the original contract, it was found necessary to seek a further 17 local subcontractors. The site agent was managing his last contract before retirement. From the outset progress was disappointing. Subcontractors were in short supply due to competing local projects and the architect was described as vague and slow. In all 109 drawings were produced plus many amendments (double the number that would be typical for a project of its size). Only when the client intervened after 5 months, realizing that the project was badly behind schedule, was a work programme produced. Even then possession of the factory was taken 9 months late and the office completed 14 months behind schedule, with neither finished to the client's expectations.

According to NEDO, this was a classic example of 'how not to' for three main reasons. First, the client had no experience of construction and was in a hurry, with expensive equipment on order to satisfy his market. As one machine alone cost about half as much as the buildings, from a financial perspective submitting the project to competitive tender represented something of a false economy. Second, the architect was inexperienced and located too far away to supervise the project properly. Greater on-site control was needed. Third, the contractor used a large number of subcontractors, requiring a higher level of supervision than could be administered by a contract manager simultaneously overseeing several other projects.

By comparison, a case study of a new food processing factory and office in the Midlands provided an illustration of an efficiently organized development. On the face of it, this project ought to have run into difficulties. The client had a preliminary design produced that proved too expensive and had to be rejected, compressing the time available for redesign and construction to only 12 months. Because of the short time scale the contractor, a large multinational firm, opted to subcontract all the work and this inevitably caused problems, in this instance with the subcontractors for cladding and electrical work. A number of changes in the revised design also had to be made, to please the client and meet statutory requirements.

Yet the project was completed on time. In fact, the client obtained limited access ahead of completion which resulted in production commencing just 1 week after the end of the contract. In NEDO's assessment, the close cooperation between the project manager, design consultants and contractors overcame problems and produced a successful scheme. The project manager had previously worked alongside the consultants, and the contractor had been selected not just on the basis of their budget but also on the 'soundness' of their operation. There had been a willingness to overlap preconstruction activities — e.g. 'bills of quantities' had been drawn up while the design was still being finalized. Finally, a high level of on-site supervision had been exercised.

Concluding remarks

What we have described about the way industrial property development is organized in Britain in no way adds up to a condemnation. Certainly there are problems. The inconsistency in achieving acceptable construction times is one, and the narrow terms on which private finance is available for advance units is another. But on the whole, if the property industry has not in recent years built very much new factory space, and if the stock is ageing as a consequence, this is not due to structural rigidities in the development process itself. These failings owe much more to the adverse trends in the national economy, described in chapter 2.

So in the development process, at least, we find only limited cause for concern. When we look at the way that manufacturing firms use their existing factory buildings, in the next chapter, it quickly becomes apparent that the problems are more serious.

4 Property, efficiency and growth

The relationship between a manufacturing firm and the buildings it uses is undoubtedly important. On the one hand the growth of output, changes in technology and competitive pressures within an industry define a firm's property requirements; on the other hand, the premises in which the firm operates impose constraints on the nature of its operations and may limit its growth and efficiency, and even influence its long-term strategy. The ways in which these links operate are likely to vary from industry to industry and from firm to firm.

Economic theory is strangely silent on this whole subject. How are land and buildings supposed to fit into the production process? All we can glean is that land and buildings are an input to production just like labour and capital and that, in the profit maximizing firm, additional land and buildings will be taken on until the point is reached where their marginal productivity no longer exceeds their marginal cost. Also, depending on the prices of the different inputs, techniques of production will be adjusted so that the optimum quantity of land and buildings is used.

These smooth, marginal adjustments might occur in some markets, but certainly not in the use of industrial land and buildings. Of all inputs to production, buildings are the most indivisible. A new factory building is almost always a very large investment, and extensions tend also to require a major financial commitment. Buildings and sites are therefore rarely amenable to marginal adjustments, year by year, as needs change. Sometimes, on a very cramped site in a densely built-up area, no adjustment at all is possible. Furthermore, each building has particular design features — ceiling heights, floor loadings, layout and so on — which short of extensive rebuilding remain fixed until the day it is demolished, irrespective of how a firm's needs evolve over the years. Added to this, firms are not so mobile as always to be able to hop from building to building to maintain the ideal balance between their requirements and the space they actually use. The option of moving to more suitable premises tends to be embarked upon reluctantly because of the effort and costs involved.

So traditional economic theory, with its emphasis on marginal adjustments, is particularly unhelpful. The existing empirical literature does not help much either. Most existing studies reflect the way that the property industry is organized and look at factory buildings from the point of view of the speculative developer or the financial investor. These people need information on what can be sold or let to firms, and at what rate of profit. The effect is to focus attention on the supply of new industrial property, and more specifically on new property for rent, which caters mostly for small firms. Studies by CALUS (1979) and the Building Research Team (1982) of the suitability of new, speculatively built, standard factory units are good examples. Unfortunately, this focus ignores the vast majority of firms who operate in older property of varying ages, and also the larger and medium sized firms that own their buildings. To get a proper view of the relationship between property, growth and efficiency we need to look at these firms, too.

At any particular point in time a firm's property needs are not difficult to identify: most managers have a clear idea of the sort of building that would best suit their firm. The problem is that firms' needs change, so that buildings that were once well suited to their occupants can become inappropriate, and in doing so they can act as a brake on growth and efficiency. This is what we call 'mismatch', and the largest part of this chapter is structured around this concept. We explain the origin of mismatch, the nature of the problems it creates, and firms' capacity to respond.

The discussion of mismatch is based largely on the findings of a survey. During 1985, we interviewed the managers of 126 factories in the East Midlands. The factories were drawn in roughly equal numbers from four industries: electronics, hosiery, food and drink processing, and engineering. Within engineering — a broad category — the factories were mainly in the vehicles sector, such as commercial vehicle body manufacturers. The survey thus included contrasting industries: a high technology sector, a traditional textile industry, a process based industry and a metal-bashing industry. Within each industry the sample was structured to include some firms in old buildings on cramped sites, some in modern buildings on spacious sites, and some in intermediate categories (e.g. old buildings on spacious sites, buildings of mixed age). The factories varied in size, though firms employing fewer than 25 people were excluded because of their distinctive needs (see chapter 7). They included single plant firms, headquarters and branch plants. Some factories were purpose built, others second-hand or speculatively developed. The length of time for which the firms had occupied their present site and buildings also varied.

The purpose of the interviews was to find out how far firms were satisfied with their premises, and if not why not, how it affected them and what they planned to do about it. What quickly became apparent is that there is a complex and often idiosyncratic pattern of interrelationships between firms and their buildings. For this reason the discussion of mismatch concentrates on the main influences at work and illustrates these mostly by reference to examples rather than statistics. Indeed, since the sample of firms was in no way random or representative the proportions we quote do not necessarily apply to the factory stock as a whole. Also, where examples are used the names have been changed to preserve confidentiality.

Firms' property requirements

But first let us look at what determines a manufacturing firm's property requirements, ignoring for the moment the fact that those requirements evolve through time. Broadly, a firm's property needs are determined by a combination of economic and technical factors.

On the economic side, firms vary in their ability to pay for factory space. For some the ideal property is a cheap second-hand or converted property, which will absorb the minimum amount of their available resources and allow them to concentrate their limited investment in other more important directions.

Closely related to the ability to pay is the choice between rented and owner occupied property. Rented property ties up less of the firm's capital, and may allow greater mobility as the firm grows and needs larger premises. These advantages are especially relevant to small firms. A disadvantage of rented property, however, is that firms are not normally able to adapt or extend the premises to match their specific needs. Many firms therefore have clear views about whether they prefer to rent or own their premises.

The management's expectations about growth are a further economic consideration. If growth is anticipated, the ideal site and premises should have the capacity for expansion.

The technical aspects of a firm's property requirements are more numerous. Foremost among these is the size of building. This depends not only on the size of the firm, in terms of turnover or employment, but also on the technology employed, so that a labour-intensive firm may employ twice the workforce of its neighbour on only a quarter of the floorspace. But in general the larger the factory in terms of output or jobs, the larger the amount of space required.

The design of factory space matters a great deal. The *Architects Journal*, in a handbook of factory design, put forward a useful way of specifying the technical factors that affect the sort of space firms require (*Architects Journal*, 1977). This concerned four variables: the production plant intensity, the production plant rate of change, the mechanical handling intensity and the services intensity.

Production plant intensity is the extent to which the manufacturing floor area is taken up by production equipment. A high intensity implies a machine-intensive system, often fully or partly automated. An example is bulk process manufacture in the chemical industry and in food industries such as grain milling. A low production plant intensity usually involves an assembly area with some equipment, e.g. bending presses and shears for light sheet metalwork, and the manufacturing process is usually under manual control. Most production-line technology comes somewhere between these extremes.

The production plant rate of change is the frequency of significant alterations to machinery, services and fixed path mechanical handling equipment. This is important because it determines the level of adaptability required of factory space. In electronics, the *Architects Journal* suggested that significant changes in production plant sometimes occur each year or more frequently; in most processing industries a longer cycle of between 5 and 15 years is the norm.

Mechanical handling intensity is the extent to which special equipment is needed to move goods or materials around the factory. Some factories rely almost entirely on manual handling; these are generally the ones with light, high value products made in small batches or as one-offs. Fork-lift trucks, overhead cranes and conveyers are more mechanized means of moving goods, but the most intensive are those where items are moved automatically, often along fixed paths, by equipment integrated into the building structure. The motor car assembly line is a classic example of the latter type of mechanical handling.

Services intensity is the extent to which facilities such as air conditioning, heating and heat extraction, dust extraction, high intensity lighting, and the supply of power need to be integrated into the factory structure. Some electronics factories are especially demanding in this respect, requiring special areas with sophisticated environmental control, but in most engineering industries the standards are generally lower.

Taken together, these variables define the design requirements for a firm's manufacturing area. They define the requirements with respect to floor loadings and ceiling heights, the layout of spaces in relation to each other and the provision for moving goods between them. They also determine whether a multistorey layout is a practical option. Certain combinations of requirements may lay down rigorous design criteria. For example, services like heating, ventilation and power supply are mostly carried within roofs and ceilings, so a high intensity of services for the production plant combined with a rapid rate of production plant change necessitates considerable flexibility to be built into roof structures.

In particular, the design requirements determine whether a firm can be accommodated in a standard factory unit or whether the building must be purpose built. In its survey of industrial construction, NEDO found that in one-third of factory developments the design of the buildings was determined by the process they housed, though other projects built for manufacturing companies also had some special features such as crane gantries, special floors, ventilation systems, services and superior office finishes. Fundamentally, however, most standard and purpose built new units were of similar construction: steel framed, with brick or metal cladding and asbestos cement roof covering, and planned with flexibility in mind (NEDO, 1983).

Two final technical issues are the balance between production space and other space (offices, for example) and the ratio between the total floor area and the area of the site.

Table 4.1 presents data from our survey of four industries. In each case, production accounts for the majority of the floorspace. The office content in electronics — 25 per cent of total space — is higher than in the other industries, bearing out the conventional wisdom that because of its high proportion of professional and other white-collar workers (in design, development and testing, for example) the electronics industry's property requirements differ from those of traditional industry (Henneberry, 1984). For comparison, offices account for only about 10 per cent of the floorspace in most new, speculatively built factories. Storage of materials, components and finished goods takes a significant minority of space in all four industries, especially food and drink and hosiery. In these two industries the high proportion of storage space in part reflects retailers' pressure on suppliers to hold large and varied stocks at the factory rather than at the shops themselves. Vacant floorspace accounts for only a very small proportion of the total. 'Other' uses shown in the table include such things as canteens and 'cash and carry' shops attached to factories.

| | % of total floorspace | | | |
	Food and drink	Electronics	Engineering	Hosiery
Production	57	57	71	60
Offices	10	25	13	11
Storage	28	14	13	25
Vacant	—	3	2	1
Other	5	1	1	3
	100	100	100	100

Table 4.1   *The use of factory space in four industries, 1985*

Source: Survey data

The ideal ratio between floorspace and total site area varies from firm to firm as well as between industries. Commercial vehicle body manufacture (one of the industries in our survey) requires an unusually low site coverage in order to provide space for the parking and movement of the lorries that are being worked on. A site coverage of only 25 per cent is often preferred for this reason. In hosiery and other branches of the textiles and clothing trade, high site coverages are generally acceptable, not least because they predominantly employ low-paid women who travel to work by public transport, so the need for on-site car parking is reduced. Aside from the issue of land for expansion, a firm's ideal site coverage depends on its need for car parking space, room for loading and unloading and the circulation of lorries, and for outdoor storage.

An issue of particular interest is the extent to which the property needs of high technology industry differ from those of more traditional sectors of British industry in terms of building design, use of internal space, and use of the site as a whole. Herring, Son & Daw (1982) argued that high technology sectors such as electronics and biotechnology require a flexible mix of high quality office, laboratory and production space in an attractive environment. However, their evidence was selective and anecdotal.

Coopers & Lybrand Associates (1986) undertook a fuller study of this issue. They looked not only at emerging high technology sectors, which account for only a small proportion of all industrial activity, but also at 'modern' industries that apply advanced methods and technology to more traditional products. The findings highlighted the availability of appropriate highly trained labour as a locational constraint, and the advantage in this respect of sites in the more rural parts of southern England. So far as the buildings themselves were concerned, the findings indicated that most modern industry can operate without any handicap in standard industrial units. Modern industry prefers a rather higher office content than normal, generous car parking for its employees, room for expansion on-site and a good quality surrounding environment. But none of these preferences is sufficiently unusual or specialized to distinguish it from the rest of manufacturing industry. In the cases where high technology firms have built architecturally distinctive buildings this has usually been to enhance their corporate image rather than to meet special needs arising out of their production processes.

The origins of mismatch

We defined mismatch as a situation in which a firm's buildings no longer correspond to its needs. In our survey, we asked firms how different they would want their buildings to be if they could start again from scratch, and the answers give a good indication of the extent of mismatch. Less than a quarter said no different, while almost another third pointed to only minor details. Significantly, these firms included ones that had only recently moved or completed major alterations to their site and buildings. The remainder of the firms in the survey — nearly half the total — said they would like something quite different, ranging from an extra two or three thousand square feet to a radically different design and size of property. In some instances they were actively seeking alternative premises or planning to make important modifications to their buildings or the way they were used. Obviously, if firms are satisfied with their premises there is no problem. The question that needs concern us is why so many appear to be in premises that for one reason or another are unsatisfactory, not just in minor details but in fundamental ways.

It is a reasonable assumption, and one borne out by the survey, that firms do not move into premises that are unable to meet their needs as they perceive them. Of course, there may be instances when a firm's choice is constrained and the premises selected are less than ideal. But by and large a mismatch is something that develops over time, as circumstances and needs change.

The pressures generating a mismatch can be either 'internal' or 'external' to the firm. Internal pressures are those that are specific to a particular firm; external pressures are those that affect all firms in a particular industry. In both cases the pressures are constantly evolving, generating new mismatches as fast as old ones are overcome.

Taking the external pressures first, the three main ones are technical changes in methods of production, changes in the nature and design of the product, and changes in the level of demand for the product. All firms in an industry experience these pressures to a greater or lesser extent, though their relative importance varies from industry to industry and from time to time. At present the most striking change is, of course, the introduction of microprocessors into both products and production processes. This was evident in many of the firms we spoke to, not just in electronics. But the major influence of product demand should not be ignored. The recession between 1980 and 1982 was a traumatic experience for many companies, from which some have not recovered or finally adjusted their use of property. At the time of the survey — mid 1985 — a modest upturn in the UK economy was also putting pressure on the productive capacity of some factories.

External pressures generating mismatch could be observed in all four industries in the survey, and can be illustrated by some examples.

Tights

The manufacture of women's tights and stockings is a specialized branch of the hosiery industry with its own distinctive machines and commercial pressures. It is going through a major period of mechanization. A new generation of computer controlled knitting machines is being introduced. Each of these produces three or four times more than an older machine, so that fewer are required and knitting occupies less floorspace. On the other hand, computer controlled knitting machines generate vast quantities of heat and require a controlled temperature, so that sophisticated ventilation and environmental control equipment needs to be installed, and they are also very noisy and therefore best segregated from the rest of the production process. Further down the line, new automated machines are being introduced in three areas: making-up (e.g. sewing on the toes), checking and packaging. Formerly these tasks were performed manually, almost exclusively by women seated at row upon row of work benches. The new machines occupy less space. Knitting machines have traditionally been operated round the clock on shifts, and the new ancillary machinery also needs to be used as fully as possible in order to pay its way, so shift working is rising in these parts of the production process. Again, this means more output from the same floorspace. But just because production is becoming more efficient the amount of warehousing space needed does not fall. If anything, more is required because the spread of retailers' own brands means that more varied stock (in packaging at least) must be carried, and there has been an increase in the factoring of cheap imported tights. The net effect of technical change in this industry is thus to reduce overall floorspace requirements (and labour requirements) and increase the proportion used for warehousing.

Telecommunications equipment

This industry is at the forefront of the shift from electro-mechanical to electronic technology. The transformation is embodied in the product itself, but has ramifications for the organization of production. Electro-mechanical technology required a whole range of metal-working skills such as stamping, plating and wiring. The labour needed was mostly manual, and the space requirement considerable. Electronic technology is lighter and dispenses with almost all traditional engineering skills. More of the work is white collar, in design for example. Less space is required even though output has generally increased, and the space needs to be of a higher environmental quality. Larger firms in this industry have therefore mostly been under pressure to shed space, and to upgrade the quality of that which remains, or even to replace old buildings with entirely new 'high tech' facilities.

Commercial vehicle bodies

Two major external pressures have altered the property needs of this industry since the 1960s. The first is the increase in the size of the lorries and trailers in use on British roads. Larger vehicles require larger sheds and fabrication areas to house them. The appropriate building now has larger doors, scope for heavier lifting gear, and fewer pillars obstructing the internal space. The second change is the major contraction (something approaching half) in the size of the UK market from the start of the 1980s onwards. Many firms therefore need less space in total than they did previously, divided into fewer, larger production areas.

Food processing

The standards of hygiene in food processing have become more rigorous. The growing influence of the major retail chains, who inspect their suppliers' factories on a regular basis, has reinforced this trend. The change has been gradual, but cumulatively adds up to a major redefinition of standards of acceptable factory space. Ventilation and dust control have had to be improved; tough, high quality flooring that is easy to keep clean is increasingly essential. When new food processing factories are built they therefore invariably need to be of a different design from the more traditional factory buildings they replace, and periodic replacement of process plant usually requires extensive refurbishment of existing factory space to bring it up to modern standards.

All these are examples of external pressures, affecting whole industries. The internal pressures creating a mismatch between a firm's buildings and its property requirements fall into three main groups: changes in the function of the factory within a larger organization, changes in the firm's product or product mix, and the competitive success or failure of the firm within its industry.

Whereas changes in the external environment are often gradual and continuous, the internal pressures creating a mismatch can arise quickly and unexpectedly. Corporate reorganization, for example, may lead to the closure of a factory and the sudden transfer of machines and production to a sister factory where the additional machinery and production may not easily be accommodated. Again, examples illustrate the processes.

Universal Radiators, Leicestershire

This is an example of corporate reorganization. This factory is the firm's main manufacturing centre, producing exchange radiators for motor vehicles. The firm had recently taken over one of its competitors, whose production was being transferred to this site, resulting in considerable pressure on space and an urgent need to reorganize the factory layout. One response had been to subcontract production, and the firm had obtained outline planning permission for a new factory on this site.

Hi-Tech Controls, Leicestershire

This factory illustrates the consequences of competitive success. A subsidiary of an American conglomerate, it is the principal production centre for a range of process control equipment, and also the UK and European headquarters for certain management and marketing functions. The present site, part of a larger factory that is rented from another company, had been occupied for only 4½ years but despite the addition of 12,000 ft^2 of portakabins it had become too small to cope with the growth in business. The firm was therefore building a purpose designed factory on a nearby site.

Brand Foods, Lincolnshire

In the case of this factory there had been a product change. The firm had formerly operated it as a vegetable canning plant but the new owners of the company, faced with declining profits, switched to producing frozen fruit, vegetables and chilled salads. This necessitated the total refurbishment of part of the factory to accommodate a new freezer unit, and to complete the changeover, other buildings on the site were going to be demolished and a second freezer unit constructed.

All three of these firms had encountered mismatches, arising from internal pressures, that to a large extent they were overcoming through substantial investment in new and refurbished buildings. They are not exceptional, but as we will explain there are a great many firms that fail to respond so swiftly or successfully. Also, in many cases the internal pressures generating a mismatch are overlain on existing external pressures, complicating the problems and the difficulty of finding a satisfactory solution with the resources available.

In general, the likelihood and severity of a mismatch between a firm's needs and its buildings depend on the length of occupation by the firm and the rate at which its needs change over time. Thus firms that have only recently moved into old factories usually find them satisfactory, while a newer factory can become totally inadequate after a short while if a firm's output or technology is changing rapidly. Each individual change in a firm's products or processes may not greatly modify its property needs, but cumulatively, through time, such changes can add up to a significant shift. This was borne out by the survey. For example, we asked firms whether their premises were the right size. Three-quarters of the firms that had occupied their present buildings for less than 5 years thought that they were the right size. But this proportion fell with increasing length of occupation. Of the firms who had occupied their present site for over 20 years, more than 40 per cent said their buildings were too small or becoming too small, and a further quarter said their buildings were too big, leaving only a third who were reasonably satisfied with the amount of space they had.

Further questions probed firms' satisfaction with their layout (which is constrained by the nature of the buildings) and the flexibility of their buildings for accommodating change. The same pattern emerged: the longer the period of occupation, the more likely that firms consider their layout unsatisfactory, their buildings inflexible, and their premises generally unsuitable for present production methods.

The way in which mismatch increases with length of occupation is illustrated by the following four firms.

Electrodynamics, Leicestershire

This electronics firm had occupied its four storey, Victorian textile mill for just 3 years and was delighted with it. There was ample space — and it was cheap — and since the product was light there were no serious difficulties arising from the movement of materials between floors. They had the potential to double production within the building without any adaptation.

Avon Hosiery, Derbyshire

This knitwear firm had occupied its two storey factory, built in the 1920s, for the previous 7 years. Essentially the building comprised two large, square floor areas, one used for knitting and the other for making-up — a reasonably efficient layout. The problem was that production from two other factories had recently been transferred here following their closure, something that had not originally been anticipated, and this factory was now tight on space, though the firm was not yet at the stage of turning away business because of this constraint.

Walker & Jones, Derbyshire

This firm produced animal feeds. The main mill building had been constructed when the firm moved to the site 40 years before, and a number of smaller buildings had subsequently been erected. Over the last 15 years demand for the firm's product had risen by 70 per cent, and increasingly their market was for customized feeds suited to individual farmers' needs. Production has therefore increased and switched to smaller batches, with a consequent need for more storage space. New processes to manufacture feeds had also been introduced. The net effect was that the firm's premises were substantially too small, and further infilling between existing buildings would have provided only marginal respite. The yard was already congested with parked vehicles, offering no possibility of adding to the production space. Potential expansion into a range of new feeds was being prevented.

United Engineering, Lincolnshire

This factory had been purpose built 73 years before to make large items of agricultural equipment. The same firm now produced braking systems for commercial vehicles. The building was very long and narrow, and was intended for volume production, but with today's batch production methods, materials and work in progress had to be moved back and forth. Layout was regarded as totally unsatisfactory, and ideally the firm would prefer a single storey building.

Apart from length of occupation, three other general factors influence the severity of mismatch and the rate at which it develops.

One is the rate of change in the product and production technology. In baking, for example, the product changes little if at all, and fundamentally the production methods, too, have changed relatively little over the years. Therefore in this industry purpose built premises put up in the interwar years can remain suitable so long as there is periodic and modest updating. At the other extreme, the products and processes in electronics change rapidly, with consequences for firms' property needs.

A second influence on mismatch is the size of firm. Small firms — those with fewer than 50 employees — are the most volatile. Their success often depends on just one or two products or markets, and some firms experience rapid growth. It is not uncommon for a small firm to outgrow its factory very quickly indeed. An example from the survey is a firm making agricultural machinery that had been established in 1977 in rented premises. It quickly outgrew these, and became acutely constrained by a lack of space. The firm had always intended to build its own factory on a suitable site, but a purpose built factory was not completed until 1980. The firm continued to grow, and by 1984 had found it necessary to further extend its new buildings from 17,000 to 36,000 ft^2.

A third influence on mismatch is the profitability of the product. There is always a cost attached to acquiring or holding more land or floorspace than is needed for current production. That cost is felt as capital tied up in property, e.g. in rates and possibly in rent paid on surplus space. On the other hand most firms are aware that their property requirements change over time, and many value the flexibility of having room for expansion within their buildings and on their site, so there is some incentive to resist the financial pressure to equate present buildings with present needs. But how far firms are able to resist these pressures, and to hold on to space that is surplus to immediate requirements, depends ultimately on the profitability of their market.

Hosiery and knitwear illustrate this latter point. More than three-quarters of the firms we talked to in this industry were operating at or near to the capacity of their buildings, an apparently odd finding considering that the textile trades were hit so badly during the recession of the early 1980s. Although by 1985 there had been an upturn in business (though to nothing like pre-recession levels) the main reason for the high capacity utilization was probably the industry's low profitability. The industry is severely squeezed by cheap imports, epecially from the Far East, and firms must therefore minimize costs to survive. Property related overheads are one set of costs, and hosiery and knitwear firms typically aim to maximize the use of all their assets and to shed any 'fat' in the system. In practice this meant that during the recession firms often closed their smaller, peripheral factories, sold the buildings and machines, and concentrated production at their main sites which they kept fully utilized. The capacity to meet upturns in demand by simply using spare capacity had therefore disappeared. Indeed, the recession had been such a trauma that some firms were unwilling to increase their capacity, by opening new satellite factories, until they were convinced that the growth in demand would be sustained.

The problems created by mismatch

The problems that arise in a mismatch can be grouped under two headings: those related to the quantity of space, and those related to design or layout. These are two conceptually distinct problems. A firm may find itself with too little or too much space, but the design of that space may be perfectly satisfactory. Conversely, a firm may have the right quantity of floorspace but of the wrong design. There are cases where both the quantity and design are wrong but the difficulties which arise from the two problems can be quite different: lack of space may constrain output; poor design may constrain efficiency.

First, let us consider shortages of space. The relationship between output and floorspace is not a simple mechanical one. A given amount of floorspace ultimately sets a ceiling to the production that can be achieved at a factory, but there is usually a range of output over which lack of space is a problem but one which can to a greater or lesser extent be circumvented. The introduction of shift working is one way in which more output can be obtained from the same floorspace, though obviously this approach is possible only if shift working is not already the norm. In the survey, 50 of the 126 firms said they had no room for expansion within their existing buildings, and 21 said this was a serious problem at the present time.

We found few instances of firms adapting their machinery to provide more output from the same space. A bakery which introduced a three-tier oven in place of a horizontal arrangement was a notable exception. But generally, if new machinery gives more output from the same space this is a fortuitous by-product of adopting best-practice technology rather than a deliberate tactic to overcome a shortage of space.

With few exceptions, firms prefer to expand production at their existing sites wherever possible, taking full advantage of economies of scale. Over half the firms that had encountered a shortage of space had responded by extending the buildings on their present sites. This avoids the duplication of management structures and resulting problems of coordination, facilitates consistency in quality control, and makes best use of ancillary and support facilities, such as stores and maintenance staff.

The main exceptions to the preference for on-site expansion arise when additional labour cannot be obtained at the present site, or when the firm has a deliberate strategy of keeping production units small for labour relations reasons. Shortage of labour is something which we found affects the making-up end of the hosiery and knitwear trade. The workforce is made up almost wholly of women who, it is said, are unwilling to travel far, and certainly cannot easily afford to do so. The labour markets in this trade are therefore highly localized, and firms locate where labour is available, establishing several small branches rather than one large unit. For example, several knitwear firms commented that a shortage of women workers in central Leicester meant that their preferred strategy would be to divert expansion elsewhere.

Once an existing site and building is full, a common approach is to acquire immediately adjacent land and buildings. Of course, the right quantity of land or floorspace is unlikely to be available in the right place at the right time, especially in densely built-up urban areas. Nevertheless, nearly a quarter of the firms in the survey had extended their sites in the last 10 years. Firms vary a great deal in their approaches to site extension and the acquisition of neighbouring property. For some it is a long-term strategy. These are the firms, usually single site, that are committed to a particular location and have expectations of long-term growth. They acquire more or less anything that becomes available next to their sites, and if it is surplus to their immediate needs they may let it on a short-term lease. Other firms adopt an *ad hoc* approach. They may not plan to acquire adjacent property, but if some happens to become available it may be purchased as a fortuitous solution to a space problem. Another group of firms try to acquire adjoining property only when they already face severe problems in their present buildings.

But despite efforts to expand on-site, some firms do encounter space constraints that limit production at their factories. In a postal survey of manufacturing establishments undertaken in 1982, roughly 25 per cent of the 2,000 respondents said that lack of space had at some time limited the growth of output at their factory (Fothergill, Kitson and Monk, 1983). In the interview survey, 51 firms (two-fifths of the total) said that production at their factory had been limited by lack of space at some time or other, either now or in the past.

If an individual factory's output is constrained there need not be a loss of business to the company as a whole if some activities are diverted to another existing factory or to a new branch factory. Throughout a large part of British industry, a widespread short-term response to a space constraint is the diversion of warehousing to rented property nearby, thereby easing pressure on storage space on-site or freeing space for additional production. Of the firms we spoke to that had encountered a shortage of space, half had followed this route. It is an especially easy option if the firm operates on a large trading estate where there is a high turnover of tenants and thus a regular supply of units to let. In some firms, off-site storage becomes permanent. It reached its logical conclusion at two biscuit factories we visited. Both factories were on sites that lacked room for expansion, and the respective companies aimed to maximize production with the available capacity on-site. All ingredients were kept off-site, and delivered only a matter of hours before they were needed. The biscuits were packaged on-site, but then removed to warehouses elsewhere prior to distribution. The disadvantage of this strategy is that it adds to transport costs, compared to keeping everything on one site, and in the case of these biscuit factories it made production vulnerable to disruption in supply, e.g. if a lorry-load of ingredients turned out to be substandard. The advantage is that to a large extent warehousing and production can be run independently of each other.

Hiving-off part of the production process to another site is more problematic. Within a multiplant company a space constraint at one factory can sometimes be managed by diverting orders to an existing factory elsewhere: in the interview survey, a sixth of the firms that had encountered space constraints had done this. One of the biscuit factories, for example, had diverted production to the company's Liverpool and London factories. However, this sort of diversion may involve losses in efficiency: in this instance the East Midlands factory claimed to be the most productive and profitable in the group. There may also be a loss of potential economies of scale. Furthermore, it would be wrong to assume that the diversion of production between factories is always possible within multiplant firms. Sometimes individual factories within a group function as more or less autonomous enterprises, with their own production and marketing strategies and their own distinctive products. Where factories operate in this way the possibility of diversion between them is less likely. The technology to produce some goods may be unique to a factory, especially where the production process involves a large quantity of specialized equipment.

Opening a new branch to take the overspill is easiest if there is no loss of economies of scale. In the interview survey, 28 of the 51 firms that had run up against space constraints had opened a new branch. A firm may opt either to hive off part of the production process to the branch factory, or to replicate all the production facilities there. Both strategies are evident in hosiery and knitwear. In this industry there is a major divide between the knitting, which is machine-intensive and usually employs men, and the making-up of finished garments, which is labour-intensive and employs women. Some firms therefore choose to operate two sites — one knitting, one making-up. Goods need to be transported between the two, which also means that more is tied up as work-in-progress, but this is not usually perceived as a major handicap. At the making-up end of the business, the diversion of growth into branch plants is a widespread feature, as already noted. It does not lead to important diseconomies because making-up requires no major centralized facilities.

The most radical response to a shortage of space is complete relocation, and many firms (especially smaller ones) do take this step. On the face of it, relocation to more spacious premises is the obvious solution. However, the fact is that financial, managerial and technical constraints mean that for many firms this is not a realistic option. So instead they muddle through in other ways. Relocation, and the conditions that allow it, is discussed at greater length later when we look at firms' capacity to respond to difficulties with their premises.

The point in outlining all these possible responses to a shortage of space is to emphasize that it is not an insurmountable obstacle. Many firms do use their buildings to the limits of their capacity, yet at the same time avoid ever losing or turning away business because of lack of space. They get round the problem by adopting different permutations of the solution just described. But it is inevitable that in some cases there is a loss of business to the firm. Sometimes the loss may be only temporary, arising from delays in opening a new branch or new extension, for example. On other occasions the loss of business is permanent.

Subcontracting is one method by which physically constrained firms maintain their sales but lose production and employment — in this case to their subcontractors but not their competitors (unless the two happen to be the same). We encountered six firms that were subcontracting work because of shortage of space, and a further ten that had done so in the past. Subcontracting may involve just components or part of the production process, or whole batches of the complete product, in which case the company's role becomes one of marketing a product designed by them but manufactured by someone else.

A not greatly dissimilar strategy is for the firm to specialize in a particular product or stage of the manufacturing process. The logical one to choose is the one that the firm finds most profitable. In such cases the growth of profits may not suffer greatly, but the potential growth of production and employment at the factory will none the less be constrained. A total of 15 firms in our sample had opted to specialize to overcome lack of space at their factories.

There are plenty of cases of straightforward loss of business to competitors, though firms only rarely turn down orders through lack of capacity. The actual mechanisms are more subtle. One is that they lengthen their order books and quote longer delivery times: seven firms we spoke to said they had done this. In some trades lengthening of delivery dates effectively adds up to turning away business. The customers go elsewhere, where they can get quicker deliveries. A variant on the same theme is that firms price their goods a little less competitively; this, too, runs the risk of losing potential customers. The commonest way in which potential business is lost through lack of capacity is by not chasing business which the firm could otherwise expect to obtain. Fourteen firms (more than a quarter of those which had experienced a shortage of space) said they had done this. Not chasing business may involve staying clear of a particular segment of the market, pursuing only a low-key marketing policy, or simply not tendering for a possible contract.

So far we have looked only at shortages of space, but some mismatches involve too much rather than too little. Many firms occupy space that is surplus to their immediate or anticipated needs but do not find the cost of holding onto this — rates, rents, insurance, maintenance and possibly heating — unduly large or worrying. As a consequence, too much space is rarely seen to be as serious a problem as too little.

In practice, firms with 'surplus' space often find a use for it. Plant layouts can be more spacious, and the storage of materials, spares and finished goods can be less tightly controlled than it might be. In other words, activities expand to fill the space available. Because of this process, some firms become aware of the extent to which they have been carrying surplus space only when they need to increase production or introduce new machines: in these circumstances a careful examination of plant layout and judicious reorganization usually release the space required.

When a discrete area does become vacant a firm faces three options: it can leave it empty, it can rent or sell it, or it can demolish it. We encountered examples of all three responses. The options differ in their attractions. Financially, renting or selling the surplus space is usually the most attractive, and leaving it empty the least. The decision is nevertheless likely to depend more on the age, design and physical condition of the buildings, and their relationship to the remaining occupied space.

Now let us turn to the difficulties arising from the design of factory buildings, the other dimension of mismatch. Design problems pose quite different obstacles from those arising from a shortage or excess of space.

One of the clear conclusions to emerge from the survey is that firms are less satisfied with older buildings. They are also, on average, less satisfied with multistorey buildings for anything other than offices. Old buildings are more likely to be multistorey, so the two problems often go hand in hand.

The problem with old buildings is not their age as such. Some old buildings provide space that differs little from that in modern factories, in terms of dimensions, flexibility and working environment. Older buildings usually require rather more maintenance — though they are sometimes built to higher standards than modern units — but offsetting this they can usually be bought or rented more cheaply. The problem is that old buildings are often of a design that is poorly suited to modern production methods. Partly the problem is one of ceilings that are too high (leading to heating problems) or too low (making installation of some machines or movement of work-in-progress difficult). The excessive number of pillars supporting the roof or the next floor can constrain plant layout, and lead to a wasteful use of space. The most common 'design' problem with old buildings is, however, that they are likely to have been enlarged over time. The additions take the form of extensions to the original building and the construction of new buildings on the same site. In each case the addition was no doubt made for sound reasons. The cumulative result, however, is the development of a highly complex site including a wide range of sizes and types of building. The range of structures on such sites offers flexibility in space utilization because there is usually some building or part of a building that is the right size to accommodate a new or modified activity. However, most present-day occupants find these sites highly inefficient, and express a strong preference for one large, single storey unit instead.

The main inefficiency is in the layout of plant and machinery, and in the workflow that results. Different functions tend to be allocated to the parts of a site that are best able to accommodate them, but they may not then be in the best place in relation to each other. Work consequently has to be moved to and fro, from machine to machine, often manually. Goods coming in and out may have to be stored at the wrong place in relation to the start and finish of the production line. Supervision of shopfloor workers and monitoring of production flows and bottlenecks becomes problematic because there are too many nooks and crannies, making it impossible for management to get an overview of what is happening. Such inefficiency is reflected in lower labour productivity. Time has to be spent moving items from one part of the factory to another, for example. Some managers said that they employed people specifically for this purpose, and that they would be able to do without them if the buildings and workflows were more logically organized. Inefficiencies of layout also encourage poor machine productivity. Partly this is because additional, special machines have sometimes to be installed to move items around the factory. And in particular, an inefficient layout leads to a high level of work-in-progress as goods wait to be moved from machine to machine around the factory.

Although one of the immediate effects of an inefficient layout is to increase employment, in the long run this can be expected to sap a firm's competitiveness, by adding to costs, and eventually lead to lower growth and lower employment. An association between old factory buildings and above average job losses is confirmed by data on employment change in a thousand manufacturing establishments in the East Midlands (Fothergill, Kitson and Monk, 1985). This showed that between 1968 and 1982 the average rate of job loss was lowest among firms that occupied premises built wholly or mostly during the postwar period. The average job loss was largest among firms that occupied buildings of mixed age — precisely those sites that have been developed in a piecemeal fashion over the years, that so many firms now find unsatisfactory and inefficient.

The gradual process of addition and modification that occurs on many factory sites need not always lead to inefficiency. Much depends on the way it is done. This can be illustrated by two contrasting factories.

Blackwell Electronics, Nottinghamshire

This firm employed 250 people in the manufacture of electronic equipment for telecommunications, and carried out a full range of activities on-site, including woodworking (for cabinets), plating and electronic assembly. It also manufactured some components, such as transformers, and previously manufactured a range of other electrical goods. It had occupied the site for more than 50 years. The original building was a stone built, multistorey mill dating from 1833 and recently refurbished as offices. There were interwar buildings on a site across the road, and extensions dating from the 1940s and 1960s. The present layout and complex of buildings was, according to the manager, the result of *ad hoc*, short-term decisions. The resulting movement of materials and people between different parts of the complex on either side of the road was regarded as haphazard and inefficient.

P.L.C. Foods, Leicestershire

This large factory employed over 1,000 people, producing more than 10 per cent of all the biscuits consumed in the UK. The site dated from 1928 but the buildings were gradually being extended and redeveloped to a masterplan laid down in 1957. A number of extensions had been built, and when the final phase (underway·in 1985) is completed all the pre-war buildings will have disappeared. The resulting factory, comprising several linked units of varying ages, was regarded as well suited to the firm's products and production processes. There were no important problems with plant layout and workflows.

The differentiating factor between these two examples is the extent to which the development and extension of the factories has been carried out in accordance with a long-term plan. Having such a plan, and sticking to it, appears to avoid the inefficiencies that arise from *ad hoc* decisions. However, not all firms are able to take such a strategic view of the development of their site. P.L.C. Foods was able to do so partly because its product and production process are relatively unchanging, whereas Blackwell Electronics had changed its product a number of times. Also, the manufacture of biscuits requires a great deal of fixed process plant and a continuous flow of materials, and layout leaves little room for discretion. In a sense, P.L.C. Foods had little alternative but to adopt a strategic plan for its buildings.

Very large factories — those employing, say, over 1,000 workers — almost always comprise a range of buildings developed at different times for different purposes, but such layouts are often not as inefficient for this size of establishment as for smaller and medium sized factories. Very large factories often have several distinct product lines, each housed within a separate building on-site, so that in effect each building functions as a 'factory within a factory'. The need to move work-in-progress from building to building is minimized in such cases. We encountered this form of organization at a telecommunications factory employing 4,500 workers and at a factory producing breakfast cereals employing 1,400. In both cases, management described their ideal site as a series of free-standing units — in contrast to so many managers of smaller firms who preferred one large factory unit with materials coming in at one end and finished goods going out at the other.

The physical layout of a factory is thus a potentially important influence on its efficiency. But it should be stressed that many firms do operate successfully for many years in inefficient buildings. They may have other attributes which offset the inefficiencies: a good product, an adept management team, a highly skilled workforce. And if a firm in a rambling old building becomes unprofitable, loses markets and sheds jobs, this is not necessarily because of the building in which it operates. The point is simply that the efficiency of a firm's buildings, in terms of layout, is one factor contributing to the overall efficiency of the firm.

Whether a factory was purpose built for its present occupant does not appear to be a very good guide to its current suitability. One reason is that a firm will not move into second-hand or new speculatively built property unless it comes reasonably close to meeting the firm's particular needs, perhaps with some modifications prior to occupation. A further reason is that firms' requirements change through time, as has been explained: they may need more or less space, and they may need a different kind of space, or a different layout. When a purpose built factory is regarded as highly satisfactory by its occupant, this is usually because it has not been occupied for very long.

In two of the industries we looked at — hosiery and engineering — investment in new machinery is rarely, if ever, constrained by the design features of buildings. Whether new machines fit in, in a technical sense, does not appear to be a problem. Small adaptations are sometimes necessary — foundations for a heavy press or ventilation for computer controlled knitting machines, for instance — but that is all. A more serious problem, in multistorey factories, is manoeuvring new machines into upper storeys, but even this difficulty is surmountable with the help of a mobile crane.

Most of the electronics industry also finds no difficulty in accommodating new machinery in old buildings. The high and rising proportion of white-collar staff in this industry (associated, for example, with the changeover from electro-magnetic to electronic technology) usually requires an upgrading in the quality of space, to provide an office-like environment, but there appear to be few limits to what can be achieved by refurbishing even the oldest of buildings. However, segments of the electronics industry that require highly controlled and very clean environments (e.g. for the manufacture of microchips, or highly sensitive calibration) usually require investment in new machines to go hand in hand with substantial building work. Some of the factories we visited had chosen to build special units within existing, older buildings; others preferred to build an entirely new factory to meet their specialized requirements.

The food and drink industry displays a very different relationship between investment in machinery and buildings. Large quantities of process plant are typically required. When it is being installed, the buildings frequently need extensive modification to accommodate it physically. The opportunity is usually taken to raise the standard of hygiene in the factory at the same time, and this alone can require significant expenditure. The link between plant and buildings is not all one way either: sometimes the design of the plant itself is modified to fit the buildings, though this is not necessarily a major step since much process plant is anyway tailored to the requirements of individual customers.

To conclude the discussion about the nature of the problems created by mismatch it is worth describing three cases which illustrate how bad things can become. In each case, the firm is a small independent company with a good record of growth and apparently good market prospects. The fact that all three were having considerable difficulties with their buildings gives lie to the myth that it is just inefficient firms that end up in inefficient buildings.

Fancy Fabrics, Nottinghamshire

This company, which employed 110 people, occupied the largest part of a five storey mill built in 1887. Each floor was on two levels, with steps between, in two wings bordering a courtyard. The intention of the original design had been to move goods between floors using outside hoists, and there was only one lift — in one of the two wings, so physical handling of goods was required to the other. The firm had produced fashion knitwear until 1981, when it almost went bankrupt after years of decline. New management and a shift to knitted industrial fabrics saved the company. The firm saw plenty of potential for expanding its sales, and was increasing output and employment again after contracting into only part of the building to weather the 1981 crisis. In 1984 alone, production grew by 45–50 per cent. But the building remained spectacularly inefficient in the movement of materials. The problem was exacerbated because the new product is made in heavy rolls. A special hoist had been installed to lift these through the floors, and several workers were employed as 'humpers'. Numerous pillars constrained plant layout. The floor loadings were not good enough to put knitting machines anywhere but on the ground floor. The ceiling was too low in the knitting shop. The heating was expensive. Maintenance was an ongoing problem. Office space was tight, and the firm had to rent additional ground floor storage space nearby to take overspill. Perhaps the only things that could be said in favour of the building were that it had genuine character and that it was cheap to occupy because it was owned outright.

Northbrook Bodies, Leicestershire

This company employed 90 people making commercial vehicle bodies on a modern trading estate. It occupied three sites, one of which was used purely for parking lorries and the other two, about 400 yards apart, comprising four main buildings (two rented, two owned) all less than 20 years old. The main office was located on the smaller of these two sites. The company also occupied another rented property about a mile away. This complex arrangement had arisen as the firm expanded after moving to the estate in 1967. The present layout was grossly inefficient. Vehicles had to be moved too often, communications between different parts of the operation were poor, and the layout led to excessive reliance on the foremen since the senior management could not keep an eye on the whole site. The management costed these inefficiencies at more than £20,000 per year. In winter the movement of vehicles between buildings led to serious heat loss through the very large factory doors, and management had taken to keeping a company car handy just to get to and fro between the buildings. Management were acutely aware of these difficulties, and were seriously considering contracting into smaller premises from which they could operate more efficiently. The firm had an option to buy the second half of the buildings (currently used by another firm) on the smaller of its present sites, giving them 16,000 ft², in one unit, with sufficient parking space. The other sites would then be vacated. Profitability would be increased by raising efficiency and by concentrating on the firm's most profitable lines, but production and employment would be cut.

Maritime Technology, Northamptonshire

This company employed 135 in the design and production of navigation equipment. It had moved 8 years previously into a modern, speculatively built unit on a trading estate and had expanded to occupy four contiguous units in a terrace (albeit broken by an open space between units 3 and 4) with the walls knocked through. With continuing growth the company was experiencing a severe shortage of space and could have readily filled a 30 per cent addition to its production floorspace. Some production had to be subcontracted as a consequence (about 10 per cent of annual output) though the firm would have liked to keep more in-house. Because the buildings were rented the company had made only limited investment in them, principally involving temporary partitioning and the addition of mezzanine floors. Temporary structures had been added at the rear to provide a canteen, storage and maintenance facilities. Certain investments had even been abandoned: e.g. the restricted drainage and water supply capacity prevented the firm becoming self-sufficient in the production of circuit boards. Space constraints had produced a 'terrible' plant layout, with highly congested production and a criss-crossing of production flows.

The capacity to respond to mismatch

The problem of mismatch is constantly being generated throughout industry, creating difficulties and constraints for the firms involved. Some firms successfully adapt and respond to restore a balance between their property needs and the buildings they occupy. What is clear, however, is that some firms fail to do so, and the mismatch persists for prolonged periods. Why does this occur, and what determines a firm's capacity to respond?

It is useful to start this discussion with a caveat: property considerations are only one of the factors that firms take into account in reaching strategic decisions, and they are rarely the most important. Frequently, other considerations overrule questions of the size and design of buildings. For example, a major hosiery group we spoke to had implemented a programme of closures in which it retreated to its sites in Derbyshire, which comprise old, rather inefficient buildings. A modern, purpose built factory in a New Town had been closed. The reason, it was stated, was that there were greater difficulties with the workforce in the New Town.

It should also be stated at the outset that the disruption of relocating, extending on-site or significantly refurbishing existing buildings is not usually an important consideration. It is striking how much can often be achieved without a break in production. Entire factories can be re-roofed during the summer holidays, or over the Christmas or Easter break, or a second floor can be added while production continues below. For smaller firms a complete relocation can be achieved over a weekend, and for larger firms particular sections can be transferred one by one to a new site, in a planned way with minimum disruption. There is, of course, a financial cost to all this, e.g. payments to specialist industrial removal contractors, but this is generally not so large as to deter the whole venture. Among the industries we looked at, food and drink is the only one in which disruption is a significant consideration. The problem here is the large quantity of fixed plant. In practice, this means that a move to a new building is often associated with the installation of new plant; the old plant and equipment would not be transferred. The problem is accentuated by the perishable nature of some products, such as bread, which prevents the stockpiling of supplies to overcome the disruption that would be involved in relocating plant and machinery.

Several factors determine a firm's ability to respond to a mismatch. The most important is the physical surroundings in which it operates. If a firm operates on a densely developed site, hemmed in by other development, the option of extending the existing premises will not normally be available. A site does not have to be wholly covered by buildings for this situation to arise. The need for outdoor storage, circulation space and car parking limits the extent to which a site can be developed. Some local authorities, for example, particularly in congested areas, lay down strict guidelines on the number of parking spaces per unit of floorspace or per capita. Some industries, like commercial vehicle body building, also need considerable land for outdoor storage. The layout is important too: a building is less easily extended if it occupies the middle of a site, with relatively little space on each side, than if it is to one side, leaving a large clear area for expansion.

The crucial influence of room for expansion is confirmed by the data, mentioned earlier, on employment change in 1,000 individual factories (Fothergill, Kitson and Monk, 1985). This showed that, on average, between 1968 and 1982 employment grew only in those factories where the premises had been substantially extended. This in turn meant that, on average, employment growth occurred only where there had been room for on-site expansion. Indeed, the data revealed a continuous and predictable relationship between average employment change and the extent to which sites are built-up: the smaller the proportion of the site covered by buildings at the start of the period, the better the subsequent growth in employment.

A factor closely related to physical surroundings is the operation of planning controls. On the whole, firms did not indicate that these were a major obstruction. The refusal of planning permission had proved to be a serious problem for only two of the firms we spoke to.

One of these, a bakery in Derbyshire, had extended its building over the last 10 years and needed to extend further to cater for storage and packing. Space was available adjoining the factory and on a site 200 yards away but planning permission had been refused because the factory was in a residential area. The local authority preferred a complete relocation to a trading estate but the firm considered the costs and disruption prohibitive.

The other firm, an electronics company in Nottinghamshire, had moved to its present site with the intention of redeveloping the existing buildings to provide a modern unit with potential for easy expansion. It was prevented from doing so by the refusal of planning permission because access was via a residential area. Consequently it continued to operate in a string of buildings on this site and elsewhere in the locality. Many problems had resulted from this situation, notably additional costs from having to staff, maintain and run many small buildings over several sites. Ideally the firm wanted a single 250,000 ft² unit.

A more widespread planning constraint is the use of listed buildings that cannot be demolished or substantially modified. The firms we spoke to appeared to accept this as an unfortunate fact of life, about which they could do nothing, and planned their property decisions accordingly. One firm overcame the restriction by buying a strip of land along the side of the factory, wide enough for large vehicles, and completely rebuilt their packing and dispatch departments at the back of the factory while leaving the listed façade intact. The production required greater ceiling height, and this, too, could be accommodated behind the listed façade. But another firm occupied a corner site with all its façades listed, and further alterations at the back were impossible. It was therefore about to relocate, though the constraint of a listed building was only one of several factors leading to the move.

Once a decision to relocate has been taken, few firms find the availability of an alternative site or building a serious problem — at least not in the East Midlands, where we carried out the survey. This may reflect the high level of vacant industrial floorspace created by the recession at the start of the 1980s. The main shortage that came to our attention appeared to be for factories of 15,000 to 20,000 ft², enough for a firm with about 30 to 50 employees. Firms of this size appear hesitant to build their own factory, to their own specification, partly because they usually have no experience of doing so and partly because of the delays involved. However, few units of this size are built on a speculative basis. Also, at this size a firm's property requirements are sometimes fairly specific — an overhead crane may be needed for instance, or an unusual ratio between office and production space. They are thus less likely to find what they need in a standard off-the-peg development. And when looking to relocate, their field of search is often highly localized — within a couple of miles of the present site — in order that the majority of the workforce can move with them. The consequence is that firms looking for factories of this size tend to experience delays in obtaining what they want. In the meantime, the mismatch in their existing buildings is perpetuated.

The tenure of a factory building is a key determinant of a firm's response to a mismatch. Most of the firms we spoke to were medium sized and larger businesses and, typically, they owned their sites and premises. Decisions about investment in extensions or relocation therefore tended to revolve around the capital cost. For firms in rented property the considerations were different. In some ways the occupation of rented property makes it easier to overcome mismatches, while in others it creates more difficulties. Rented property is easier to move in and out of, as a firm's requirements change, because a lease need not be renewed and the firm has no capital tied up in the building. But rented property is less easily adapted to meet a firm's specific needs. The problem here is that firms are reluctant to invest in building work that will ultimately revert to the owner. The owners, too, are usually unwilling to allow this work because it may make the building too specialized and harm its subsequent marketability. The outcome, in many cases, is that firms adopt short-term solutions, such as the erection of portakabins, prior to relocating to a more suitable building.

If a firm owns its premises, a major difficulty it faces in relocating is getting an acceptable price for the old site and buildings. Often the factory will have been added to and modified over the years, in ways that were particular to that firm's needs, and many of the buildings may therefore be of no value to a new occupant. An old factory might thus fetch only a quarter or a fifth of the cost of a new factory of the same size, and only this much because of the residual value of the land on which it is built. Faced with the need to find such large sums for new premises, most firms opt for smaller incremental investment on their existing sites.

This is one of the main mechanisms through which firms get 'locked in' to unsuitable sites and buildings. If they need additional space, for example, they face a choice. Should they put more money into a site which they already know is unsuitable? Or should they take the plunge and move to an entirely new site? If they take the latter option and move, they will probably be abandoning at least some buildings that are modern, purpose built and efficient, even if the rest of the site is hopeless. The investment in these newer buildings will effectively be discarded, because the site as a whole will be difficult to let or sell. But an entirely new factory would be so expensive. So many firms end up investing a little where they are and muddle through. In doing so they reinforce the case for staying put because there is yet more relatively recent building on-site.

This problem mainly affects larger firms. Small firms are more likely to operate in rented premises, so if they move when the lease expires the disposal of the redundant buildings is not their responsibility. Also, where small firms own their premises the sites and buildings are neither so extensive nor so complex. Invariably, when a small owner occupier relocates the whole of the firm's operations are transferred to better premises, and the potential gains are thus proportionally greater than for a large firm that has to discard recent investment on its old site.

For all firms there is an important distinction between relocation to facilitate expansion and relocation to improve efficiency. If a firm moves in order to expand it spends money on land and buildings but gets a quick return in the form of extra output and profit; if it relocates simply to obtain a more efficient building it spends a lot but usually gets only a very long-term gain. Relocation to a more efficient building therefore tends to occur only when firms are expanding at the same time.

This was a tendency noted by NEDO (1978) in a survey of industrialists' investment in new buildings during the early and mid 1970s. They found that out of 299 firms that had invested in new buildings, 170 cited the need to meet additional demand as one of their reasons. The need to accommodate new machinery was another important motive, but only a third of the firms cited a desire to achieve a better production layout. However, what also emerged from the survey was that in the event more than two-thirds of the firms were able to improve their production layout as a result of their building investment. Three-quarters also noted an improvement in the working environment, and 40 per cent a reduction in maintenance costs. The net effect was that of the 299 firms, 204 said their productivity had increased, and 172 claimed that their profitability had improved.

These are impressive gains in efficiency, but the striking thing is how often they were unanticipated. This led NEDO to conclude 'that investment in industrial buildings by many firms is inadequate, in that they are unwilling to replace obsolescent buildings', and they went on to comment that 'many industrialists are insufficiently aware of the contribution which well-designed buildings can make to production efficiency and profitability because it is more difficult to measure than that of new machinery'.

In the NEDO survey, lack of finance was cited by more than a quarter of the firms that had not invested in new buildings. Finance for relocation or on-site expansion is, of course, essential if a mismatch is to be overcome. Firms' access to capital varies considerably, and not simply because of their profitability or prospects. As a general rule, factories that belong to a larger group (e.g. a multinational company) are in a stronger position than single plant firms because funds can be allocated by their parent company or by headquarters. They do not have to rely on internally generated finance or bank loans. For the smaller firm, the construction of a new factory can be a make-or-break move because of the scale of investment. It therefore proceeds very cautiously indeed, investing only if there is proof that its markets are set for long-term growth. In contrast, the larger firm's activities are more diverse, allowing it to take a greater risk when considering building a new factory.

Yet it would be wrong to view investment in new property as just a drain on capital. A modern, owner occupied building may, for example, be the principal asset against which a company secures its bank loans. The more valuable the premises, the bigger the potential loan to finance day-to-day activities. An electrical and electronic engineering firm, employing 200 people, stressed this point. Their modern spacious buildings were worth £800,000 and were appreciating all the time; the total value of their plant and equipment (an alternative security for a loan) was only just over £300,000. Furthermore, modern buildings have the advantage that they are more marketable than older ones, so that if a firm does hit severe difficulties and needs to contract, the modern buildings can be sold or rented out. We encountered firms that in the aftermath of the recession of the early 1980s had decided to dispose of units they had built in the 1960s and 1970s and retreat to their older, original buildings. This strategy for shedding space appears to be at least as popular as the one which in terms of long-run efficiency usually makes more sense, namely concentrating production in the newest buildings and disposing of the old.

Old inefficient buildings sometimes reinforce the lack of capital to finance relocation. The savings which old buildings offer in rent and rates may be more than offset by higher running costs. The cost of inefficiency arising from poor layout in an old building is potentially even greater. These financial difficulties are compounded if the old building has become too big for current needs, because many of the costs of occupation are overheads which do not vary with the scale of production. Costs per unit of output are thus higher, and profitability lower.

Managerial capability and discretion do, of course, play a part, so that firms do not all respond in the same way when faced with a given set of problems, constraints and opportunities. The interaction between managerial strategy and difficulties with premises is illustrated by the contrast between two firms we interviewed. Both these companies had been involved in the manufacture and repair of commercial vehicle bodies. By the late 1960s both faced the same problem: their existing premises were too congested and cramped to cope with the increasing size of vehicles. One of the firms opted to relocate to more suitable buildings and remain in this market; the other opted to stay put and to concentrate instead on the restoration of veteran and vintage cars, an activity compatible with their existing building. The decisions were a reflection of managerial preference and discretion, and in particular one of the managers' pre-existing interest in old motor vehicles.

Managerial competence is reflected not just in firms' response to mismatch but in the perception of the problem itself. It is apparent that some are unaware of the extent to which the efficiency of their buildings falls below the best that is available in their industry. One hosiery company we spoke to, for example, recycled the heat from its knitting machines to the rest of its factory, a practice which is probably never contemplated by many more traditional managers. We were shown shopfloor layouts that were considered satisfactory, yet appeared chaotic and worse than layouts that had been condemned by other firms. It is difficult to assess managerial competence, but in general the most dynamic managers appear to be those who have the most complaints about their buildings. They are also those most likely to be tackling the problems.

Finally, to illustrate the varied responses to difficulties with sites and premises, and the factors which condition those responses, it is worth looking at five examples. The first two are especially interesting because the firms faced almost identical problems.

Lion Breweries, Leicestershire

This is a privately owned brewing company, employing 150 at a brand new surburban site. Previously they operated at two small sites, but the sustained growth in the market for 'real ale' meant that by the late 1970s they had nothing like the capacity they required. They opted to develop a new 12 acre site, where they constructed 100,000 ft² of purpose designed accommodation and installed the most modern computerized plant. A development of this scale could not have been accommodated at their old sites, which were physically congested. The development was financed by a £10m bank loan; they were able to raise this money because as owners of a chain of pubs they could offer security against the loan. The old brewery, now sold off, continues to produce beer for them under licence.

County Ales, Leicestershire

This is also a privately owned brewery, employing 110, that has been transformed by the boom in real ale. They had room for expansion on-site, and being located in a village they were able to acquire farmland at the rear. They also had a strong preference to stay put because their 'rural' image is important to their marketing strategy. Unlike Lion Breweries, County Ales' growth has therefore been contained on-site. It involved the reconstruction of older buildings (though their external appearance remains more or less unchanged) and the construction of new units. This major expansion was financed by selling off their tied houses; they now rely predominantly on sales via supermarkets and retail chains. Thus for County Ales, as for Lion Breweries, the unusual position of brewers as property companies was again crucial to financing such a substantial investment in new plant and buildings.

St Andrew, Leicestershire

This is an independent hosiery and knitwear company with six factories and more than 1,000 employees. The headquarters site employs 300 and has been occupied for more than 50 years. It comprises a range of buildings, including some very old, listed buildings, developed in a piecemeal way adjacent to a canal. The management viewed this site as their least efficient, with all the classic problems of workflow and materials handling. However, their cumulative investment on the site (including a recent new dyehouse) had created a barrier to relocation to more suitable premises. The cost of acquiring new premises (or even suitable second-hand premises, which were available in the town) was too great in relation to the sum they would get for the old buildings and site. So further incremental investment went on there. Their response to the inherent unsuitability of the buildings had been to transfer production to the other factories and to concentrate warehousing, administration and some specialist activities on this site.

Tudor & Stuart, Leicestershire

This is a dynamic and profitable firm producing tights, stockings and socks. It employs 250 at its main factory and operates two other factories nearby. Over the years the business has expanded — hence the opening of additional branches — and

the firm had numerous complaints about the unsuitability of its main factory, especially with regard to materials handling and warehousing. The buildings were leased,
which deterred the firm from making modifications that would lead to an increase in
rent on renewal, and prevented them from utilizing the modest room for expansion at
the rear of the building. The outcome was that they decided to build a 50,000 ft²
factory on a separate site nearby, to which production from the main factory and one
of the other two would be transferred. Unlike many hosiery companies, they were
able to afford such a bold move because they had found a profitable market niche.
This financed their computerized knitting machines, and profits from these were in
turn financing the new building.

J. Brown & Sons, Leicester

This is a long-established, family owned knitwear firm, employing 120, in a multistorey, inner city mill that it built in 1914 and extended during the interwar period.
The firm's market had contracted, and it had not diversified into new products. The
premises were now much too big, and not especially efficient because of the multistorey layout. Smaller, single storey premises would have been more appropriate. The
firm had opted to stay put and rent out about a quarter of the building, though a
further quarter remained vacant. The decision reflected a number of pressures: the
sale of the present building and site would not raise enough finance for a new,
purpose built factory; production was in any case not very profitable; and the firm
was reluctant to abandon its traditional base since the factory had been developed by,
and indeed was owned by, the managing director's own family. The result was that
the mismatch between the firm's building and its present-day needs was perpetuated.

Some conclusions

Judging by our findings, probably at least half of British manufacturing
industry has few difficulties with its factory buildings. Or rather, when it does
encounter difficulties it is capable of solving the problems quite adequately
without special help. For another chunk of manufacturing industry the
buildings are less than ideal but not so serious a problem as to warrant public
concern. But that still leaves a great many firms and a large proportion of the
manufacturing sector for whom difficulties with sites and buildings pose, to
varying degrees, an obstacle to growth and efficiency. For these firms,
suffering from a mismatch between their property needs and the sites and
buildings they occupy, there is abundant evidence that market adjustments
in the supply and use of factory space do not function sufficiently well, if at
all.

When property begins to impinge on growth and efficiency it effectively
becomes one of the factors that allocate a given amount of business among
competing firms. A firm may secure an order not because it is the most
efficient or because its product is the best, but simply because its competitors
do not have the physical capacity within their sites and buildings to handle

that order. This is surely not a sensible way in which to allocate production. Furthermore, where antiquated and inappropriate buildings undermine efficiency and pose constraints that cannot easily be overcome, the beneficiaries are not necessarily going to be competing UK companies. In virtually all segments of manufacturing, imported goods now take a large slice of the market, so that a potential market share lost by a UK firm is just as likely to go to a producer abroad. If mismatches between firms' property needs and their buildings impede growth and efficiency, they therefore help undermine the performance of the UK economy.

For this reason, there is a good case for redefining the way that firms' property needs are understood. At the present time, they remain largely in the private domain: with a few exceptions, it is left to firms themselves to find the buildings they need, to finance them, to organize a move if necessary, and to cope with the consequences of an emerging mismatch. Not all firms do this very well, especially in a property market where much of the factory stock is very old. What we would argue, from the evidence we have presented, is that difficulties with Britain's industrial buildings are sufficiently serious and widespread to warrant bringing issues of industrial property supply firmly into the domain of public policy. They are too important to be left to chance and the market.

In the final chapter we set out what we see as the proper function of central and local government in relation to the industrial property market, and put forward specific policies. Before that, however, it is useful to explore (in chapter 5) some of the locational consequences of the relationships between property, growth and efficiency, and (in chapters 6 and 7) the extent and consequences of existing public sector involvement.

5   Property's role in location

So far we have identified a number of important relationships between industrial property and economic growth. For instance, chapter 2 showed how national trends in output and productivity have a major impact on the demand for factory space and the intensity with which it is used. Chapter 4 showed how the sites and buildings that manufacturing firms occupy can have a significant influence on their growth and efficiency.

However, we have not yet looked at how these relationships are differentiated across space. Is the decline in employment density occurring equally in all areas? Is the fall in the stock of industrial floorspace evenly spread? Do the inefficiencies associated with older buildings impede firms in some areas more than others? Are barriers to physical expansion widespread or concentrated in just a few places? And what is the net effect on the location of jobs?

This chapter takes up the locational issues. The first part explores theoretically the possible links between industrial property and the location of jobs. Two dimensions of employment change in Britain are then examined — the variation between regions and that between urban and rural areas — and the corresponding trends in floorspace are investigated. The second half of the chapter looks in detail at the influence of land supply on industrial location.

The role of property in the location of manufacturing

Land and buildings are a necessary input to the production process though, as the introductory chapter explained, theories of industrial growth and location often ignore this fundamental point. Because property is an essential input, a broad correspondence between the location of manufacturing jobs and manufacturing floorspace can be expected. At the very minimum, there can be no jobs in an area if there is no floorspace. The interesting issue is the extent to which locational shifts in jobs and floorspace are tied to each other, and the direction of the causality. Do jobs follow factory floorspace; or does floorspace follow jobs? How much is the pattern of industrial location determined by the preferences of manufacturing firms and how much by the supply of suitable land and buildings?

Neo-classical economics postulates a complex, fluid relationship between the location of floorspace and jobs in which price adjustments act as the mediating mechanism, bringing the supply of and demand for floorspace into balance. If there is a 'shortage' of factory space in an area, rents will be bid up. As rents rise, the provision of factory space becomes more profitable, so the market responds by constructing new space or by changing space from other less profitable uses. Higher rents also force some firms to move away or to reduce the scale of their activity. Demand and supply thus move back into balance in the area. A shortage of factory space, in the sense of an unsatisfied demand at a given market price, only arises as a strictly transient phenomenon as the market moves from one equilibrium to another.

This is textbook stuff, and a poor approximation of the real world. Price adjustments do occur in the property market, but the neo-classical model does not get us very far in understanding the relationship between floorspace and the location of jobs.

One reason is the rigidity in patterns of industrial location — the inertia which firms so often display. Sometimes the obstacle to relocating to more suitable premises is the potential disruption to production, or fear of loss of skilled and reliable workers in the case of longer distance moves. As we saw in the last chapter, often the problem is financial: the low market value of large, specialized, second-hand buildings and the prohibitive cost of new, more suitable alternatives. Moreover, buildings are fixed overheads rather than a variable factor of production, so that marginal adjustments to the amount of space a firm uses are often impossible. The result is that firms remain in buildings and locations that would not have been chosen in the light of their current requirements and contemporary market signals.

Another reason is that the market rarely operates as neo-classical theory suggests. In theory, if urban land is worth more in industrial use than in other uses market forces should ensure a change in favour of industry. In practice, many urban land uses — schools, roads, parks, hospitals and churches, for example — are not allocated by market forces and often cannot be bought out at any price. Private housing might be more easily purchased by firms to make way for their expansion, but the cost and difficulty of acquiring numerous small plots of land from individual vendors would almost always be prohibitive. Added to this, in Britain there is a highly sophisticated system of planning controls so that even if land can be acquired by industry there is no guarantee that permission for development will be forthcoming. Indeed, it might be more accurate to say that in Britain land uses are allocated by administrative mechanisms rather than the market; the availability of land rather than its price is the important concept.

At one extreme it is possible to postulate a city where none of the traditional neo-classical adjustment mechanisms operate — a city where there is a fixed quantity of land and property for industry (e.g. because of green belts, planning controls and the scarcity of undeveloped land) and where each firm's space requirements are dictated by the prevalent technology in its industry. In these circumstances what would be the relationship between the location of floorspace and the location of jobs?

One consequence would be that manufacturing employment in the city would fall through time. We saw in chapter 2 that as labour productivity increases with the rising capital intensity of manufacturing production, the number of workers per unit of factory floorspace — the employment density — is falling. Where the supply of industrial floorspace is fixed, the reduction in employment density would thus lead to a loss of jobs.

Another consequence, if there were sufficient pressure on the stock of floorspace, would be that firms' decisions would interact because of the competition for space. The expansion of one firm into bigger premises, for example, would displace the potential growth of another, with little net effect on the city's employment. A closure might release buildings that would then accommodate the expansion of an existing firm, again with little net effect on employment. Similarly, an entirely new firm might occupy buildings that would otherwise have been used by an existing firm.

The example may be extreme, but it illustrates the point that where the supply of premises is fixed the level of employment is best understood by reference to the stock of industrial floorspace. This stock, together with the prevailing employment density, sets a ceiling for manufacturing employment. Employment may fall below the ceiling in a recession because of under-utilization of capacity, but it cannot rise any higher. The example also illustrates the point that where there are significant constraints on the supply of premises it is less essential to understand the behaviour and preferences of individual firms. Individual preferences will determine which firms remain in a city where land and premises are scarce and which move elsewhere — the fewer the ties with the city, the greater the likelihood that a firm will move — but the supply of land and buildings, not firms' preferences, ultimately sets the ceiling for the city's industrial employment.

At the other extreme we can postulate a location where the supply of land and property for industry is highly 'elastic' — where industry can obtain additional space quickly, easily and without bidding up property rents and values to any significant extent. This might arise where there are no important physical constraints on the quantity of land that can be made available, or where the supply adjusts rapidly in response to marginal changes in price. In these circumstances the relationship between the location of floorspace and the location of jobs would be quite different. The supply of floorspace would pose no important constraint, so that firms would locate or expand in the places which best suited them. An area where manufacturing profits were above average, for example, might expect to experience above average growth in manufacturing production, and probably in employment, too. The focus in understanding locational patterns would need to be on the factors that made areas more or less attractive to firms, not on the capacity of areas physically to accommodate manufacturing activity.

The actual situation in late-twentieth-century Britain falls between these extremes. The supply of land and property for industry varies markedly from place to place, and market adjustment mechanisms operate in only a partial way. This can be expected to influence the location of jobs. So too can institutional factors, such as the availability of private finance and the involvement of the public sector, in so far as they discriminate against some locations in favour of others.

Regional growth and decline

Let us look first at the relationship between floorspace and employment at the regional level.

Table 5.1 shows the change in manufacturing employment in each region between 1967 and 1985. There is no special significance in the use of 1967 as a starting date, except that it is the earliest year for which comparable floorspace statistics can be obtained. The dominant feature of the table is the loss of jobs in all but one region, reflecting the loss of over a third of all manufacturing jobs in the country as a whole. Within this context the experience of regions varied greatly: in East Anglia the number of jobs increased very slightly, whereas in the North West there was a fall of more than half a million, or over 40 per cent.

The regional pattern of change was complex. The three regions that lost

	Employment (000s)		% change
	1967	1985	
East Anglia	174	176	+1.1
South West	423	347	−18.0
East Midlands	621	479	−22.9
South East	2,316	1,519	−34.4
Wales	311	202	−35.0
North	450	288	−36.0
Yorkshire and Humberside	813	502	−38.3
Scotland	691	422	−38.9
West Midlands	1,162	682	−41.3
North West	1,216	693	−43.0
GREAT BRITAIN	8,176	5,310	−35.1

Table 5.1   *Manufacturing employment by region, 1967–85*

Source: Department of Employment

jobs much more slowly than average (East Anglia, South West, and East Midlands) all belong to the more prosperous southern half of Britain, but in Wales and the Northern region the loss was close to the national average, and the South East fared little better. Partly this complexity arises because the period from 1967 to 1985 is really an amalgam of two different periods: the years up to the mid 1970s, when regional policy was moderately success-ful in raising manufacturing employment in the peripheral assisted regions and in restraining potential growth in the South East (Moore, Rhodes and Tyler, 1986); and the years since the mid 1970s when regional policy has been less effective and the North–South disparity has been more pro-nounced. The complexity in the regional pattern also reflects the urban–rural contrast in employment change, discussed later. The three regions at the top of the 'growth league' all lack a large declining conurbation; the regions at the bottom all include one.

The comparable changes in industrial floorspace are shown in Table 5.2, excepting Scotland for which data are not available. There are important differences between the changes in floorspace and those in employment. The most noticeable is that in most regions a decline in manufacturing employment has gone hand in hand with an increase in industrial floorspace. Only three regions — the South East, Yorkshire and Humberside and the North West — actually experienced a reduction in industrial floorspace over this period, and then only a small one. While at first sight this disparity might seem odd it is readily understood by reference to the large reduction in

| | *millions m²* | | *% change* |
	1967	1985	
Wales	6.8	10.0	+47.1
East Anglia	5.8	8.3	+43.1
South West	11.1	15.3	+37.8
North	10.9	14.3	+31.2
East Midlands	19.1	23.4	+22.5
West Midlands	34.0	36.9	+8.5
South East	53.2	52.7	−0.9
Yorkshire and Humberside	31.4	28.4	−9.6
North West	48.0	42.9	−10.6
ENGLAND AND WALES	220.1	232.2	+5.5

Table 5.2   *Industrial floorspace by region, England and Wales, 1967–85*

Sources: Commercial and Industrial Floorspace Statistics
      Statistics for Town and Country Planning

employment density, discussed in chapter 2, which means that fewer workers are now employed per unit of floorspace.

The other important difference between trends in floorspace and employment is the ordering of the regions. Although there are broad similarities, the increase in floorspace in Wales and the North, for example, has been greater than might be expected given their decline in employment. In the South East, the growth in floorspace has lagged behind what might be expected on the basis of employment change. Indeed, at the regional scale the differences between trends in floorspace and employment are sufficient to illustrate that there is not a rigid link between the two. Real economic processes and purely definitional points both have something to do with this.

The first reason for the differences in trends is the variation in regional industrial structure. The large decline in employment density has undoubtedly proceeded at different rates in different industries. Because these industries are far from evenly spread across the regions, the average employment per unit of floorspace will not have declined at the same rate in all regions.

The second reason is the impact of the recession at the start of the 1980s. This was sufficiently severe to have a major effect on manufacturing employment in all regions, but its impact was greatest in the northern and western half of Britain. By 1985 — the end of the period we are looking at here — the stock of industrial floorspace in the regions had not fully adjusted in response to this massive shock to their economies so that there were still large regional differences in the amount of vacant floorspace.

Third, the floorspace and employment statistics are not strictly comparable. In particular, the floorspace statistics exclude industries like steel, heavy chemicals and shipyards, whose floorspace is difficult to measure. These industries form an important component of employment change in some regions but are negligible employers in others, and consequently generate a contrast between regional floorspace and employment trends. The Northern region and Wales are the best examples: the very large loss of jobs in their heavy industries, especially steel, is not reflected in the floorspace figures. In these two regions, the statistical disparity between overall trends in floorspace and employment is therefore quite misleading.

The urban–rural contrast

Cutting across the variation in manufacturing trends between regions is a second dimension of spatial variation. This is the contrast between cities, towns and rural areas. Throughout most of the postwar period there has been a tendency for cities to lose manufacturing jobs more quickly than the country as a whole. Small towns and rural areas have lost manufacturing jobs more slowly, and in many instances have actually experienced an increase.

This urban–rural contrast is well documented (see, for example, Keeble, 1980; Fothergill and Gudgin, 1982; Fothergill, Kitson and Monk, 1985). It has occurred in every region and if anything has been a more powerful influence on the geography of employment change than the broader shifts in employment between whole regions.

Table 5.3 shows the change in manufacturing employment by type of area between 1967 and 1981. Again, 1967 is used so that the data can be compared with figures on floorspace change, and 1981 is (at the time of writing) the latest date for which statistics are available for employment in local areas. Two features of the table should be noted. The first is the scale of the urban–rural contrast. London, at one end of the urban hierarchy, lost almost half its manufacturing employment during this period. The other conurbations lost 40 per cent of their manufacturing jobs. In contrast and despite the large contraction in employment nationally, manufacturing employment rose a little in rural areas. The second point to note from the table is the consistency of the urban–rural contrast. Across the whole urban hierarchy, manufacturing employment change has been related to settlement size. As a general rule, the bigger the settlement the greater the decline.

Prior to the recession at the start of the 1980s, small towns experienced

| | Employment (000s) | | % change |
	1967	1981	
London	1,223	650	−46.9
Conurbations	2,167	1,295	−40.3
Free-standing cities	1,353	950	−29.8
Large towns	961	756	−21.3
Small towns	1,863	1,609	−13.6
Rural areas	609	655	+7.6
GREAT BRITAIN	8,176	5,916	−27.6

Table 5.3 *Manufacturing employment by type of area, 1967–81*

Notes:

Conurbations = Manchester, Merseyside, Clydeside, West Yorkshire, Tyneside, West Midlands

Free-standing cities = other cities with more than 250,000 people

Large towns = towns or cities with 100,000–250,000 people

Small towns = districts including at least one town with 35,000–100,000 people, plus coalfield areas

Rural areas = districts in which all settlements have fewer than 35,000 people

Source: Department of Employment

steady growth in manufacturing employment and the growth in rural areas was much faster. But despite the recession, by the 1980s the location of manufacturing jobs differed markedly from that in the 1960s. In just a couple of decades, Britain's cities lost much of their pre-eminence as industrial centres. By 1981, for example, the number of manufacturing jobs in rural areas had overtaken the number in London; only 15 years earlier there had been two manufacturing jobs in London for every one in rural areas.

This striking trend in the location of employment is matched by trends in the location of floorspace, shown in Table 5.4. Between 1967 and 1985 the stock of factory space fell by more than 20 per cent in London and 10 per cent in the conurbations. At the same time it rose by 30 per cent in small towns and 50 per cent in rural areas. As with employment, the urban–rural contrast was remarkably consistent: the smaller the settlement, the faster the growth in the stock of factory space. Indeed, the growth in small towns and rural areas was so great that it is questionable whether similar proportional increases could ever have been accommodated in Britain's largest cities.

| | millions m² | | % change |
	1967	1985	
London	26.7	20.5	−23.2
Conurbation	65.8	58.0	−11.9
Free-standing cities	37.2	38.8	+4.3
Large towns	29.7	32.8	+10.4
Small towns	44.3	57.0	+28.7
Rural areas	16.5	25.1	+52.1
ENGLAND AND WALES	220.1	232.2	+5.5

Table 5.4 *Industrial floorspace by type of area, England and Wales, 1967–85*

Sources: Commercial and Industrial Floorspace Statistics
Statistics for Town and Country Planning

As at the regional scale, in urban Britain the stock of floorspace has not fallen anything like as steeply as the number of jobs, and in rural areas the percentage increase in floorspace has been greater than the increase in employment. The difference again reflects the decline in employment density.

The impact of the decline in employment density can be examined more closely with the help of a simple calculation. Table 5.5 divides the change in manufacturing employment in each type of area into two components: the loss of jobs associated with the fall in density, and the change in employment associated with changes in the stock of floorspace. Together, these components add up to the net change in employment in each area. To undertake this calculation it has been assumed that additions to the stock of floorspace are occupied at a density 25 per cent higher than the average for the stock as a whole. This assumption is derived from data on 163 new factories built on English Estates land between 1970 and 1976 (Fothergill, Kitson and Monk, 1985, p. 20), and probably reflects the more efficient use made of new buildings. The loss of jobs associated with the decline in employment density has been calculated as a residual (i.e. net change in employment less the jobs associated with the change in the stock of floorspace).

| | Jobs associated with: | | |
	Change in stock of floorspace	Reduction in employment density	NET CHANGE IN MANUFACTURING EMPLOYMENT
London	−16	−31	−47
Conurbations	−2	−37	−39
Free-standing cities	+8	−38	−30
Large towns	+14	−35	−21
Small towns	+22	−36	−14
Rural areas	+45	−33	+12
ENGLAND AND WALES	+8	−36	−28

Table 5.5 *Floorspace and employment trends by type of area, England and Wales, 1967–81 (as % of 1967 manufacturing employment)*

Source: Authors' estimates

The results of this exercise, for 1967–81, show that the large reduction in employment density has affected all types of area to roughly the same extent: the loss of jobs due to the fall in employment density was between 30 and 40 per cent in both urban and rural Britain. The important factor differentiating areas is the change in the stock of floorspace. At the extremes, it is estimated that the loss of industrial floorspace in London was associated with a 16 per cent reduction in manufacturing employment, while the increase in rural areas was associated with a 45 per cent gain in employment.

This analysis can be taken a step further. Table 5.6 looks at the components making up the change in the stock of floorspace. It compares cities with towns and rural areas, for England between 1974 and 1985. It shows, first, that the urban–rural contrast in floorspace trends is almost entirely the result of additions to the stock. During this period, demolitions and other losses together accounted for almost the same proportion of the stock in cities as in towns and rural areas. In contrast, additions accounted for a 20 per cent gain in cities, but a 36 per cent gain in towns and rural areas.

	Cities*	Towns and rural areas
STOCK IN 1974 (millions m²)	129.2	97.8
	as % of stock	
New units	+6.5	+13.6
Extensions	+8.1	+15.6
Change of use	+5.0	+6.4
ALL ADDITIONS	+19.6	+35.6
Complete demolitions	−6.9	−4.8
Other	−21.1	−22.3
ALL REDUCTIONS	−28.0	−27.1
NET CHANGE	−8.4	+8.5

Table 5.6   *Components of change in industrial floorspace by type of area, England, 1974–85*

*London, conurbations, free-standing cities

Source: Commercial and Industrial Floorspace Statistics

Second, the urban–rural contrast in additions to the stock is largely the result of the location of new units and extensions to existing buildings. Changes of use differentiate urban and rural areas to a much smaller extent. Very roughly, the rate of addition through new units and extensions is twice as high in towns and rural areas as in cities. At the extremes of the urban hierarchy this disparity is even larger. In rural areas the rate of addition through extensions was four times higher than in London, and the rate of addition through new units three times higher.

The picture for urban and rural areas is thus fairly straightforward. The loss of jobs associated with the reduction in employment density does not differentiate urban from rural areas to any significant extent; the change in the stock of floorspace is the main factor. This in turn mostly reflects the location of new units and extensions to existing factories. These are important conclusions because they mean that in order to explain the urban–rural shift in manufacturing employment it is necessary to understand why new units and extensions are more likely to be located in towns and rural areas than in cities. Let us consider extensions first.

On-site expansion

Once a firm has become established at a particular site there can be powerful reasons for remaining there. Some of the reasons were discussed in the last chapter: e.g. the difficulty of disposing of old factory buildings and financing new ones, the technical difficulty of splitting production between sites, and sometimes the potential disruption of a move. Firms usually relocate or open an additional factory only when there are irresistible reasons for doing so. The locational inertia of larger firms is particularly marked: their property requirements are often specialized, in design and size, and not adequately met by the sorts of new and second-hand buildings coming onto the market. Consequently, many firms prefer on-site expansion as a way of accommodating growth.

Whether or not on-site expansion actually occurs depends principally on three influences. The first is the performance of the firm. Whatever the physical opportunities for expansion, a firm will not extend its premises unless its competitive performance — in particular, the growth of its output — is sufficient to justify expansion. The second factor is the corporate strategy of the company. In multiplant organizations decisions about expansion at one factory are unlikely to be taken in isolation from what is happening at the firm's other factories. We saw in chapter 4, for example, how the transfer of functions between plants can often be the stimulus for new investment on-site, and also how some multiplant companies prefer to maintain several medium sized factories rather than one very large one. Third, whether on-site expansion occurs depends on firms' physical surroundings. This determines the locational options that they face. Put simply, if there is no room for adding to existing premises an extension cannot go ahead.

Several aspects of the physical context are potentially important: the age and design of the existing buildings, including whether production is on more than one floor; the room for expansion within the site; the availability of immediately adjacent land; and the tenure of the buildings. Evidence has been presented on how each of these affects a factory's growth and efficiency. From a locational point of view they are important because the physical context is likely to vary from area to area, and thus influence the extent of on-site expansion occurring in different parts of the country.

But just how much do factory sites and premises vary from area to area? The difficulty here is that there are no comprehensive data other than on quantities of floorspace. To get round this problem we have combined the results of two surveys for specific areas.

The first is a survey of 2,447 factories in the East Midlands, carried out in 1982 (Fothergill, Kitson and Monk, 1985). This covered all manufacturing establishments in the region with 25 or more employees, excluding certain industries (e.g. steelworks, cement works) which use unusual and highly specialized buildings and structures. The survey was carried out by a postal questionnaire which obtained a response rate of 79 per cent, and the non-respondents were surveyed by site visits, allowing information on items such as the age of buildings and site coverage to be obtained for all the firms in the survey.

The second survey, carried out in 1979, covered all industrial premises in the inner area of Birmingham — roughly 80 per cent of the industrial buildings in the city (JURUE, 1980). The information was obtained by visiting each factory site. The original data related to individual buildings rather than whole factories, which often include several buildings on one site, so to be comparable with the East Midlands we converted it from a dataset on buildings to one on whole factories. Also to maintain comparability, non-manufacturing firms and vacant premises were excluded, as were factories of less than 10,000 ft^2 (corresponding on average to those with fewer than 25 employees). The remaining data cover 1,292 establishments.

Combining the two surveys gives information on a total of 3,739 manufacturing establishments. This is the largest amount of information that has so far been available on the quality of Britain's industrial building stock. It includes factories in the inner area of a conurbation, in medium sized cities like Derby, Nottingham and Leicester in the East Midlands, and in small towns and rural areas. The extent to which the survey areas are typical of similar areas elsewhere in the country is difficult to assess, but it should be noted that they contain a diverse range of industries and that industrial development in the Midlands has neither been as actively promoted as in the assisted areas nor as tightly squeezed by planning controls as in the South East.

Table 5.7 presents statistics on the industrial building stock in the survey areas. The first part deals with the age of buildings and reveals a marked urban–rural continuum. Almost two-thirds of the floorspace in Birmingham's inner city was built before 1945, and nearly 30 per cent before 1919. Conversely, in rural areas in the East Midlands over two-thirds of the stock of industrial floorspace is postwar. The cities and towns of the East Midlands have an industrial building stock which falls between these extremes.

The second part of the table shows that a substantially higher proportion of manufacturing jobs in cities, and the inner city in particular, is in factories with production on more than one floor. Over 80 per cent of the manufacturing

	Birmingham, 1979 inner city	East Midlands, 1982		
		cities	towns	rural areas
Age of floorspace (%)				
Pre 1919	29	21	17	13
1919–45	34	27	20	18
Post 1945	37	52	63	69
Factories with production on more than one floor (% of jobs)	82	52	33	27
Factories with less than half the site covered by buildings (% of jobs)	12	28	26	41
Factories with vacant land adjacent to site (% of jobs)	14	44	50	57
% of jobs in owner occupied factories	n.a.	84	85	83

Table 5.7   *The industrial building stock by type of area*

Sources: JURUE (1980); Fothergill, Kitson & Monk (1985).

jobs in the inner area of the Birmingham conurbation are in multistorey premises, compared with just over a quarter in the rural East Midlands.

The third and fourth parts concern room for expansion. The proportion of jobs in factories where less than half the site is covered by buildings — where on-site expansion will normally be practicable — is lower in cities than elsewhere. An alternative to the extension of premises within an existing site is the acquisition of adjacent land to accommodate expansion. Many firms on the fringes of built-up areas expand onto adjacent agricultural land (which we class as 'vacant') and within urban areas land next to existing factories can become vacant or available from time to time, allowing physical expansion. However, firms in cities again appear to be at a disadvantage: only 14 per cent of the manufacturing jobs in inner Birmingham are in factories with vacant adjacent land, compared with 57 per cent in the rural East Midlands.

Urban industrial sites may be more densely developed because of the high costs of urban land, which encourages firms in cities to restrict the amount they acquire initially and to dispose of parts of their sites for which they have no immediate use. In addition, because industrial sites in cities are older on average (as indicated by the age of premises) they are more likely to have been filled up to capacity by extensions over the years. In cities, too, the land adjacent to factories is more likely to be in existing urban uses, rather than undeveloped or agricultural. The net effect is that factories in cities have less room for on-site expansion than their counterparts in rural areas.

The final part of Table 5.7 concerns the tenure of industrial buildings. As chapter 4 explained, this is a potentially important influence on growth because firms in rented premises are less likely than owner occupiers to be able to extend or otherwise adapt and improve their premises to meet changing needs. However, in contrast to other indicators of the building stock, tenure shows no important variation between urban and rural areas, the majority of jobs in all types of area being in owner occupied factories.

Three characteristics of the industrial building stock — age, layout and room for expansion — thus reveal potential handicaps to growth and efficiency in Britain's cities. Other things being equal, we would expect these characteristics to lead to an urban–rural contrast in the rate of on-site expansion. Because the physical context is less favourable in cities, firms there will be less likely to extend their premises than similar firms in small towns and rural areas.

How much of the urban–rural contrast in the growth of factories can be accounted for in this way? One approach to this question is by using multiple regression analysis. For those unfamiliar with this technique, it should be explained that multiple regression generates an equation measuring the relationship between a number of independent variables (in this case site coverage, age of buildings, etc.) and a dependent variable which needs explaining (the expansion or contraction of individual manufacturing establishments). The strength and direction of the relationships can be measured and it is possible to assess whether the independent variables are statistically significant — in other words whether they are measuring real relationships in the data rather than just random variation. In an application of this sort the important results to look for are coefficients on the independent variables that are significant, have the expected sign, and are reasonably stable.

The analysis has been carried out on a subset of the East Midlands data, comprising 1,000 factories that were open in 1968 and still operating at the same site in 1982. These factories account for nearly 60 per cent of the region's manufacturing jobs. By combining data on employment and premises, it is possible to examine how the sites and buildings occupied by firms affected the expansion or contraction of their employment. The data are described in full elsewhere (Fothergill, Kitson and Monk, 1985) and the main results are presented in Figure 5.1.

Equation 1 confirms that the differences in the growth of manufacturing establishments between cities on the one hand and towns and rural areas on the other are statistically significant — that they are not the arbitrary outcome of random variation between factories. The statistical significance of the variables is indicated by the 'standard errors'. As a rule of thumb, the standard error should be less than half the value of the coefficient above in order for that variable to be significant.

(1) $E = 11.0 + 15.1 D_1 + 22.2 D_2$
      (5.0)   (7.4)   (10.8)
       **   **   **

(2) $E = 241.5 - 18.1 \log S - 0.2 A - 24.8 \log F + 0.6 I$
      (23.9)   (4.2)   (0.07)   (2.9)   (0.2)
       ***   ***   ***   ***   ***

(3) $E = 231.5 - 17.0 \log S - 0.2 A - 24.8 \log F + 0.7 I + 9.7 D_1 + 11.5 D_2$
      (23.9)   (4.2)   (0.07)   (2.9)   (0.2)   (7.1)   (10.3)
       ***   ***   ***   ***   ***

standard errors in parentheses
** = significant at 95–99 per cent
*** = significant at more than 99 per cent

E = % change in employment, 1968–82
S = % of site covered by buildings in 1968
A = % of buildings in 1968 which had been built before 1945
F = employment in 1968
I = % change in GB employment, 1968–82, in the firm's industry
D_1 = towns (dummy)
D_2 = rural areas (dummy)

Figure 5.1   *Multiple regression analysis of establishment growth*

Equation 2 measures the relationships between employment change and firms' physical context. A number of points should be noted. First, the size of the establishment and the national growth of its industry are included in addition to site and buildings variables because these are important influences on employment change in individual factories. Second, whether a factory is single or multistorey is not included in the equation because this variable was not statistically significant. In other words, in this sample of factories a multistorey layout does not appear to exert an independent influence on growth. Third, the variable included in the equation are all statistically significant. Fourth, the relationships between employment change and size and between employment change and site coverage are non-linear.

The magnitude of the relationships identified in equation 2 is as follows. For every 10 per cent increase in the proportion of a factory built before 1945, employment growth declined by 2 per cent. The effect of site coverage on employment change (measured by the 'logged' variable) shows that an increase in coverage from 10 to 40 per cent reduced employment growth by

25 per cent, an increase from 40 to 70 per cent by a further 10 per cent, and an increase from 70 to 100 per cent by another 6 per cent.

Equation 3 considers whether a factory's location still helps explain its employment change. It does this by reintroducing the variables for town and rural locations. If employment in factories in towns and rural areas grows faster than employment in city factories, after allowing for the age of buildings, site coverage and so on, the location variables ought still to be statistically significant. In fact, both coefficients are positive but neither is significant, and the magnitude and statistical significance of the coefficients on the variables measuring site coverage, age of buildings, size and industry all remain largely unaffected.

This third equation is especially important because the statistical insignificance of the location variables suggests that a factory's employment growth is not affected by whether it is in a city, town or rural area. The important influences are its size and industry and the physical constraints of its site and premises. Thus, in so far as factories in cities on average grow more slowly (or decline more rapidly) than in small towns and rural areas, this is because they are more likely to operate in older, physically con-strained premises, not because there is something else inherently inefficient in urban locations.

There is a different way of interpreting the same evidence. That is that firms with potential for growth make sure they have sites with room for expansion, whereas stagnant or declining firms willingly accept physically constrained sites because room for expansion is not required. The reason for the poor growth of firms on constrained urban sites would thus be the nature of the firms themselves.

However, the evidence presented in chapter 4 does not support this alternative interpretation. The mismatch between firms' needs and the property they occupy can be considerable. It is certainly not the case that firms' potential for growth is neatly matched by the capacity of their sites to accommodate it. Moreover, to some extent this alternative interpretation of the data misses the point. Adequate space is a prerequisite for on-site expansion, and many sites and premises in cities are physically constrained so firms cannot grow there. If dynamic firms were therefore to move to spacious sites in rural areas this might leave cities with a moribund popula-tion of firms, but the cause of lower rate of expansion in cities would still be the inadequacy of sites and premises, which forced the dynamic firms to move out.

The view that inadequate sites and premises are an obstacle to expansion in Britain's cities is strengthened by the findings of several surveys.

The Department of Trade and Industry (1973) looked at factories that opened at new locations between 1964 and 1967. Of the 159 factories with a London origin, 70 per cent said the new factory had to be opened in order to expand output, and half mentioned the need to reorganize production space and avoid congestion at the existing London site. Another survey by the Department of Industry, reported by Dennis (1978), covered 53 firms that relocated from London to New or Expanded Towns in the South East and East Anglia between 1970 and 1975. In over 85 per cent of cases, difficulties with existing premises in London were a major reason for relocation.

A survey by IFF Research Ltd (1980) covered 500 firms in manufacturing and services in inner city, suburban and other locations. It asked managers to comment on a range of issues relating to the growth and performance of their firms. Labour difficulties, such as problems in recruiting skilled workers, were mentioned frequently. However, the main factors differentiating the responses of inner city firms concerned sites and premises, including the room for on-site expansion, the suitability of buildings, and parking and loading facilities. All these appeared to be worse in the inner city. Firms that had moved from the inner city, or were considering moving, stressed the physical condition of buildings, their suitability, and the cost compared with alternatives.

Further surveys of manufacturing firms in London by Keeble (1968) and Leigh and North (1983) highlight the problem of lack of room for on-site expansion.

New factories

The influences on the location of entirely new factory buildings are more complex than those on the location of extensions to existing factories. One reason is the greater diversity in sources of supply. Extensions to existing factories are almost always purpose built by manufacturing firms for their own use. New factory units, in contrast, are provided by three different groups, each with its own locational criteria.

The first group comprises manufacturing firms building for their own use. The distinguishing feature of this group is that manufacturers intend to make profits not so much from investment in buildings as from the subsequent use of those buildings. The construction of a new building is a means to an end, rather than an end in itself. Its location is therefore determined not by the need to maximize capital gain on the completed development but by what is most profitable or convenient from the point of view of production.

The second group is the private sector development industry, examined in chapter 3. This group starts with the opposite criteria. The building itself is the source of profit — in the form of capital gain from its sale, or rent if ownership is retained. It will therefore be located where adequate and secure profits can be made, and the most profitable locations will normally be the first to be developed. In theory, the need to maximize profits should mean that private developers build in the areas where industry wants to go, because a plentiful supply of potential occupants is necessary to maintain high rents and high capital values. If this were the case, the geography of private sector speculative development would merely mirror those production orientated considerations which determine the location of factories built by manufacturers. In practice, the need to achieve a minimum rate of return means that private developers steer entirely clear of some areas where manufacturers still find it worthwhile to build for themselves.

The third group supplying new factory buildings is the public sector. The public agencies involved in the industrial property market are examined in chapter 6. They are similar to private developers in that they mostly build factories on a speculative basis but differ in that the scale and location of their activity are not determined by the profitability of development. Financial criteria may have to be met, but factories are built mainly with a view to promoting economic development in specific places.

What all these groups have in common is that they require land on which to undertake their developments. The availability of industrial land, its price and quality are therefore likely to have an important influence on the location of the factories they build.

The supply of land for industry in any locality depends first and foremost on the total amount of land in the area and the intensity of competition from non-industrial uses. Cities are small areas containing thousands of people and businesses, so land is a scarce commodity; in large, sparsely populated, rural counties, land for all uses is more plentiful. The effect of competition between alternative land uses is to bid up prices, and in a market economy land will be allocated to the highest bidder. Thus in a city we would expect industry to occupy land only if it is able to outbid other potential land uses. In fact, market mechanisms do not operate smoothly, as we explained. Once allocated, some urban land uses are almost impervious to market forces, and the reallocation between uses that does occur is always small in relation to the total stock of land. Furthermore, administrative structures and procedures mediate between competing land uses. The system of town and country planning controls, for example, may protect one land use against the advances of another, and the behaviour of public and private institutions may mean that surplus land is hoarded rather than brought onto the market.

The supply of land for new industrial development is therefore the result of the interplay of several, sometimes conflicting forces. It is partly determined by the market, and partly by planners and politicans. Within local areas the supply may be coordinated and regulated by the local planning authority, but over the country as a whole it is not.

No public or private agency collects comprehensive data on the availability of industrial land. However, most local authorities keep records of land available in their areas, and in some cases the information is highly detailed. The information is usually collected either as part of the service many county councils provide in promoting economic development, or by planning departments in the course of preparing and monitoring structure plans.

Where the county council does not compile information on land availability, figures can often be obtained from districts, boroughs and development corporations.

During 1982 we collated statistics on industrial land availability from local authorities (Fothergill, Kitson and Monk, 1985). Tables 5.8 and 5.9 present the statistics by region and by type of area. In order to provide a comprehen-

	Ha	Ha per 1,000 manufacturing employees
Wales	3,550	15.0
Scotland	6,350	13.0
North	3,850	11.3
South West	2,650	7.0
East Anglia	1,250	6.9
Yorkshire and Humberside	3,850	6.8
East Midlands	3,400	6.5
North West	2,850	3.6
West Midlands	2,600	3.3
South East	3,200	2.0
GREAT BRITAIN	33,550	5.7

Table 5.8 *Available industrial land by region, 1982*

Note: 1 hectare = 10,000 square metres

Source: Local authorities

	Ha	Ha per 1,000 manufacturing employees
London	750	1.2
Conurbations	4,650	3.6
Free-standing cities	5,100	5.4
Large towns	4,850	6.4
Small towns	11,200	7.0
Rural areas	7,000	10.7
GREAT BRITAIN	33,550	5.7

Table 5.9 *Available industrial land by type of area, 1982*

Source: Local authorities

sive picture, estimates have been included for the few districts and counties (mostly in Southern England) for which figures could not be obtained. The figures include both public and private land, and sites that required substantial investment in infrastructure or reclamation, as well as sites that could be developed more or less immediately. They exclude land earmarked for specific firms, land within the curtilage of existing factories, and land reserved for warehousing. However, it should be noted that there are inevitable variations between local authorities in what they consider 'available'. Details were obtained on definitions in order to try to maintain consistency, but the process by which land becomes available is nevertheless likely to vary. In some places it may be designated for industry only where there is perceived demand; in others it may be designated well in advance of demand.

The first column of each table shows the quantity of available industrial land, in hectares. In Great Britain as a whole, in excess of 30,000 ha were available in 1982. Of the ten regions, Scotland had the largest supply — more than 6,000 ha. The South East, with roughly a third of the country's people and jobs, had just under a tenth of the available industrial land. Over half the land available was in small towns and rural areas, whereas London and the conurbations together had about one-sixth.

The second columns of Tables 5.8 and 5.9 show the number of hectares available per thousand manufacturing employees in each area. In some respects this is a more useful measure because it shows how much land is available in relation to the existing size of each area's manufacturing sector.

Using this second measure of supply, the regional variations are especially marked though not difficult to interpret. The three regions most assisted by regional policy — Wales, Scotland and the North — have the most industrial land available. This is to be expected, because regional policy has deliberately created a plentiful quantity and range of sites for in-coming firms and for local expanding firms. Next on the list come the South West and East Anglia, primarily rural regions where the pressures from competing land uses are not as great as in more urban regions. The regions with the smallest supply of industrial land are the North West, the West Midlands and the South East, each of which contains a large conurbation. Bottom of all, the South East also has a restrictive planning regime towards industry in many areas, partly to protect environmental and residential quality and partly to restrain the overall growth of the region.

The urban–rural differences are equally striking, and consistent. In relation to manufacturing employment, small towns and rural areas have substantially more land available than cities. Over the country as a whole, rural areas have three times as much land available per employee as the conurbations, and nine times as much as London. Despite years of industrial decline, Britain's largest cities therefore have modest quantities of land available for new industrial development compared with other areas. This is a situation which on the whole has not previously been recognized, except perhaps by some planners in urban authorities who have found difficulty in assembling suitable land for industry. What has probably occurred is that prominent areas of derelict land within cities — in London's docklands, for example — have created a misleading impression of the opportunities for new industrial development.

Statistics on the price of industrial land, from Inland Revenue records of transactions, show that there are large regional differences, principally between the North and South of the country (Fothergill, Kitson and Monk, 1985). In 1982, for example, land available for immediate development in Northern England generally fetched less than £100,000 a hectare, while it fetched £1m a hectare in parts of the South East. However, within each region there is a tendency for cities to form centres of high prices compared with immediately surrounding areas.

Statistics on the quality of available industrial land are partial. In 1982 just under half the total was classed by local authorities as available for development immediately or within 12 months. This proportion was slightly higher in London, but did not vary much between urban and rural areas in the rest of the country. Detailed figures for Merseyside, Leicester and Norfolk showed that less than 10 per cent of the sites were of more than 10 ha, but these larger blocks accounted for between a third and a half of the total land available. In Merseyside, very small sites of less than 1 ha made up a higher proportion of the number of sites available and of the total supply of industrial land.

Small sites are more limited in their uses because they cannot accommodate large factories or the sorts of large trading estates favoured by the property industry. Obviously, if the pattern in Merseyside is repeated in other cities, it represents an obstacle to employment regeneration. Also, in inner city areas much of the available land is likely to be re-cycled from firms that have closed, from public utilities and from other uses. In some cases it will require considerable expenditure on reclamation, even involving the clearance of abandoned buildings and structures. In a few cases the land is contaminated to an extent that imposes limits on its future use. Derelict Land Grants are available from central government to help tackle these problems, but the process of reclamation introduces a time lag into the development process, and often considerable uncertainty, deterring many potential users. Such difficulties are not encountered on greenfield sites.

On a number of counts — the quantity, price and quality of industrial sites — Britain's cities are therefore disadvantaged. The way this affects the location of new factories now needs to be considered.

The supply of land is certainly important in that it sets a ceiling on the amount of new factory building in an area. This is illustrated by the shortage in London. A typical new development might consist of a single storey building with a site coverage of 30 per cent, implying that each hectare of industrial land might accommodate 3,000 m² of floorspace, enough at average densities for 75 employees. If all the available industrial land in London (roughly 750 ha) were to be fully developed it would therefore accommodate an extra 55,000 jobs. Although a welcome boost to employment, this number is small by comparison with the 600,000 manufacturing jobs lost in London since the mid 1960s. Furthermore, the potential employment capacity of available industrial land must be considered in the light of the continuing decline (at between 2 and 3 per cent a year) in the number of workers on existing factory floorspace as employment densities fall. Even if all the available industrial land in London were developed immediately, the resulting increase in employment would be entirely offset within only 5 years by the decline in employment density on existing floorspace.

London is an extreme example, though it illustrates the constraint on manufacturing activity and employment, which would become particularly acute during a period of sustained economic growth. To breach the ceiling imposed by the current supply of industrial land would require either the release of peripheral greenfield sites (as in the 1920s and 1930s), the transfer of land from other urban uses to industry, or substantial expenditure to make derelict or marginal land usable. The political acceptability of the first two of these policies is doubtful to say the least.

Nevertheless, most firms could find suitable sites in Britain's cities. If the firm is small or medium sized and if its site requirements are not particularly demanding, each of Britain's cities can probably offer at least one if not several suitable plots of land for a new factory. The potential sites may not always be available in the preferred part of the city — especially in London — but at least there will be some to choose from. Only a firm requiring a very large site will encounter serious difficulty. A new car plant, for example, needs such a large site that it would almost certainly have to be located on the fringes of a city or in a small town rather than within an existing built-up area. A property company seeking a large site on which to develop a new trading estate is also likely to be forced to look outside cities to find a suitable piece of land that does not require significant reclamation. However, on balance it is difficult to argue that few new factories are built in cities simply because there is no suitable land.

It is nevertheless still likely that the greater supply of land for industry in small towns and rural areas exerts an important influence on the location of new factories. Two mechanisms are important.

The first concerns the price of industrial land, which as we noted is usually higher in cities than in surrounding areas. Many firms have no compelling reasons to locate within a city, and for these the price of land will tend to attract investment to small towns and rural areas where sites can be acquired more cheaply.

The second and probably more important mechanism concerns the way that site selection enters firms' decision making. The decision to open a new branch plant is one of the best-researched questions in industrial geography (e.g. Luttrell, 1962; Townroe, 1971; Department of Trade and Industry, 1973) and the findings can be summarized as follows. Once a firm has decided to open a new factory it first chooses the area that would be suitable. This may be defined quite loosely (e.g. 'Scotland') or more specifically (e.g. 'somewhere within 20 miles of Glasgow'). The second stage is the search for a suitable site within that area which meets its detailed requirements (e.g. size, preparation costs, tenure, access). Some firms stop their search as soon as they find somewhere satisfactory; others do a thorough evaluation of alternatives. At this second stage in the location process the availability of land is likely to be important because within an area that includes urban and rural locations a disproportionately large share of the sites on offer will normally be in small towns and rural areas. If a firm simply opts for the first suitable site it finds, the chances are it will therefore not be in a city. If a firm evaluates a range of possible sites, a large number of small town and rural sites are likely to end up on the shortlist because there are more of them to choose from. In this way, it is reasonable to assume that if firms have no special preference for either an urban or a rural area the availability of land will direct a large share of new factories to more rural locations.

The Department of Trade and Industry's survey of firms opening at new locations supports the view that the availability of land and buildings steers firms to particular locations within a broad area. Of the 242 firms in the survey that had considered alternative locations within their chosen region, 56 per cent rejected the alternatives because of the lack of a suitable site or building. This proportion rose to 66 per cent for firms locating in non-assisted regions (Department of Trade and Industry, 1973).

But although we are suggesting that greater availability favours small towns and rural areas, the rates of take-up of available industrial land indicate that, in relation to the sites on offer, firms and developers actually prefer city locations. In 1982, for example, London and the conurbations had 16 per cent of the available industrial land in England. Yet between 1974 and 1982 these areas received 28 per cent of all floorspace in new factory units. This is lower than their share of the total stock of floorspace — 39 per cent in 1974 — but suggests that in London and the conurbations industrial land is developed more quickly than elsewhere.

An important reason why some firms favour city sites is the proximity to their existing urban factories. Savings on the transport of materials between plants can be achieved, and two or more nearby factories can often be administered as one, without duplicating management structures. However, many firms have no pressing reasons for locating new factories near existing factories in the same company, or near existing major centres of population and employment. There is thus no reason why the geographical distribution of new factories should mirror and perpetuate the existing distribution of factories. Instead, the way in which firms select new locations gives the availability of suitable sites a prominent role in diverting factories away from major urban areas.

It is less clear that the variations in land supply between whole regions — e.g. between the assisted areas and the South East — have an important influence on the location of new factories. The processes just described, linking land supply to location, operate at the local level, directing new factory building away from some places and towards others within the same region or subregion. Firms' choice of region probably depends on factors unconnected with land availability, and a plentiful supply of sites for new factories is thus no guarantee of a region's success. Though having made this general point, there are undoubtedly a few firms — perhaps those needing land quickly or in large quantities — for whom the generous land supply in the assisted areas is a significant attraction.

The exact extent to which land availability influences the location of new factory buildings probably depends on whether other factors constrain decisions. For example, if an adequate supply of labour can be found in some areas but not others, new factories will be located where the labour is available and the amount of land available may have little if any influence. Individual firms may have preferences for either urban or rural sites. A number of factors pull in each direction. On the one hand, city locations are accessible to large and diverse labour markets, which will be important if a new factory needs large numbers of workers or if a wide range of specialized skills are required. Proximity to suppliers and markets may also be an attraction of an urban location. On the other hand, urban land is costly to acquire, there are frequently problems of parking and access for heavy lorries, and managers may in any case prefer to live and work in the countryside. Individual firms reach decisions on the basis of the importance to them of each of these factors.

Within the broad categories of cities, towns and rural areas, some places secure more new factories than others. Sometimes this can be attributed to land supply. Surrey in particular, and Hertfordshire to a lesser extent, have received less new factory building than comparable areas or than outer parts of the South East because green belt controls have severely curtailed the supply of industrial land. Conversely, a plentiful supply of serviced land, together with good road links and energetic industrial promotion, enables the New Towns to attract a substantial volume of new industrial development. In other cases the amount of new factory building in an area may have little to do with the availability of land: the success of the 'M4 corridor' in attracting high technology developments is a case in point. The link between the supply of land and the location of new factories therefore ought not to be regarded as mechanistic, especially in understanding the decisions of individual firms or trends in specific areas.

Property and industrial location: some conclusions

The introduction to this chapter raised doubts about the applicability of neo-classical economic models to the role of land and buildings in industrial location. The subsequent evidence has confirmed these doubts. The supply of land and buildings does exert an important influence on location of manufacturing firms' activity, and this influence operates not so much through the price mechanism as through physical constraints and availability. The effect is to favour economic development in some areas and to disadvantage others.

The effect on the geography of employment change has little to do with variations in the way buildings are used: the decline in employment density has been a powerful influence but appears not to have differentiated areas to any great extent. Instead, the main effects on the location of jobs arise because of constraints in the supply of land. More extensions to existing factories and more entirely new factories are built away from major urban areas than inside them. In both cases the supply of land — for on-site expansion and for new factories — is much more limited in cities than in small towns and rural areas. This undoubtedly plays a major role in generating the urban–rural contrast in manufacturing employment trends.

6   Public sector intervention

The provision of industrial premises by the public sector is a long-established dimension of policy to promote economic development, and until recently it was uncontroversial. The public sector built only a small number of factories, concentrated in the most depressed parts of the country — North East England, Scotland and South Wales for example. Few politicians questioned the usefulness of this modest intervention.

In the 1970s things began to change. As a response to rising unemployment the rate of factory building by central government agencies was stepped up and local authorities became more involved in property provision, many for the first time. The scale of public intervention increased even more rapidly in relation to private sector activity, which fell off as economic growth slowed. In the 1980s the political context also changed. The Conservative Government began to question the wisdom of public intervention in a sector which it believed ought to be regulated by purely commercial considerations. Manifestations of this scepticism were tighter financial guidelines for the main public agencies, and research into the cost-effectiveness of factory building. The Labour Party, too, grew weary of factory building programmes. Instead, it began to favour more direct intervention in companies, e.g. through local enterprise boards, to tackle obstacles to industrial regeneration such as inadequate investment and poor management.

Government factory building has invariably been regarded as part of regional policy, which itself has come under pressure in the 1980s. The deindustrialization of the economy has added many previously prosperous regions to the casualty list and militated against the possibility of diverting mobile, job creating investments northwards and westwards from the shrinking islands of prosperity in the South East. The failings of traditional regional policy have been exposed: advance factory provision, in particular, has been associated with one of the prime weaknesses of some regional economies, namely the development of a branch plant economy too unstable to weather all but the mildest economic storm. And like so many other areas of public expenditure, in the 1980s spending on regional policy has been severely squeezed.

This chapter looks at factory building by the public sector. The first part examines the potential benefits. The main factory building agencies are then introduced and their quantitative contribution is assessed. This is followed by a closer look at two of them — English Estates and local authorities. The final part of the chapter discusses the evaluation of public factory building, including the impact on private sector development.

The benefits of public provision

There are four main mechanisms through which public sector factory building might raise an area's level of economic activity.

The first is by improving the availability of industrial property — measured in terms of the number, tenure, size and design of premises for rent or sale at any point in time. This might enable local companies to expand faster than would have been the case, by providing suitable premises into which they can quickly and easily relocate, or premises which they can use to open a new branch plant. The ready availability of premises might also attract firms to an area for the first time, again because their additional production can be swiftly and easily accommodated.

The second mechanism through which public sector factory building might raise an area's level of economic activity is by lowering industrial rents. Lower rents reduce firms' costs, and thus potentially increase their profitability or improve their price competitiveness. This in turn may help secure survival or growth. Some local authorities pursue a policy of not charging full market rents, and the practice of granting an initial rent-free period is widespread throughout the public sector. But even when public agencies charge 'what the market will bear', in the areas where they are the dominant suppliers of new industrial property, market rents are not independent of their actions. In particular, if the public sector creates a surplus of property in order to improve the availability of factory space, it removes the scarcity which elsewhere bids up rents. Market pressures then transmit the low rents across the whole of an area's factory stock, including older and privately rented space, because firms are reluctant to pay substantially more for private floorspace than they need pay for comparable public floorspace nearby. Indeed, these downward market pressures are held in check only by the willingness of the public sector to hold large stocks of vacant floorspace rather than cut rents still further to try to secure more lettings.

The third mechanism through which public sector factory building might raise an area's level of economic activity is by creating 'vacancy chains' which diffuse the benefits among a larger number of firms in an area. For example, if a new factory is occupied by an existing firm relocating in order to expand, this releases older existing premises for occupation by another company, which in turn may consequently be able to expand and release its previous premises for yet another firm. The chain carries on until the premises remain vacant, are demolished, or an entirely new firm occupies them. The total job gain arising from the construction of the new factory, it could be argued, is the sum of the job gains at each stage in the vacancy chain.

The fourth mechanism through which public sector factory provision may promote economic development is by improving the quality of the industrial building stock in an area. Even if no new jobs were attracted in the process, the transfer of firms from old to new buildings is likely to bring gains in operating efficiency and costs, as chapter 4 indicated, and this in turn is likely to promote their survival and growth.

The relative importance of each of these four mechanisms depends to some extent on the segment of the property market in which the public sector is intervening. The provision of larger advance factories intended to attract firms from outside the area is unlikely to set off local vacancy chains, for example, and likewise may do little to upgrade the average quality of premises occupied by firms already in the area. The provision of small factory units and workshops, on the other hand, probably does little to attract firms from outside the area but may remove an obstacle to the formation and growth of local businesses.

Many of the jobs which public factory building generates in an area may be at the expense of other areas. This is particularly true of jobs in branch plants and transfers from outside the area. For these to represent a gain in employment to the country as a whole it would have to be shown that the expansion could not have occurred in the areas of origin and that, in the absence of public factory building, the jobs would not have gone elsewhere in the country. Alternatively, it would have to be shown that the new location and premises are inherently more efficient so that the survival of the companies is assured and growth enhanced.

Although a higher proportion of the jobs created by fostering the formation and growth of local companies may be genuinely additional, new jobs, some of the same considerations apply: in the absence of public factory building many of the jobs might have gone elsewhere, often within the same locality. However, if public intervention creates a more favourable industrial property market than otherwise would have been the case, some expansion is likely to occur that would have been frustrated by the difficulty of obtaining suitable premises. Whether this growth is an addition to economic activity then depends on where the firms' competitors are located: the growth 'unlocked' by public factory building may displace competitors and jobs in the same local area, elsewhere in Britain, or abroad.

The precise extent to which public factory provision creates new jobs or merely shifts them from place to place is an empirical matter. Factory building does nevertheless have the advantage that it can steer jobs to specific places within a wider area. As explained in chapter 5, for many firms the location decision is a two stage process: they select the broad area which they prefer, and then they look for an appropriate site or building within that area. The availability of suitable premises is crucial at this second stage. For the new or very small firm, the area of search may be small — say within a few miles of the owner's home. For the branch plant of a large company, the final search for a suitable site and building may extend over the whole of a region. In both cases, public sector factories can steer the firms to one location rather than another by influencing the choice of suitable buildings that confront the firms.

A word of caution should be added, however. Although the public provision of factory floorspace is potentially a useful adjunct to urban and regional policies, it is not by itself sufficient to create economic development. If for whatever reason an area is seen as an unsuitable location — e.g. because it has acquired a reputation for labour militancy — no amount of public factory building can be expected to revive it. The main effect would simply be to increase the amount of empty factory space in the area. Public factory building is at its most effective when it is working in the same direction as other influences: when it is easing a bottleneck in the supply of premises for small firms, for instance, or when there is a plentiful supply of mobile industrial investment eager to tap a plentiful local supply of labour.

Moreover, it would be wrong to see public factory building as a purely economic tool. Advance factories are useful political tools, too, as local councillors and Westminster politicians are only too aware. Irrespective of the real impact on a local economy, advance factories provide an immediate and visible expression of concern about the problems of depressed areas. By comparison, training programmes or grants towards the capital cost of machinery are harder to 'see', and less likely to win votes.

The public developers

The range of public agencies involved in building factory space reflects the essentially uncoordinated way in which this branch of government activity has developed. From central government's point of view, factory building has never been an end in itself but a tool used to pursue other, wider policies: the regeneration of depressed regions, the decentralization of people and jobs from overcrowded cities, and the strengthening of rural economies. Each of these policies has been implemented by separate agencies, each with a factory building arm. Likewise, many individual local authorities have begun to provide factory space, each with their own motives and programmes. Indeed, even in the mid 1980s the provision of factory space by the public sector remains uncoordinated to the extent that the figures presented here are, we believe, the first to assess the overall scale of its involvement. First, however, it is appropriate to say a few words about each of the main public suppliers of factory space in Great Britain.

English Estates

English Estates is the trading name of the English Industrial Estates Corporation, the factory building arm in England of the Department of Trade and Industry. The present corporation and its predecessors have been building factories in the assisted areas since the 1930s, with the aim of promoting regional industrial development. Its activities include the provision of serviced industrial land on which firms build their own factories as well as the construction of publicly funded advance factories, and it also builds a small number of factories to firms' own specifications. Over the years it has assembled a very large and diverse portfolio of sites and premises. Changes in the boundaries of the assisted areas and its role as property developer and manager for the Development Commission (see below) have in recent years extended its activities from its traditional heartlands in North East England, Cumbria and Merseyside.

Scottish and Welsh Development Agencies

These two development agencies, founded in 1975 and 1976 respectively, took over the functions of the Scottish and Welsh Industrial Estates Corporations, and within their areas perform a similar role to English Estates as the government's main factory building arm. However, in both cases site preparation and factory building are only a part — though an important one — of a wider range of development activity, including the provision of loans, grants and investment capital to companies, promotional work to attract mobile investment and, especially in the case of the Scottish agency, extensive involvement in 'area renewal'.

Development Commission

The Development Commission, dating from 1909, is Britain's oldest development agency. Its original objectives — to reduce rural depopulation, to improve the economic and social structure of rural areas, and to create jobs — remain intact but the range of its activities has changed with the evolving character of the rural problem. In economic development the commission began by supporting traditional rural crafts and industries, but from the mid 1970s onwards its factory building role was expanded with the aim of creating 2,500 new jobs a year. Programmes are agreed between the commission, local authorities and other organizations, and the acquisition and development of factory sites are carried out by English Estates using the commission's funds. The factory and workshop programme now absorbs over half the commission's development fund. The commission operates throughout rural England, but is especially active in the far South West, upland areas in northern England, and the Welsh border counties. The units provided are almost all very small.

Highlands and Islands Development Board and Development Board for Rural Wales

These two agencies, established in 1965 and 1977 respectively, undertake a wide range of activities in the remote rural areas for which they are responsible. The amount of new factory space they provide is small in absolute terms but important in relation to their overall budgets and the volume of industrial activity in their areas. Both can provide loans, grants and equity capital for firms. The Development Board for Rural Wales also oversees the development of Newtown, a 'new town' in Powys. Unlike the Development Commission, these rural development agencies also build bespoke factories to meet specific firms' needs.

New Town development corporations

The first New Towns were established in the late 1940s, followed by more in the 1950s and 1960s. They were intended to be new centres of population and employment to divert growth away from Britain's cities, London in particular, which were seen as congested and overcrowded. In all, 28 New Towns were established in Great Britain (excluding one very short-lived New Town in Scotland). Some of the later ones (e.g. Northampton and Peterborough) were planned expansions of existing towns. The development corporation acquires land — at existing use value, a power unusual among factory building agencies — and then provides serviced sites for firms to develop, or builds its own factories for sale or rent. The finance comes from central government, from private institutional investors, and from the corporation's internally generated funds. The development corporations are being gradually wound up as the New Towns programme comes to an end, and their assets are being sold directly or transferred to the Commission for the New Towns, which is primarily concerned with property management and disposal. The Commission for the New Towns undertakes new factory building only in exceptional circumstances, for example to help offset the steel closure in Corby, where it built 130,000 m² of new space between 1980 and 1984.

Local authorities

There is no statutory obligation upon local authorities to build factory space but an increasing number of counties, boroughs and districts have taken this step. For many, it is an extension of their traditional activity of providing serviced industrial land. It is estimated that by 1982, 52 per cent of all English local authorities and 70 per cent of Welsh local authorities had become industrial landlords (Perry, 1986). The funds for factory building come from local authorities' own resources, including inner city and other special programme grants from central government, and in some cases from partnership arrangements with private sector institutions. The criteria on which local authorities decide to build and the terms on which they make premises available to firms vary enormously from authority to authority.

Table 6.1 shows the stock of industrial floorspace in England and Wales belonging to each of these public developers in 1984. Because the figures have been compiled from several sources they are not fully comparable, and a number of definitional points should be noted. First, they include factory space owned by the public sector but exclude owner occupied space on publicly owned land, except in the case of the active New Towns where private development under the aegis of the development corporations is included. Second, factories built by the public sector but subsequently sold are excluded. These are especially important in some New Towns in favoured locations: e.g. half of Northampton Development Corporation's industrial floorspace was sold between 1980 and 1984. Third, the figures for the active New Towns include warehousing floorspace, while the others refer only to industrial space. Fourth, the figures for local authorities are estimates based on surveys of all English and Welsh local authorities carried out in 1982 (Perry, 1986). These asked local authorities to supply details of their small-factory building activity (up to 5,000 ft²) during the previous 5 years, and achieved response rates of 76 and 80 per cent respectively. The

	Stock of floorspace (millions m²)	% of total
English Estates		
Development Commission	0.2	0.1
Other	2.0	0.8
Welsh Development Agency	1.0	0.4
Development Board for Rural Wales	0.2	0.1
Active New Towns	5.8	2.5
Commission for the New Towns	3.0	1.3
Local authorities	1.8	0.8
TOTAL PUBLIC SECTOR	14.0	5.9
Private Sector	221.6	94.1
TOTAL STOCK	235.6	100.0

Table 6.1 *Public sector industrial floorspace, England and Wales, 1984*

Sources: Annual reports
Authors' estimates
Commercial and Industrial Floorspace Statistics

estimates for 1984 assume that non-responding authorities built at the same rate as those which replied, and that after 1982 local authority building carried on at the same rate as before. No allowance is made for local authority units of more than 5,000 ft² — they build few larger than this — or for local authority units built prior to 1976, when councils were less heavily involved in factory building.

Bearing in mind these definitional points, Table 6.1 presents some interesting conclusions. In particular, the privately owned factory stock continues to dwarf the public sector, which accounts for only about 6 per cent of the total in England and Wales. The extent of the gulf between the public and private sectors reflects three major influences: the limited geographical areas to which the major public agencies are tied; the public sector's emphasis on the speculative provision of premises to rent, mainly to small and medium sized companies, rather than on larger, custom built factories; and the comparatively recent large-scale involvement of some of the public developers.

Definitional problems exaggerate the lead of the New Towns in the league of public providers, but their premier position is probably still justified. They have a long history of involvement in the supply of industrial property and have been much more active than local authorities. The cumulative growth in the New Towns means that they now house over 2m people and provide nearly 1m jobs, many in newly developed factories. Further down the league of public providers, English Estates and local authorities own broadly similar amounts of industrial floorspace (around 2m m² each), despite their very different histories and English Estates' geographic concentration. The two development agencies in Wales own smaller property portfolios, reflecting in part the smaller size of the Welsh economy.

In Scotland the five New Towns remain active and in 1984 held 1.4m m² of industrial floorspace. The Scottish Development Agency owned 2.4m m², and by 1984 the Highlands and Islands Development Board had built just over 0.1m m², principally in small speculative units but also in a number of larger purpose designed premises.

The data are not available to measure the contribution of public agencies to the total stock of industrial property in Scotland. However, assuming that the average employment density is the same in Scotland as in England and Wales, in 1984 the 440,000 manufacturing workers in Scotland were probably accommodated in approximately 20m m² of industrial floorspace. The combined holdings of the public sector account for 20 per cent of this. The Scottish Development Agency alone probably accounted for some 10 to 12 per cent. For comparison, the Welsh Development Agency accounted for just under 10 per cent of the stock in Wales, and English Estates for 8 per cent of the stock in the seven counties in which it has been most active (Tyne and Wear, Durham, Cleveland, Cumbria, Northumberland, Merseyside and Cornwall).

The broad similarity of these figures for central government's main factory building agencies owes a great deal to their common history. All have antecedents in the estate companies established in the 1930s, and although at times they have made significant investments in bespoke factories their markets have been broadly the same. The economies of the assisted regions share many common characteristics in terms of industrial structure, regional policy and levels of local entrepreneurship, and this is mirrored in their industrial property markets. Each agency has concentrated on supplying standard speculative units for small and medium sized companies, to suit both local and in-migrating businesses. The similarity between the three agencies is also a reflection of the selective basis on which they act: they meet the needs of companies willing to move into unsophisticated rented accommodation, but provide little for companies with special requirements and a preference for owner occupation.

Turning from the overall stock to just the supply of new factory space, Table 6.2 shows the amount of industrial floorspace completed by the public sector in England and Wales during the 1983/4 financial year. The same definitional points apply as in the previous table, and in addition the public sector figures exclude floorspace in custom built units for owner occupiers, in

	Floorspace in new units (000s m²)	*% of total*
English Estates		
Development Commission	30	1.9
Other	80	5.1
Welsh Development Agency	60	3.8
Development Board for Rural Wales	8	0.5
Active New Towns	220	14.1
Commission for the New Towns	30	1.9
Local authorities	230	14.7
TOTAL PUBLIC SECTOR	658	42.0
Private Sector	907	58.0
ALL NEW UNITS	1,565	100.0

Table 6.2 *New factory units built by the public sector, England and Wales, 1983/4*

Sources: Annual reports
        Authors' estimates
        Commercial and Industrial Floorspace Statistics

extensions and in refurbished property. Local authorities emerge as the largest single supplier. The remaining 13 active New Town development corporations were close behind, though as we noted, this is an overestimate because it includes some private sector and warehousing space. English Estates continued to be an important supplier, though the balance of its provision reflected the growing importance of Development Commission funding.

In Scotland, the five New Town development corporations completed 100,000 m² of industrial floorspace in 1983/4. The Scottish Development Agency completed 85,000 m² of which 16,000 m² was purpose built for specific occupants. The Highlands and Islands Development Board built just 15,000 m².

The public sector's contribution to the supply of new floorspace is undoubtedly much larger than its share of the overall factory stock, though by how much is difficult to assess. In Table 6.2 the public sector's contribution is expressed as a percentage of all the floorspace built in new industrial units, and the figures indicate that the share was over 40 per cent. However, as we explained previously, most medium sized and small industrial units are suitable for warehousing as well as manufacturing, so it is unfair to compare the public sector's contribution just with the supply of new 'industrial' space. In England and Wales in 1983/4, 2.9m m² of 'warehousing' space as well as 1.6m m² of 'industrial' space were built in new units. The public sector supply, in relation to the combined total of new warehousing and industrial space, was 15 per cent. Moreover, it should be borne in mind that 1983/4 was a period in which the level of private sector factory building was very depressed.

There is one important respect, however, in which the aggregate statistics hide the significance of public investment in industrial property. In the restricted geographical areas and typically depressed local economies where public agencies are active, they are now often the dominant if not the only provider of new floorspace. This becomes clearer when we look more closely at the activities of English Estates.

Case study: English Estates

The history of English Estates can be traced back to the Special Areas Act of 1934, the first legislation to provide funds and powers to tackle the regional problem. At an early stage the Commissioner for the Special Areas — a post created by the Act — identified a need for modern trading estates:

The small industrialist seeking a site for a new factory is attracted by the admirable facilities provided so freely on estates like those at Trafford Park and at Slough, where among other advantages, he is able to obtain suitable factory premises on lease, and he is repelled from the Special Areas by the lack of such facilities and by the expense of the preliminary work which he realises is necessary in their absence. (Quoted in Slowe, 1981, p. 15)

As a result, in 1936 the first government sponsored industrial estate company, North Eastern Trading Estates Ltd, was established. Its first estate was a 700 acre site at Team Valley, Gateshead, intended eventually to accommodate 400 factories and 15,000 jobs, where the headquarters of English Estates remain to this day. This estate company was followed by others in West Cumberland, Merseyside, Scotland and Wales. The estate companies were responsible not only for acquiring and preparing land for new industry but also for attracting the firms in the first place, and for ensuring that the estates would eventually pay their own way. Only 18 advance factories were built under the Special Areas Act, but by the outbreak of war Team Valley alone accommodated 100,000 m² of factory space and provided employment for 4,000 people.

In 1945 responsibility for the attraction of industry was transferred from the estate companies to the Board of Trade. The late 1940s witnessed a major expansion in the scale of activities, as central government pursued an active regional policy. The 1950s were a period of relative inactivity, as regional policy was allowed to lapse. From 1951 to 1959, although the legislation permitting the building of government advance factories remained on the statute book, none were built.

The English Industrial Estates Corporation was formed in 1960, at a time when interest in regional policy was reviving, by a merger of North Eastern Trading Estates with the estate companies covering West Cumberland and Merseyside. By that time the North Eastern company alone was already responsible for 38 estates and sites, and 1.1m m² of factory space. The new corporation was to implement the government's factory building programme in the assisted areas in England, and during the subsequent two and a half decades the scale of its activity fluctuated, depending on the emphasis given to regional policy and on changes in power at Westminster. As a general rule, Labour governments gave higher priority to advance factory building. An important extension to its activities occurred in 1966, when it began to build and manage small factories and workshops in the rural parts of the assisted areas on behalf of the Development Commission. In 1981 it also took over responsibility for these activities outside the assisted areas, thus widening its involvement in the industrial property market to include many new parts of England.

English Estates' activities are an important element of the regional policies administered by the Department of Trade and Industry. The aim of English Estates, in determining the balance and location of its activities, is to promote economic development in depressed areas rather than merely to maximize the financial return on its investments. It pursues this goal in a number of ways: by acquiring and preparing sites for subsequent development either by itself or by private sector owner occupiers; by providing custom built premises for specific clients; and in particular by building advance factory units and workshops, for sale or rent.

At the end of March 1984, English Estates owned 422 separate sites totalling 1,756 ha, and 3,813 units totalling 2,166,900 m² of floorspace and accommodating 42,500 employees. A further 385 units totalling 102,600 m² were under construction. The vast majority of this portfolio and the new investment is industrial property, despite some diversification into the provision of advance offices, high technology 'incubator' units and 'craft homes'. Until the 1980s English Estates did not look favourably on warehousing tenants, so most of the industrial property is occupied by manufacturers.

It is estimated that in 1983 half of the tenants of English Estates' factories were branch plants, mainly with origins in other regions and abroad. Just over a third were new business start-ups, and the remainder were transfers from other locations, mainly within the same region. The average branch or transfer employed more than 60 people, more than four times as many as the average new start-up, so in terms of employment the figures looked rather different: branches were estimated to employ two-thirds of the workers in English Estates' factories and new start-ups only one in eight (Cambridge Economic Consultants, 1985). Since 1983 the provision of very small premises has been expanded considerably, so the proportion of tenants and jobs accounted for by new start-ups has increased.

The capital to finance English Estates' development work (£39m during 1983/4) has traditionally come from the Department of Trade and Industry, though funding from the Development Commission to pay for the rural factory programme has become more important. English Estates' revenue comes from the sale of completed factories (£12m in 1983/4) and other receipts, mainly rent (£16m).

At the start of the 1980s, English Estates began to collaborate with the private sector, which financed some of its developments. In the peak year of 1981/2, private funding accounted for a quarter of the new floorspace built by English Estates, mainly through Beehive Workshops Ltd, a wholly owned subsidiary. The individual financial arrangements varied considerably, but all made provision for the long-term risks and rewards of development to be shared by English Estates and the funding institution. These arrangements were expedient for both parties. The financial institutions needed to be seen to be investing in desirable industrial projects in depressed areas, at a time when they were criticized for transferring funds abroad and into non-productive investments, and English Estates was under pressure from the Conservative Government to reduce its dependence on the public purse. More recently, the financial institutions have been reluctant to fund further investments which bring them a low rate of return and the private funding of English Estates' factories has all but come to an end.

There have been other changes in English Estates' activities. Until 1980 the overall scale of its programme was a political decision and the location of the factories was determined largely by the distribution of existing and anticipated unemployment within the assisted areas. New guidelines, effected in 1980, introduced target rates of return and an obligation to take account of likely demand, vacancies and the rate of take-up of completed property. The guidelines were introduced just as the onset of recession greatly reduced the demand for industrial property, and led to an immediate fall in the amount of space built on a speculative basis. They also reinforced a marked shift towards the provision of smaller units.

Table 6.3 shows the size of factories built by English Estates since 1974. In the mid 1970s about 80 per cent of the floorspace was in units of 1,000 m² or more. At the average employment density at the time, factories of this size might have been expected to employ at least 30 people. Just over 40 per cent of the new floorspace was in units of over 2,500 m² (big enough, at average densities, for firms with at least 75 employees). During the late 1970s the shift towards smaller property began. After 1980, the proportion in units of less than 500 m² rose to over 60 per cent, of which nearly half was in units of less than 200 m². This shift towards smaller property led to an explosion in the number of units owned and managed by English Estates.

| | % of total floorspace completed in each period | | |
	1974–7	1977–80	1980–3
Less than 200 m²	0.2	5.6	28.0
200–499 m²	7.3	22.7	34.2
500–999 m²	10.6	18.1	24.0
1,000–2,499 m²	41.0	35.5	6.1
2,500 m² or more	40.9	19.0	7.7
TOTAL	100.0	100.0	100.0

Table 6.3   *Size of factories completed by English Estates*

Source: English Estates

The move towards the provision of small factory units and workshops reflects the takeover of the Development Commission's factory building and the fashion for small firms, as well as the 1980 guidelines. However, in the 1980s very small factory units are more easily let than larger ones, so the guidelines mean that English Estates is effectively locked in to the provision of predominantly small units.

This represents a major shift in function. Previously, the factory pro-gramme was orientated to the in-migrant branch plant. The aim was to provide ready built premises into which firms from Southern England or abroad could move quickly when they needed to open a new production unit. Now, English Estates mostly provides property for new firms, young firms and very small firms, the overwhelming majority of which are local in origin. The change in orientation has to a large extent evolved as a result of decisions such as the introduction of the guidelines; it seems not to have been a strategic political decision, nor the outcome of debate about English Estates' proper role in the industrial property market.

Nevertheless, the shift towards smaller property has not solved the prob-lem of vacancies. In March 1985, 1,210 of the premises managed by English Estates were vacant. These accounted for 32 per cent of English Estates' properties and 22 per cent of the floorspace. The vacancy rate for small units was higher than for large units, reflecting in part the recent competition of so many of the small units. By way of comparison, data compiled by the estate agents King & Co. indicate that at the time roughly 4 per cent of the total stock of industrial floorspace in England and Wales was vacant and on the market. The English Estates and King & Co. figures are both higher than before the recession of the early 1980s, but even during the late 1970s between 10 and 12 per cent of English Estates' stock of floorspace was vacant.

Whether high vacancy rates should be a cause for concern is debatable. The important point, perhaps, is that a high vacancy rate is inherent in English Estates' role. Its aim is not to maximize its profits but to promote economic development by maintaining a stock of good quality, vacant property for swift occupation by any firm that may require it. To do this, it ensures that there is always a sufficient stock of vacant property of different sizes in a wide range of locations. And when that stock begins to be taken up it must build more to maintain the supply of vacant property. In other words, although the level of vacancies may be unnecessarily high, if English Estates did not hold a large stock of vacant property it would not be fulfilling its role as an economic development agency.

As we showed earlier, English Estates' share of the total stock of indus-trial floorspace remains small. However, the global figures hide English Estates' importance in certain areas and segments of the market. Table 6.4 looks at the seven counties where it has been active for longest — mainly North East England, but also Merseyside, Cumbria, and Cornwall. Here it accounted for 12 per cent of the stock of industrial space in 1983, of which floorspace owned by English Estates accounted for two-thirds and owner occupied floorspace on English Estates' land the remaining third. In the industrial parts of North East England — Tyne and Wear, Durham and Cleveland — English Estates' involvement was nearer the 20 per cent mark.

Looking just at additions to the stock of floorspace, English Estates' contribution is still more significant. As we have explained, additions to the

	EE floorspace (000s m²)	Other floorspace on EE land (000s m²)	Total as % of county stock of industrial floorspace
Tyne and Wear	734	406	18.8
Durham	396	203	20.3
Cleveland	253	135	20.5
Merseyside	190	170	4.1
Cumbria	161	93	12.2
Northumberland	77	83	12.3
Cornwall	49	2	6.6
MAIN ASSISTED COUNTIES	1,860	1,092	12.3
Rest of England	283	154	0.2
ENGLAND	2,143	1,246	1.5

Table 6.4   *English Estates factory floorspace, 1983*

Sources: English Estates
   Commercial and Industrial Floorspace Statistics

stock of industrial floorspace occur through three channels: the construction of new units, the extension of existing premises, and changes of use. Although English Estates builds a few extensions for specific occupants, its contribution is mainly through the construction of new units. The first column of Table 6.5 shows the floorspace in new units completed by English Estates between 1974 and 1982 (including units subsequently sold, but excluding custom built property). This totals 900,000 m² in England as a whole and 600,000 m² in the seven main assisted counties. This comprises 12 per cent of all additions to the stock of industrial floorspace in the seven counties, and 30 per cent of all the floorspace in new units.

Finally, Table 6.6 expresses the floorspace built by English Estates as a percentage of the total floorspace in new units of different sizes, again for 1974–82. Larger industrial premises are more likely to be built by firms for their own use and English Estates has reduced its involvement at this end of the market. Not surprisingly, therefore, English Estates' importance is greatest at the smaller end. In the seven counties nearly 60 per cent of all floorspace in new units of less than 2,500 m² was built by English Estates. Even in England as a whole, English Estates built 12 per cent of the floorspace in new units of less than 500 m², and 8 per cent of the floorspace in units between 500 and 2,500 m².

In the seven counties, provision by English Estates is supplemented by

	EE new floorspace (000s m²)	as % of all additions to stock	as % of floorspace in new units
Tyne and Wear	192	15.4	37.6
Durham	43	4.8	10.6
Cleveland	130	21.2	80.0
Merseyside	129	11.2	25.3
Cumbria	36	7.4	21.4
Northumberland	39	10.7	33.3
Cornwall	33	11.0	26.0
MAIN ASSISTED COUNTIES	602	11.9	30.1
Rest of England	307	0.7	2.3
ENGLAND	909	1.9	5.1

Table 6.5   *New floorspace completed by English Estates, 1974–82*

Sources: English Estates
        Commercial and Industrial Floorspace Statistics

	Size of unit (m²)		
	less than 500	500–2,499	2,500 or more
Tyne and Wear	54.3	78.8	12.1
Durham	48.5	20.2	2.6
Cleveland	80.0	96.9	66.2
Merseyside	53.6	58.3	3.8
Cumbria	92.3	45.5	8.4
Northumberland	68.2	59.4	4.8
Cornwall	40.6	32.3	14.1
MAIN ASSISTED COUNTIES	57.0	59.0	10.4
Rest of England	6.5	2.7	0.4
ENGLAND	12.5	8.1	1.6

Table 6.6   *English Estates' share of floorspace in new industrial units, 1974–82 (percentages)*

Sources: English Estates
        Commercial and Industrial Floorspace Statistics

other public agencies. The local authorities are involved to varying degrees in building small factory units, and there are active New Town Development Corporations at Washington in Tyne and Wear, and Aycliffe and Peterlee in Durham. These together probably account for a large part of the remaining 40 per cent of new, small industrial units in these counties. The remaining development of small units, by the private sector on a speculative basis or by firms for their own use, must therefore be small, negligible or even non-existent in the main areas where English Estates is active. In effect, the figures show that in the assisted areas of England the provision of new industrial property for small firms is a nationalized industry, of which English Estates is the main component.

Case study: local authorities

During the postwar years of large-scale slum clearance, city centre redevelopment and highway schemes, a number of local authorities provided land and occasionally new factories for displaced businesses. The provision of alternative sites was not a legal requirement, but local councils recognized the importance of maintaining their economic base where this did not conflict with the primary objectives of redevelopment and comprehensive planning. Only a few county councils, typically in depressed regions, pursued more active economic development policies, and their factory programmes were mainly limited to the construction of large premises suitable for migrant businesses (Camina, 1974).

Following the Bolton Report on small firms (Bolton, 1972), many local authorities accepted the criticism that their policies and attitudes had been harmful to small businesses, particularly in respect of their basic need for accommodation, and they were urged by central government to play a more positive role in the provision of suitable premises. The Inner Urban Areas Act 1978 introduced measures to support small businesses, including the power to declare Industrial Improvement Areas within which local authorities were supposed to stimulate the rehabilitation of older premises and provide accommodation for small firms. In 1980, further government advice to local authorities criticized the rigid application of land-use zoning because of its supposedly damaging effect on small businesses and called on planning authorities not to restrict small firms in residential areas where there are no specific and convincing objections.

Initially the government therefore fostered local authorities' concern for firms' property needs. By the 1980s, however, local authority involvement in factory provision had developed a momentum of its own, as the deterioration in the economy prompted a wave of building work intended to alleviate the job losses that were occurring. Indeed, now that central government has tightened the restrictions on councils' capital spending, local authority factory building continues in spite of government actions rather than because of them.

The impetus for building factory units may come from a variety of sources within a local authority. Many now have industrial development officers who take a leading role in the initiation of factory building because they see the availability of industrial accommodation as important for the promotion of the area. Elsewhere, factory building is usually the responsibility of the planning or estates department. Planners' objectives are generally to mitigate the worst impact of economic change and they view the provision of speculative units as an important tool, even if current lettings are slow. By comparison, estate departments are usually more concerned with the efficient management of property, and they tend to be more cautious about supplying premises without evidence of strong demand (Perry, 1986). However, according to Chandler and Templeton (1980), 'the problems of co-ordinating departments within compartmentalised authorities may deter officers from strongly promoting this element of employment creation as opposed to more easily implemented activities'.

Whichever department takes the lead, it is rare for provision to be based on research into the local industrial property market. A local authority may undertake a development in phases, so that the extent of demand can be assessed before embarking on the next phase, but typically the impressions and perceptions of individual officers are more important than market research or an analysis of experience to date. However, this informal approach need not produce less satisfactory results. Malvern Hills District Council, in the West Midlands, was exceptional in its market investigations. The industrial development officer contacted local businesses that had previously inquired about the availability of premises and subsequently designed the district's programme to suit their needs. When the factories were completed, he despairingly reported to his councillors that none of the businesses were now interested in taking new accommodation (Perry, 1985).

The units built by local authorities are mostly between 100 and 250 m² in size and take the form of purpose built terraces. They may be sold to occupants, but they are primarily available for rent. Properties of this size are rarely built by private developers and many authorities characterize their programme as 'filling the gaps' in the market left by other builders. Even so, there is some evidence that the units local authorities are building are still too large and too expensive for many small businesses, and particularly new start-ups. Thus although three-quarters of authorities claim to have provided 'starter' premises designed and managed to suit the requirements of new firms, one survey found that tenants of such 'mini-factories' predominantly have several years' trading experience (Goodrun, 1980). Cheaper, refurbished properties are typically favoured by new start-ups, but in 1982 only 12 per cent of local authority units were in this sort of scheme (Perry, 1986).

The result of the many individual programmes is a complex geographical pattern of local authority factory provision. Surveys by Urbed (1979) and the Association of District Councils (1983) covered all sizes of factory built by local authorities, but the former covered only urban areas and the latter was limited to district councils. Both identified the concentration of activity at the smallest end of the market. The most comprehensive sources of information are the surveys of local authority provision of small units, mentioned earlier (Perry, 1986). These identified an area of inactivity in the South East outside London, where a combination of restrictive industrial development policies (to protect green belt land and existing firms from competition for labour) and a willingness by the private sector to develop speculative factory units appears to account for the low provision. Nonetheless, even here some authorities had been very active: Aylesbury Vale had completed 145 units by 1982, and North Bedfordshire 68 units. Within London, two-thirds of the boroughs had supplied factory premises, and the inner London boroughs had been especially active, partly because in some areas funds from the government's Urban Programme were available.

The scale of provision in London was sufficient to ensure that more local authority factory units were built in the South East than in any other region, as Table 6.7 shows, though in relation to the size of the region (measured by population) more were built in the East Midlands, East Anglia and the

	No. of units	% of total	Average no. of factories per active authority	Factories per 100,000 population	% of authorities with factories
South East	1,706	31.5	40	10	36
East Midlands	1,260	23.5	57	33	66
North West	538	10.0	26	8	77
Yorkshire and Humberside	426	8.0	42	8	44
South West	412	7.5	21	9	54
East Anglia	372	7.0	29	20	62
North	367	7.0	19	12	82
West Midlands	295	5.5	16	5	56
ENGLAND	5,376	100.0	33	11	54

Table 6.7 *Regional distribution of local authority factory building, England, 1976–82*

Note: Data refer only to survey respondents and exclude premises of more than 5,000 ft^2

Source: Perry (1986)

North. The table also shows that local authorities in the assisted areas no longer dominate factory provision. In fact, although two-thirds of local authorities in the assisted areas (as defined in 1982) had built small factory premises compared with under half elsewhere, the authorities in the assisted areas supplied only 29 per cent of the factory units identified by the survey. Part of the reason may be that local authorities in the assisted areas take account of the factories built by English Estates. Another possibility is that the demand for small units in the assisted areas is limited by a low rate of formation of new firms.

In addition, the northern and western parts of the country do not benefit much from partnerships between local authorities and the private sector. Partnership schemes have long been common as a means of implementing town centre redevelopment, and during the late 1970s interest grew in their use for industrial projects. Between 1976 and 1982, one in three of the factory units built by local authorities was the result of joint funding arrangements (Perry, 1986). The benefits to the local authority are financial savings, because funds come from the private sector, and greater influence over schemes that in purely private hands might have taken a different form.

The most common form of partnership is a 'leaseback' arrangement. This usually involves the authority leasing a site at a nominal rent to a developer, who undertakes to build an agreed scheme. The developer then leases the completed development back to the local authority, who sublets to tenants, and normally at this stage the developer also sells his interest — at a profit — to a financial institution. The local authority and the financial institution recoup their investments as a flow of rent, but whereas the institution's income is guaranteed because the whole development is leased to the local authority, the authority bears the risk of vacancies. The only uncertainty for the financial institution is the amount of long-term rental growth. Variants on this standard leaseback arrangement generally leave the local authority with less influence over the letting and management of the factory units.

Although partnership units can be found in all regions, they are concentrated in the areas most attractive to private capital. In 1982, half of the local authorities that provided factory space had built some or all of their units in partnership with the private sector, but in the Northern region this proportion fell below a fifth and in the South East it was as high as three-quarters. The locations preferred by private developers and funding institutions are those where the balance between the demand and supply for factory space indicates that rents are likely to increase faster than inflation: the 'M4 corridor' west of London is a good example.

Assuming the location is acceptable to a private developer, cooperation with a local authority usually requires a number of other conditions to be met. Private developers prefer sites with good access, close to highways and accessible to a large labour force. The provision of 'bare shells' with minimum services is often favoured by local authorities to enable rents to be kept as low as possible, whereas the private sector seeks a long life for its investment, which can be prejudiced by low building standards. The appearance and upkeep of an estate, which affects its value, is another potential area of conflict. Local authority estate management can inhibit investors where they fear that the council's employment priorities may lead it to reject more secure and cleaner enterprises in favour of risky or 'bad neighbour' tenants that offer more jobs. This view has been expressed by the National Coal Board Pension Fund, for example, a major institutional investor in property, which has deliberately avoided partnership agreements with local authorities.

It is increasingly questionable, however, whether the scale of local authority provision of factory space can be sustained in the face of tightening constraints on local spending. The traditional source of finance, a central government allocation to local authorities in the form of a 'right to borrow', has been progressively reduced since the mid 1970s, so that factory building programmes are increasingly in conflict with other capital projects. Capital receipts from the sale of existing local authority assets have been exploited as an alternative, but the amount that can be re-cycled into new projects has been limited by central government. Partnership schemes, too, are subject to stricter guidelines laid down by Whitehall. Increasingly, therefore, local authority funding for factory building is available only on a selective and limited basis through specific government initiatives, notably the Urban Programme.

The evaluation of public factory building

At one extreme, some local authorities claim that all the jobs in factories built by them are jobs that they have created. This makes their factory programmes appear highly successful and cost–effective. At the other extreme, it might be argued that public sector factory building simply displaces an equal amount of private sector factory building, so that there is no net impact on the stock of floorspace or level of economic activity.

The detailed evaluation of factory programmes has not been a hallmark of public development agencies. Partly this reflects the difficulties of identifying the precise importance of property in generating employment: premises permit growth, but they do not cause it. It is also a reflection of the varied objectives of factory programmes. The widespread concern with job creation hides many variations in policy emphasis, and public agencies often set subsidiary objectives that are not easily quantified, such as environmental improvement and the promotion of an 'enterprise culture'.

The most difficult problem of all is to assess the impact on local unemployment. Even if job creation can be measured successfully, the effect on local unemployment depends on the types of jobs created — e.g. whether they are filled by men or women, and the level of skill required — on patterns of commuting and on the impact on migration. For instance, if a high proportion of the jobs are part-time they are likely to be taken by women who had previously not been registered as unemployed, so the impact on the published rate of unemployment will be negligible.

The most common approach in the evaluation of public factory programmes is essentially 'partial'. The direct impact on the firms occupying the new factories is assessed, but the effect on the scale of private sector factory development is ignored. However, there is no single model even for this partial approach. For example, Willis (1983, 1985) distinguishes three methods to identify the employment consequences of factory programmes.

The first compares the level of employment within firms at two points in time, one before occupying the new factory and the other a period of time afterwards. The difference in employment between these points is then attributed to the factory programme. Clearly, this method ignores the changes in firms' employment that would in any case have taken place. However, its value is enhanced if the employment gains are also traced through the vacancy chain initiated when an existing business moves into a new public sector factory.

The second method compares the employment growth in the firms moving into the new factories with the likely position had the firms not moved. The most thorough way to establish this hypothetical alternative is to collect information for a matched sample of firms that do not benefit from occupying a public sector factory. The firms should be matched in terms of product, size, location, technology and corporate status. The problem is that this sort of match is not easily achieved, rendering this particular method of evaluation very difficult.

The third method relies on firms' own judgement. Firms are asked to assess the effect of occupying the new public sector factory, compared with the alternative they faced.

These three methods for measuring the direct employment effects are not mutually exclusive and can be used in combination as a check on the reliability of the results. For example, in a study of local authority provision in Tyne and Wear by Cameron *et al.* (1982) managers were asked how many people they would have employed if they had not moved into their advance factory, and this was compared with the actual number employed. This method indicated that the factory programme had created 210 additional jobs. However, a simple comparison between employment levels before and after moving into the new factories indicated a gain of 950 jobs.

The second and third methods, which aim to establish an alternative position in the absence of factory provision, can be applied to the workforce itself. For example, Hodge and Whitby (1979) asked employees in Development Commission factories what they thought they would have been doing if factory employment had not been available. Apart from people moving from unemployment and from other local jobs, some had intended to migrate in search of work, and others who had not been registered unemployed had been drawn into the labour force.

But perhaps more relevant than a single figure for the jobs created is the cost-effectiveness of factory provision. The principal financial characteristics of a factory programme are high capital costs during the development phase, offset by low running costs (administration and maintenance) in subsequent years and by rent receipts. However, not all the costs and revenues necessarily accrue to the factory building agency. A local authority's development costs, for example, may be offset by a subsidy from central government. Regional Development Grants and Derelict Land Grants are two such subsidies. From the point of view of the public sector as a whole, the cost-per-job calculations are also complicated by changes in social security payments and tax revenue that result from any job creation. Not surprisingly in the face of these complexities, public developers usually fall back on simpler financial criteria, such as the rate of return on capital invested.

Evaluation is therefore a quagmire of competing methods, inadequate data and real-world complexity. What can be stated with some certainty, however, is that public sector factory provision has brought jobs to areas of need. This is particularly true of the factories built by English Estates.

For example, the Department of Trade and Industry (1973) surveyed firms that opened a new manufacturing plant in an area where they had previously not operated. The availability of labour and investment grants emerged as the main factors influencing the choice of location, but 18 per cent of the moves to the assisted areas cited the immediate availability of a government factory as a major factor.

English Estates' factory building has also steered jobs to specific places within the assisted areas. A study of firms moving into Devon and Cornwall between 1939 and 1967 found that the availability of government built factories was the main influence on where firms located (Spooner, 1972). The same process could be observed in North East England during the heyday of regional policy in the 1960s and early 1970s. At that time the North East's most acute employment problems were in the coalfield areas of Durham and south-east Northumberland, where mining was contracting rapidly and where there were few jobs for women. Advance factory building by English Estates was therefore addressed to the needs of these areas, and with some success. The coalfield areas, with just over 20 per cent of the North East's employment, received 40 per cent of the floorspace in advance factories and secured 40 per cent of the manufacturing jobs recorded in new openings (Fothergill, 1976). There are still not enough jobs, but within the coalfields the industrial estates developed by English Estates have become the new nodes around which local economies are organized, replacing the pits which have disappeared entirely from some areas.

The most recent and comprehensive study of the benefits of English

Estates' factory building, which also looked at provision by the Scottish and Welsh Development Agencies, was carried out for the Department of Trade and Industry by Cambridge Economic Consultants (1985). It tried to establish the extent to which jobs in government were additional to the local area and additional to the region.

One of the ways the study tackled this issue was by surveying 200 tenants of government built factories. Firms were asked not only why they had located where they did, but also what they would have done if their advance factory had not been available. A third of the branch plants from outside the region said they would have found an alternative factory in the same locality; a third said they would have gone elsewhere in the same region; the remaining third would have gone to a different region. Transfers, new start-ups and branches with origins inside the region would have been more likely to look for an alternative factory in the same area. Over 40 per cent of new start-ups said that the setting up of the company would have been delayed or cancelled.

This information, weighted by the number of jobs in different types of establishments, was used to estimate the number of jobs created in the assisted areas by the advance factory programme. The conclusion was that for every 1,000 jobs in firms occupying government advance factories, some 480 are additional to the particular local area in which the factories are built, and between 230 and 340 are additional to the assisted areas as a whole.

The same issue was also examined through analysis of aggregate data on industrial movement between 1960 and 1978. The results suggested that some 11,200 manufacturing jobs had been attracted into Wales, Scotland and the Northern region by government factory building, an estimate broadly consistent with the findings of the company survey.

The study took the analysis further by quantifying the jobs displaced (e.g. by competition) by firms in government built factories and the jobs created through linkages with suppliers. For every 100 jobs created, it was estimated that 19 others are displaced in the same local area and 38 in the same region; but 9 additional manufacturing jobs are created locally through linkages, and 13 in the region as a whole. On balance, therefore, government factory building still adds significantly to an area's employment.

Finally, the study looked at the quality and security of employment provided in government advance factories. It was estimated that for every 100 jobs created, roughly 91 are filled by existing local residents. The occupational structure of the jobs is on average of a lower quality (measured by the proportion of qualified and skilled manual occupations) than the average in the same areas and industries. The jobs also appear to be marginally less secure, measured by the closure rate of firms.

Impact on the private sector

As we explained, these partial evaluations do not take account of the impact of public factory programmes on private sector factory building. A full evaluation requires these consequences to be considered.

An important point, in this context, is that public sector intervention is concentrated in just a few segments of the industrial property market. The public sector mostly builds general purpose advance factories, for example, but the firm with special needs is unlikely to find one of these an acceptable alternative to a custom built factory. Consequently, in the assisted areas where the public sector has been most active, it is not unusual to find continuing private provision of custom built floorspace alongside a large surplus of public sector space.

But as we have seen, especially in the provision of small and medium sized units in the assisted areas, the public sector accounts for a significant proportion of the stock and the majority of the new floorspace coming onto the market. A study for the Department of Trade and Industry (Coopers & Lybrand Associates, 1984) confirmed this tendency in a number of specific areas. In Sunderland, for example, only 1,400 m² of speculative industrial space had been provided by the private sector between 1974 and 1983, compared with 58,000 m² by the public sector — in this instance mostly by Washington New Town, which falls within the boundaries of the district. In the Wirral (one of the districts of Merseyside county) English Estates had provided 80,000 m² between 1976 and 1983 but the only private sector activity involved refurbishments and a development of eight new units on a pre-let basis. In Cardiff the situation was little different: the Welsh Development Agency had built 50,000 m² of industrial floorspace on the former site of the East Moors steelworks and private provision of speculative space had all but disappeared, though the private sector had been active prior to the agency's intervention. In Bradford, St Helens and Plymouth, three further case study areas, a measure of private sector speculative provision did coexist with public provision, but here the scale of public involvement had been more limited.

In the areas where the public sector is the dominant supplier of speculative industrial floorspace any residual private supply of speculative space competes in a rather different market. Cambridge Economic Consultants (1985), in their evaluation of the advance factory programme, found great difficulty in identifying new, privately rented industrial premises in the assisted areas, which testifies to the dominance of the public sector. Where the private sector had provided space it differed in three important respects. First, it was almost always near motorway junctions or trunk roads, and close to cities. This arises because private developers perceive tenants' needs as being dominated by transport costs and travel time. Public sector factories, in contrast, are often located near to pools of available labour. Second, a higher proportion of the private sector tenants were warehousing and dis-tribution companies. The private sector usually views these as better bets than manufacturing industry, because they generally make fewer specialist demands on the buildings and do not cause as much wear and tear. Third, a higher proportion of the occupants of privately built factories were 'blue-chip' tenants — national companies with established reputations, that are unlikely to go bankrupt or default on payments. The typical tenant of a new private development in an assisted area is therefore a regional distribu-tion depot of a major national company whose choice of location has been determined primarily by accessibility and proximity to the market, rather than by labour supply, financial incentives or the character of the factory itself. In effect, the few new, privately rented factories in the assisted areas compete in a different market from those built by the public sector. Before 1980, when few non-manufacturers were eligible for government factories, this market segmentation was even more marked.

Private sector factory building appears to coexist with public provision, in the same segment of the market, only when public provision is on a small scale. However, it does not follow that large-scale public sector activity automatically displaces the private sector. One complication is that the recession at the start of the 1980s reduced the private provision of specula-tive industrial space in almost all areas: the depressed demand for property and the large quantities of second-hand floorspace coming onto the market undermined the attractiveness of new investments. Thus even in Norwich, for example, where the public sector had not been involved, private sector speculative development had come to a near standstill by 1984 (Coopers & Lybrand Associates, 1984). Furthermore, the areas where industry was hit worst during the recession were generally the ones where the private sector was already the least active.

The evaluation of government factory building by Coopers & Lybrand Associates (1984) argued that in order to assess whether displacement occurs one has to look at the criteria the public and private sectors use in appraising potential investments.

The preconditions for private sector speculative factory development were outlined in chapter 3. First, the private sector requires evidence of scarcity in order to be confident that the development will be marketable. It would normally aim to let a completed development within 6 months, and certainly within a year. Second, it must be able to secure an adequate rate of return on its investment. In the mid 1980s this would be a profit margin of at least 20 per cent if the completed development were sold, or, in the assisted areas, an initial yield as high as 10 or 15 per cent to offset the risk of the investment and poor prospects of real growth in capital values and rents.

English Estates' investment criteria in building factories for the Depart-ment of Trade and Industry are laid down in the 1980 guidelines. These require an initial minimum yield of 7 per cent in a Development Area and 8 per cent in an Intermediate Area. English Estates must also take account of perceived market need, which is interpreted as ensuring that there is no more than 2 years' stock available in the specific size group in an area at the current rate of take-up. The Welsh Development Agency operates the same 2 year stock rule, though its financial criteria are rather more complex. New Towns are required by the Department of the Environment to achieve a 10 per cent initial return on the costs of industrial development, though they can and do obtain permission to go ahead with developments showing rates of return as low as 7 per cent. Finally, local authorities do not operate any consistent financial criteria, but tend to base their decisions on wider social, economic and political considerations. Added to this, the public sector shows a willingness to let completed property on terms that the private sector is unwilling to concede. Traditionally the private sector tries to let units on 25 year leases; the public sector has undercut this by offering 'easy in, easy out' terms, with shorter leases, and for the smallest units the possibility of merely paying weekly or monthly rents.

All these public sector criteria, and especially those of local authorities, are more lenient than those of the private sector. The result is that the public sector becomes involved in factory building where the private sector will not. However — and this is the crucial point — in providing speculative factories on non-commercial criteria the public sector actually reinforces the conditions which deter the private sector. In particular, the high proportion of vacancies that the public sector is willing to accept in its property portfolio depresses rent levels and removes the scarcity which is crucial if the private sector is to become involved. Simply because of the terms and conditions on which the public sector is active, the private sector often finds that it cannot meet its minimum criteria for involvement.

But would the private sector ever become involved in speculative factory building in Britain's most depressed industrial areas? Economic theory suggests it would. If the public sector were to stop building new factories in depressed areas there would be a period when no new speculative space would be built. Eventually, because no new property was being supplied the existing stock of vacant premises would become occupied, since even in depressed areas there is some demand for new property. Conditions of scarcity would begin to be created, and rents would begin to rise. Sooner or later the point would be reached when the private sector would find it sufficiently profitable to become involved.

Against this view a number of points should be made. First, the delay before the private sector became involved might be very considerable. There is a large 'overhang' of empty, publicly owned floorspace which in a depressed economy would take some years to disappear. Second, the financial institutions are now so wary of investment in industrial property in the assisted areas that they would take much convincing that they should move into this market. No doubt investment in the assisted areas would have to become more rewarding than comparable investment in South East England before the financial institutions would overcome their prejudice and caution. Third, the track record of the private sector does not suggest it is very good at identifying market gaps and investment opportunities. Its involvement — or rather lack of it — in the provision of premises for very small factory units and workshops is a case in point: in the assisted areas this was a new market pioneered by the public sector. It is therefore misleading to think that the supply of industrial property would respond smoothly to market signals if the public sector were to withdraw from its current heavy involvement. A better characterization is that the private sector's response would be hesitant, partial and slow.

However, much of this debate about the displacement of the private sector misses the point. Even if the public sector displaces the private sector entirely from some market segments in some locations, this is not necessarily a cause for concern. The point is that public sector factory building is not intended to be a mere substitute for private sector activity. Its aim is not to replicate the sort of industrial property market that can be found in the South East, for example, where the private sector is active. Instead, the intention is to provide a better supply of property in the assisted areas than would be the case if the private sector were left to itself, and to give these areas an advantage over the rest of the country in promoting economic development.

There can be little doubt that the private sector, left to its own devices, would not have provided the quantity and range of factories that have been built in the assisted areas. In particular, it would not have provided the large stock of advance factories intended to provide immediate accommodation for mobile firms from other regions and abroad. It is an anathema to the private sector to build factories that would stand empty for prolonged periods awaiting a tenant. Yet it is precisely this sort of factory building, in advance of need, that has proved so useful in helping attract jobs to the assisted areas and in steering those jobs to the places of greatest need.

The unintended but unavoidable side-effect of large-scale public sector provision is that it does displace private sector speculative activity. The public sector therefore finds itself not only adding to the supply of property at the margin, but having to take over responsibility for the whole of the supply of speculative industrial space. And once having made this commitment there is no going back: the time lag before the private sector would get involved again would be politically unacceptable. If public intervention is going to continue to make a valuable contribution to urban and regional economic development, these inevitable consequences must be accepted.

7　Small firms

Small manufacturing firms have traditionally occupied the worst premises — the sweatshops, the backyards and the rooms above shops in the poorer quarters of town. The inner city, in particular, is frequently characterized as a prime location for workshops and small factories, often in old converted buildings never designed for manufacturing and jostling cheek by jowl with competing land uses. This image dies hard. But in the 1980s 'sweatshops' have become 'seedbeds', and public and private developers up and down the country have become energetic providers of premises for small firms. A small firm is now likely to be found on a trading estate in a unit built by its local authority, rather than working from under the proverbial railway arch. Local authorities, the traditional bugbear of small business, are now its major benefactor.

The interest in small industrial property is one aspect of the political rehabilitation of the UK's small-business sector. Sometimes, small firms are projected as a panacea for raising national economic growth and regenerating rundown urban areas at the same time. Some of these hopes are undoubtedly misplaced because there is a limit to what small firms can achieve, especially if the rest of industry continues its downward slide. But if small firms do fail to live up to expectations it is not through lack of trying. A whole range of policies and schemes have been introduced to enhance their growth. Encouragement to invest in small premises is just part of a larger package including loan guarantees, new enterprise programmes for the unemployed, business advice schemes and a favourable tax regime.

It is against this background that this chapter looks at the provision of premises for small manufacturing firms. First, we consider their distinctive needs and the ways in which they are met. This is followed by a closer look at the supply of new small units and the terms on which they are managed, including a case study of new provision in Cornwall. Finally, the chapter considers the importance of property availability for the formation and growth of small businesses.

The property needs of small firms

One of the characteristics that distinguishes independent small firms in the property market is their dependence on rented accommodation. This owes a great deal to their financial predicament. They generally have difficulty in obtaining long-term loans for investment in land and property because they cannot offer the financial guarantees the banks require, and when loans are available the owner-manager is often required to offer his or her own home as security. It is not surprising, therefore, that most new businesses rely initially on the personal savings of the founder, which are necessarily limited. And as the business subsequently develops there may not be sufficient capital to finance investment in property as well as investment in machines and materials.

Lack of finance also means that small firms usually cannot take a long-term view of their property needs. A large firm can ensure a long life from its factory by finding a site with room for expansion. A small firm, in contrast, is usually under pressure to trim expenditure to meet immediate needs. This implies premises that give sufficient space for current activities but little margin for growth. Short-term increases in production or storage needs may be met by renting additional space nearby, if such space can be found at a cost the business can afford, but sustained expansion normally means relocation.

Small firms' property needs are themselves often volatile, changing rapidly depending on the commercial success or failure of the business. Entirely new firms, in particular, are likely to be uncertain about the final scale and form of the business. It therefore makes sense to avoid investing a great deal in a property that may quickly become unsuitable. Research in Birmingham, for example, found that for firms with fewer than 25 employees the median length of occupation of premises was 8 years, compared with over 50 years for firms with more than 250 employees (JURUE, 1980).

All these considerations mean that the typical small firm prefers cheap, rented accommodation, on a lease that is long enough to offer some security but short enough to provide the freedom to move if necessary. Even among established small businesses faced with the need to relocate, only a quarter are prepared to consider buying a property (Chalkley, 1978).

Another distinguishing characteristic of the small firm is its tightly drawn area of search for premises. Few managers look beyond 2 or 3 miles from their present location and many limit the search to even more restricted areas. In the case of a firm just starting up, this is usually because the founder is reluctant to move house. For more established small firms, the preference to remain within the existing locality usually arises from a dependence on local labour, suppliers and customers. However, this means that within a given small area of search there are likely to be only a few premises available that might meet a firm's requirements. Property search procedures accentuate the difficulty. It is normally the firm's owner-manager who undertakes the selection of property and, in order to minimize disruption to the normal round of business duties, the search is often combined with other personal and work journeys. Informal contacts with employers, suppliers and customers may therefore be an important source of information on vacant properties, and this can be somewhat haphazard.

One way of looking at the property needs of small firms is to see them as a series of evolutionary steps. Falk (1978) outlined five phases in the development of a typical business: embryonic (hobby or part-time enterprise), infant (full-time employment for one or more people), youthful (several employees), established (basic work processes mechanized) and institutionalized (management and production roles clearly separated). According to Falk, business growth involves crossing thresholds which alter the balance of the company's activities and which are facilitated by an appropriate environment. Each stage in the firm's development is marked by a move on the 'premises ladder'. The first rung on the ladder is often the founder's home (e.g. a spare room or garage), followed by a small second-hand workshop, a new small unit and, finally, a high quality leasehold property or even a purpose designed factory when the needs of the company have taken a definite form.

Of course, not all firms develop in this stereotyped fashion. Indeed, many small businesses exhibit a strong disinclination to grow at all. Consequently, surveys that have tried to find evidence of Falk's property ladder working in practice have failed to do so. Rather than this idealized progression it is perhaps more useful to think in terms of broad categories of accommodation, each suited to particular types of enterprise at different stages of development. The following categorization identifies the typical forms of small industrial property being supplied and the tenants whose needs they are intended to meet.

Refurbished accommodation

The refurbishment of old premises to provide space for small firms is becoming increasingly popular. Some developers deliberately undertake a minimum amount of refurbishment to provide cheap and basic accommodation. In Devon, for example, a former army camp was made available by the local authority after little adaptation. In London, old multistorey warehouses have been converted to provide small workshops: the Clerkenwell Workshops, which contain 75 separate units, are an example. As well as providing accommodation for small enterprises, this type of scheme can bring the additional benefit of conserving a historic building. Another form of rehabilitation involves the conversion and subdivision of space under-utilized by existing occupants of larger buildings. This provides a useful additional source of income for the firm letting or subletting part of its floorspace. Rehabilitation is normally only worthwhile where the work can be carried out at a cost appreciably below that required to provide equivalent new property, and the process of conversion can be difficult if the property has fallen into disrepair or if the original layout needs major alteration. The need to conform to modern building and fire regulations adds to the cost. Nevertheless, where the costs can be kept down, rehabilitation is a feasible means of providing accommodation: Green and Foley (1982) found that conversion costs averaged just over £2 per ft^2, whereas English Estates estimated a cost of £15 per ft^2 for new units. In many cases refurbished units are associated with flexible management that allows short-term tenancies. This, combined with low rents, makes them particularly attractive to firms entering the property market for the first time.

Nursery units

Nursery units are intended to be very small premises suitable for new businesses, and are usually provided in terraces around shared parking and service areas. To minimize rents, the design and construction are usually kept simple; even so, Green and Foley (1982) found that in West Yorkshire rents in nursery units were twice those in converted premises. In practice few tenants are genuinely new firms in their first property. In Peterborough, for example, less than a quarter of the tenants of nursery units had started trading there, though the majority of the firms had been established for only a few years (Goodrun, 1980). The main role of nursery units may therefore be to foster youthful businesses rather than new start-ups.

Shared-service accommodation

The rationale behind this type of provision is that small firms, and particularly new starts, need services that they cannot afford to buy for their own exclusive use. A few developers have recognized the potential by providing accommodation plus supporting services on a shared basis. The majority of such schemes rely wholly or in large part on public sector finance (Department of Industry and Shell UK, 1982). The common services typically comprise secretarial facilities, business advice, conference rooms and a canteen, and in some schemes access to computing resources are also provided. Birmingham's New Enterprise Workshops are an example, where shared facilities are available as part of a refurbishment project. Tenants pay a licence fee which includes charges for both accommodation and service use. Shared-service schemes directed specifically at high technology firms are usually associated with a university based science park and provide access to the university's facilities as well as conventional services. An example is the 'incubator building' at Warwick University's science park, where the units are reserved for entrepreneurs from the university and for ventures in advanced technology that wish to draw on the university's resources.

Flatted factories

In some industries — textiles, furniture and clothing in particular — small firms have traditionally rented factory space in larger multistorey buildings. In the clothing industry, for example, there are many cases of flatted factories built by private developers between the wars, and of large firms building premises with the intention of letting a substantial part to smaller firms. But flatted factories are not popular with many firms, who prefer ground floor premises. Thus they are occupied predominantly by enterprises that might normally be housed in office accommodation, e.g. photographers' workshops. Flatted factories are now rarely provided by developers, except through the rehabilitation of old multistorey buildings.

Terraced factories

The most common form of new provision for small firms is a terrace of industrial units of between 100 and 400 m². Terraces reduce building costs and allow some flexibility in the partitioning of space so that the size of individual units can be changed. The idea is not new — examples can be found on some of the earliest trading estates — but the design is particularly suited to small firms looking for standard, relatively low-cost accommodation without adjoining land for expansion. Terraces are usually single storey, but the specification of units can vary widely. Public developers sometimes prefer to provide a 'bare shell', allowing the occupant to adapt the property to meet its needs. Private developers tend to prefer a high standard of unit which provides separate offices and multiple access to the property.

Detached and semi-detached factories

This type of provision is rare because of the high building costs compared with those of terraced construction, and the units tend to be individually larger. Examples can be found within the Development Commission's factory programme in rural areas. A few private developers also include small premises of this sort on their estates, aiming to attract established small businesses.

Science parks

Science parks provide buildings of flexible design and varying sizes in a high quality environment with extensive landscaping. They are intended for high technology firms involved in both research and manufacturing, and the buildings usually differ from those on a traditional trading estate by having a higher proportion of office and laboratory space. The concept of a science park was originally developed in the United States. In Britain, the Cambridge Science Park, owned by Trinity College, is the most fully developed example, but elsewhere — in Warrington and Bristol, for example — science parks have been developed without formal links with a university. 'Pure' science parks tend to rely on public finance and there are only a few successful ones; 'high technology' estates are more widespread and have attracted significant private investment, but these are often little more than high quality versions of traditional trading estates.

The supply of small premises

Let us now look in more detail at the supply of small industrial premises, which in this context we will define as premises of less than 500 m² (5,400 ft²). Buildings of this size might normally be expected to accommodate firms with up to 20 employees, though most occupants will employ considerably fewer than this.

Numerically, small premises dominate the stock of factory space: chapter 2 showed that in 1985 there were more than 60,000 industrial units of less than 500 m² in England and Wales — over half the total number of industrial premises. In terms of floorspace, units of this size were less important: they provided 13.5m m², or 6 per cent of the total. However, the number of small units has been growing and they account for a rising proportion of the total stock of floorspace. Indeed, while the overall stock of factory space began to decline during the 1980s, investment in new small units reached an all-time high.

This is illustrated in Figure 7.1. As the property boom of the early 1970s

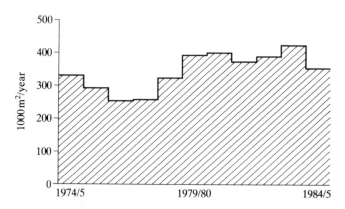

Figure 7.1   *Floorspace built in new small* industrial units, England and Wales, 1974–85*
*less than 500 m²

Source: Commercial and Industrial Floorspace Statistics

petered out, the amount of floorspace built in small units fell to around 250,000 m² a year. But as small firms became an important focus of public policy in the late 1970s the new supply rose swiftly to around 400,000 m² a year, and remained close to this new high level throughout the recession of the early 1980s. As a proportion of all floorspace in new units, small units soared from 10 per cent in the mid 1970s to over 25 per cent in the mid 1980s. In total, more floorspace is now built in units of less than 500 m² than in units of over 10,000 m².

The supply of small factory premises is geographically uneven, as Table 7.1 demonstrates. They account for a significantly higher proportion of the total factory stock in the South East than in any other region, and the proportion is generally higher in Southern England than in the North. The North–South disparity is also apparent in the supply of new space, where a consistently higher proportion in the South is in small units. It is tempting to ascribe this contrast to the behaviour of the developers of factory space, and in particular the private sector's aversion to property investment in the more depressed northern regions, but the main influence is probably the traditional dominance of the economies of the northern regions by large manufacturing establishments.

New small premises are predominantly supplied on a speculative basis by developers because, as we explained, small firms generally lack the resources to build for themselves. All the public sector factory building

	% of total factory space, 1985	New small units, 1974–85	
		m²	% of all floorspace in new units
South East	8.9	917,000	18.5
East Midlands	6.0	406,000	19.1
South West	5.9	360,000	18.4
West Midlands	5.7	679,000	18.8
Wales	5.1	273,000	12.7
East Anglia	4.8	141,000	16.1
Yorkshire and Humberside	4.2	235,000	9.2
North West	4.2	455,000	13.3
North	3.5	270,000	11.9
ENGLAND AND WALES	5.8	3,736,000	15.6

Table 7.1 *Small industrial units* by region*
*Units of less than 500 m²

Source: Commercial and Industrial Floorspace Statistics

agencies, introduced in the previous chapter, are active in the provision of small units. Some, like local authorities, concentrate almost exclusively on this segment of the market.

Table 7.2 provides an estimate of the public sector provision of new small units in England between 1976 and 1982. The figures for English Estates and the Development Commission come from annual reports, and the data for local authorities and New Towns are derived from a special survey (Perry, 1986). Local authorities emerge as much the most important of the public sector suppliers, though the New Towns, English Estates and the Development Commission are major contributors in the areas where they are active. The prominence of local authority provision reflects the view, common among councillors and officials, that small firms are susceptible to local influence, and the hope that limited council budgets can help create jobs in this sector. It also reflects the highly visible nature of factory building at a time when there is pressure on politicians to be seen to be doing something about unemployment.

	m^2	%
Local authorities	1,600,000	71.6
New Towns	380,000	17.0
English Estates		
Development Commission	125,000	5.6
Other (DTI, etc.)	130,000	5.8
TOTAL PUBLIC SECTOR	2,235,000	100.0

Table 7.2   *Public sector suppliers of new small* industrial units, England, 1976–82*
*Units of less than 500 m²

Sources: Annual reports
          Authors' estimates from survey data

The total supply of new small factory units by the public sector during this period was just over 2.2m m². In practice, many of these small industrial units are suitable for use by either manufacturers or service, distribution and warehousing firms. In the survey of local authorities and New Towns, only one in six estate managers considered it 'essential' for the tenants of their small units to be manufacturing firms, though two-thirds 'gave some priority' to manufacturers (Perry, 1986). In a survey of new small units in Cornwall, described later, just over half the occupants were engaged in manufacturing. A reasonable estimate might therefore be that of the

2.2m m² built by the public sector, roughly half — 1.1m m² — is in 'industrial' (i.e. manufacturing) use. This compares with an overall supply of new small 'industrial' units, shown in the published floorspace statistics, of 1.8m m². The difference — 0.7m m² — can be attributed to the private sector, which therefore emerges as less important than the public sector as a source of small industrial units.

Private funds for the speculative development of industrial property come mainly from financial institutions such as pension funds and insurance companies, but as chapter 3 explained, this investment is tied to a narrow range of prime property. Small factories are usually excluded from this category becaue they are expensive to manage, and involve greater risk of non-payment of rent and poor maintenance by the occupants.

To try to overcome this reluctance to invest, the Small Workshop Scheme, introduced in 1980, increased the proportion of building investment that could be offset against tax from 50 to 100 per cent. The scheme applied to industrial premises of less than 2,500 ft² (232 m²) and initially ran for 3 years. It was later extended for a further 2 years for premises of less than 1,250 ft² (116 m²) and widened to include buildings used for repairing, servicing and the storage of industrial goods as well as manufacturing.

The Small Workshop Scheme was a partial success. A review undertaken by the Department of Trade and Industry (1985) estimated that the private sector supply of workshops was some three times greater than could have been expected on the basis of pre-1980 levels of provision. But despite the overall increase, a number of limitations were noted. New developments were concentrated in the South East, particularly London, and some of the more prosperous urban areas; isolated rural communities and the assisted areas continued to depend on public developers for a supply of new small units. Also, even in the favoured areas the units were financed not by major City institutions but by small development companies, many of whom lacked any previous history of factory building. This is probably not surprising since financial institutions like pension funds and insurance companies already had special tax provisions exempting them from paying on property investments. It appears, therefore, that the scheme did not greatly affect attitudes towards the provision of small workshops, but rather attracted a wave of one-off developers looking for tax efficient investments.

Property management and allocation

Procedures regulating the allocation of factories to tenants are a feature of the industrial property market that impinge particularly on small firms because of their need for rented accommodation and their financial instability.

The small firm looking for premises is likely to encounter property management as a series of hurdles. Its initial assessment of a property will be based on the physical and locational characteristics of the building and its rental and lease terms. For some firms, this information is sufficient to preclude any further interest. For those that remain, the landlord initially considers the firm's main characteristics, such as the nature of its activities and its previous trading history. This filters out more potential tenants — e.g. those that would make bad neighbours. More detailed investigations then follow. These usually consist of at least a formal interview and the examination of references from the bank. The length of time taken by the selection process can vary from only a few days, where estate managers undertake little scrutiny or where the firm has a successful trading record, to several months if particularly searching procedures are followed.

Of course, it may not always be the case that estate managers select tenants from a range of eager applicants. In the 1970s it was reported that new small units were attracting more applicants than there were premises to allocate. Coopers & Lybrand Associates (1980), for example, quoted the case of an inner London borough where over a 6 month period there were 34 inquiries for every small unit advertised. In the 1980s the shortage of small-factory space appears to have eased and many units are now allocated on a 'first come, first served' basis. Having obtained a broadly suitable applicant, landlords do not seek further applications in the hope that other firms will offer better financial guarantees or greater employment gains. Nevertheless, the design of tenant-selection procedures remains a significant issue, whatever the strength of property demand, and differing professional and agency perspectives contribute to a diversity in estate management styles.

Most small businesses prefer short leases. Commercial failure brings the need to vacate the premises because the firm is closing or moving to smaller or cheaper accommodation; success may necessitate a move to larger premises. These pressures underline the advantages of short leases and easy 'exit' conditions. Public sector agencies recognize this by granting short-term tenancies on most of their small factories. Terms of between 1 and 5 years are commonplace. Moreover, the public sector usually allows a firm to give up its tenancy before it expires if it is moving elsewhere in the same vicinity. For the smallest units, typically up to 150 m², flexible tenancy conditions reducing commitments to only a few months are widely available. The most common approach is a 'licence agreement' which may be renewed annually or terminated by the tenant at only 3 months' notice. In the private sector, short leases are less common. Many private developers retain a traditional insistence on leases of at least 21 years, since these provide security for the landlord and minimize management responsibilities and costs, but these terms are undoubtedly at odds with the preferences of most small firms. Shorter leases are generally available in the private sector only where the demand for factory space is sluggish and short leases are necessary as a marketing device.

Other aspects of the lease show less variation. Rent reviews every 3 or 5 years are standard practice, for example. Similarly, responsibility for insurance and maintenance usually lies with the tenant. The main exception is where the building is let by a licence agreement which relieves the tenant of responsibility for insurance or repairs. English Estates also sometimes lets its small units on short leases (up to 12 years) which make the tenant responsible for internal repairs only.

It is normal for the lease to contain restrictions on the building's use. These may relate to specific businesses or potential nuisances such as toxic fumes and dangerous chemicals. Any significant change of activity requires the landlord's permission. Subletting is also strictly regulated because landlords tend to be wary of additional wear and tear and potential management problems. Usually the lease also specifies restrictions on the tenant's freedom to modify the building. Typically the tenant can claim compensation for any improvements made, whilst the landlord can ask for the premises to be reinstated to their original condition at the end of the tenancy.

All factory landlords, in the public and private sectors, try to avoid firms that are potential bad neighbours. Small factories are often built in terraces with shared access and parking, so activities that generate excessive noise, noxious fumes or wastes, or traffic hazards are problematic. There is also another group of firms, including builders, timber merchants and scrap dealers, that require relatively large areas for outdoor storage which may compromise the letting of neighbouring units or cause added wear and tear on the building fabric.

Most estate managers prefer a mix of tenants. This can be achieved by limiting the number of units a single firm occupies on the same estate, and by avoiding tenants dependent on the same market. But the types of enterprise favoured by the public and private sector do vary.

Private landlords seek tenants with a successful trading record and financial resources. New, unproven business ventures are generally considered too risky. Services and high technology companies are viewed as a growing sector, unlike traditional manufacturing, and are therefore favoured. Branch plants of well-known national companies are particularly welcome as the parent company provides good security. By contrast, local authorities tend to view branches as vulnerable to closure during recessions, and they often prefer locally owned enterprises.

At one time the public sector's concern for employment creation was associated with a preference for manufacturing tenants; service firms were less favoured because they often compete in the same market as existing local firms. Although this bias persists it is now rarely enforced with any vigour, partly because of the higher level of vacancies prevalent in new developments. There is also a recognition that many small firms start at the service end of an operation and gradually move into manufacturing. A wider range of enterprises is now accepted, though businesses with a major storage or retail component remain unpopular. Similarly, though public sector landlords are concerned about employment creation, they rarely lay down minimum employment densities or job targets.

The financial vetting of potential tenants is another area where practices vary. Private landlords usually examine firms' past accounts, often with the help of outside accountants. Evidence of successful trading, market growth potential and past profits equal to at least five times the annual rent are normal requirements. A firm without an established trading record may be accepted only if the directors personally guarantee the rent for a number of years. Public sector landlords are more ambivalent in their approach, balancing estate management caution against the need for job creation. The Development Commission has traditionally been the most demanding: it requires a full history of the business, an up-to-date balance sheet and cash flow projections, and a statement of how the tenancy will contribute to the development of the business in terms of sales, employment and productivity. At the other extreme, would-be tenants of English Estates' Beehive work-shop programme, intended to encourage new local businesses, merely have to submit financial references and sign short-term tenancy agreements. Local authority estate management practices vary between these two extremes. One authority in the North East, for example, always conducts interviews, examines firms' accounts, requests cash flow and marketing projections and asks for a personal guarantee of the rent. Conversely, a small number of authorities base their decisions on minimal investigations: two authorities in the South West rely solely on interviews with potential tenants. But a tendency common to nearly all is that the financial standards expected of entirely new ventures are less demanding than those expected of established businesses.

The rents charged for small factory units reflect the differing priorities of public and private sector landlords. In the private sector, rents are set to maximize the return on the investment, which means the highest level that the market will bear. The main public development agencies also set their rents at a 'market' level, but in many depressed areas this is below the minimum that would be required by private developers. Local authority practices, however, often diverge from the practice of market pricing because factory building is seen as part of economic development policy rather than as a purely commercial venture.

Direct comparisons between local authorities and the private sector are difficult because similar units are rarely found in the same location, but where they do exist in close proximity it is not unusual to find rent differences of £5 per m² (or £1,000 a year for a typical 200 m² unit). There are some cases of much greater disparity. In the West Midlands in 1982, Dudley council charged an average rent of only £1.10 a year per square foot, using the government's Urban Programme fund to provide a subsidy, while neigh-bouring South Staffordshire charged on average twice this sum (Perry,

1986). The use of special funds to reduce rents is rare, but many local authorities keep rents down by accepting a longer payback period than is usual in the private sector and by not incorporating full management costs into the accounts. The latter can become significant where a high turnover of tenants means additional re-lettings and extra marketing.

A further 'non-commercial' practice is the use of rent concessions. In 1982, two-thirds of English local authorities and New Towns offered some kind of concession to new tenants of small industrial units (Perry, 1986). The most common was an initial rent-free period, often aimed at enterprises whose employment potential was thought to be greatest. A 6 month rent-free period was typical in the North of England, and even longer rent-free periods were available for manufacturing firms willing to take leases of over 10 years, a concession made possible by ploughing back the Regional Development Grant paid towards the cost of building new premises. English Estates also formerly operated a widespread policy of rent concessions, but as part of the agency's new commercial emphasis this practice was restricted. Rent concessions on English Estates' factories are now limited to small units on estates with persistently high vacancy rates.

Case study: the supply of small industrial units in Cornwall

The roles played by the different suppliers of small factory units are clarified by looking at the property market in Cornwall. This essentially rural county contains new small factories built by several of the main agencies — private developers, local authorities, the Development Commission and English Estates.

During the 1960s and early 1970s Cornwall's manufacturing sector expanded as firms were attracted by regional aid. Until 1982, the whole of the county had Development Area status, and the Camborne–Redruth–Falmouth triangle in the far south west had Special Development Area status. A plentiful supply of relatively cheap labour, reflected in above average unemployment, and a pleasant environment added to the county's attractions. The county council has long been active in developing industrial estates to help diversify the economy, but the provision of small premises by the public sector dates from only the mid 1970s. Between 1976 and 1981 a total of 191 units of less than 500 m² were completed by the various developers, providing 38,000 m² of new floorspace.

As Table 7.3 shows, the private sector supplied roughly a third of these units and half the floorspace. Most of the private units were located in the more accessible eastern end of the county, near Saltash, Liskeard and Bodmin. Nearly all were let on long leases at rents above the county average.

The second largest supply arose from a partnership between English Estates and the private sector, in this instance CIN Properties Ltd. This was

	No. of units	Floorspace (m^2)	Typical unit sizes (m^2)	Typical annual rent (£ per m^2)	Typical lease (years)	Locational priorities
Private sector	63	19,000	350	24.50	21	Larger settlements in eastern Cornwall
Partnerships (EE/private)	44	3,800	70	20.00–29.00	Tenancy agreement	Special Development Area
Development Commission	41	8,950	200	21.50	3–6	Rural communities
Local authorities	27	1,650	50	19.00	3	High unemployment
English Estates	16	5,500	350	24.50	6–12	Special Development Area

Table 7.3   *The developers of small factory units* in Cornwall, 1976–81*
*Units of less than 500 m^2

Sources: Cornwall County Council
         Survey data

part of a national programme of 1,000 jointly financed small premises. In Cornwall the units were built on two estates, near Camborne and Falmouth, in the former Special Development Area, a priority area for English Estates' investment. The premises were designed to be suitable for new businesses, and the stringent letting criteria usually adhered to by the private sector were not applied. The units were let by licence agreements committing the tenants to give only 3 months' notice of their intention to vacate, but rents were towards the top end of the market to satisfy the private sector and to meet English Estates' target rate of return.

The Development Commission was the third largest builder of units. With the exception of the main towns, the whole of Cornwall was a 'Special Investment Area' for priority treatment by the commission. Its factory programme started in 1976 and expanded in three phases. As the programme was intended to assist rural communities, the factories were built in small clusters in isolated locations. However, the distribution of new premises only partly reflected the commission's priorities because suitable building sites were not always available: acquiring sites proved difficult in coastal resorts such as Looe, Fowey and Padstow. The commission set an employment target of 4 jobs per 1,000 ft^2 of floorspace, and gave priority to manufacturers with links to the local economy. Leases were typically shorter than those required by the private sector, and the rents a little lower.

Three district councils (North Cornwall, Kerrier and Carrick) supplied small premises, all workshop-type units. The very small average size of these units arose partly because the councils had limited resources, and partly because the units were intended to fill a gap left by other developers: only the English Estates partnership programme included premises as small. Kerrier and Carrick let units on 3 and 5 year leases, and both were prepared to accept termination with 8 weeks' notice and no financial penalty. Financial investigation of the tenants was kept to a minimum. The building specifications were below those of other developers, and rents were deliberately kept low.

English Estates' small units formed part of a much bigger property portfolio, including larger premises designed to attract firms from outside the county. The small units were concentrated in towns in the west where unemployment was most acute. The average size of the units was large: none was below 2,500 ft^2 (232 m^2). English Estates' small units were formerly reserved for manufacturing firms willing to sign a long lease. Since 1980 a more flexible approach has been adopted, letting small units on leases of between 6 and 12 years. At the same time, the practice of granting initial rent-free periods was dropped in favour of a more commercial approach: rents close to those in the private sector were the norm in Cornwall.

A survey carried out in 1983 provides a profile of the businesses occupying these different premises (Perry, 1986). This covered 122 of the units, including premises built by all the main developers. At the time, 81 of the units were occupied; however, some firms rented more than one so the number of businesses included in the survey was 71.

Over three-quarters were independent businesses. The remaining firms, mainly branch plants, were virtually all in either private sector or English Estates premises. Just over half the total were manufacturers, though very few were in high technology industries. The private sector units had the highest proportion of non-manufacturing tenants.

Only one in five of the firms had started life in the new units. The partnership and local authority units, being the smallest, had the highest proportions of new start-ups, but even two-thirds of the firms in these units had previously operated elsewhere for more than a year. The vast majority of all the tenants were in fact transfers from elsewhere in Cornwall, mostly over short distances. Only nine of the firms had previously operated outside the county. The single most common pattern was for the occupant to be a local firm that had moved out of older, second-hand premises; in other cases the previous property had been another advance factory, a building due for demolition, or the owner's home.

At the time of the survey there were almost 400 full-time and 130 part-time jobs in the 71 firms. Two-thirds of the jobs were held by men. The average number of employees per unit of floorspace was lowest in the private sector units. Almost half the firms had expanded the size of their workforce since moving into the new premises, contributing to a net increase of 136 jobs, and the majority anticipated taking on additional workers within the following 12 months. The strongest growth in employment was amongst the Development Commission's tenants, which may reflect the Commission's especially thorough vetting of potential tenants and its preference for manufacturing firms with good employment prospects.

The typical tenant of a new small factory unit can therefore be described as an established firm, probably in manufacturing, that employs five or six workers and has moved from an older property in the vicinity. In other words, new small premises are acting mainly as entry points into modern property for young businesses rather than as starting grounds for new ones. In moving into the new units, firms may release older premises for new start-ups, but if the intention is to provide help more directly to new firms the premises probably need to be still smaller and still cheaper. This is something that the Development Commission and Cornwall County Council have recognized, and their more recent schemes include low cost accommodation in refurbished older buildings.

It is also clear that in Cornwall, and probably elsewhere, the supply of new small premises is subtly differentiated. The various public and private sector developers do not all build for the same market. In Cornwall, private investors have concentrated in the east of the county; further west, where economic problems are more acute, the public sector dominates. Private sector units are usually larger, more expensive to rent, and available only on long leases. Not surprisingly, the dichotomy is reflected in the profile of tenants: private units, let on a purely commercial basis, accommodate more service activities and branch plants, while the employment objectives of public agencies lead them to accommodate a higher proportion of small, independent manufacturing firms.

Small factories and economic development

In 1980 a report for the Department of Industry argued that there was a serious shortage of premises for small firms: 'There is clear evidence that the shortage of premises has constrained the establishment and development of small firms; the provision of premises on suitable terms has undoubtedly itself had the effect of stimulating the formation of new firms and the growth of existing small firms' (Coopers & Lybrand Associates, 1980, p. 3). The underlying cause of the problem, according to the report, was the reluctance of private developers to build small units. But planning policies were also blamed for the shortage: the redevelopment of city centres and the elimination of 'non-conforming' industrial uses from residential areas had exacerbated the incipient crisis, it was argued.

Hard evidence on the balance between the demand for and supply of small factory premises is difficult to come by. The visible image provided by Britain's redeveloped inner cities is a powerful reminder of the loss of small business accommodation. In American cities, various studies have shown that up to 50 per cent of firms fail to relocate after their premises are demolished to make way for redevelopment (Chalkley, 1978). In Britain, however, redevelopment and compensation procedures differ. Thus in Glasgow renewal has not so much caused company closures as accelerated the suburbanization of employment (McKean, 1975). In Birmingham and Leeds, research indicates high survival rates among displaced firms with some benefiting from the move, albeit reluctantly embarked upon, to premises which give the opportunity to thoroughly reorganize production (Chalkley, 1978). So while urban redevelopment has undoubtedly led to a substantial loss of small premises, fears about the fate of displaced firms may be exaggerated.

Coopers & Lybrand based their conclusions on a number of indicators. First, they observed that the number of inquiries and applications exceeded the number of small premises coming onto the market. Second, the ease with which small units had been let and the low incidence of vacancies were noted. Finally, the ability of developers to increase rents without dampening demand was taken to indicate a shortage of small factories.

All these indicators have limitations. The level of inquiries about premises always runs way ahead of accepted applications: some firms find the property specification and terms unsatisfactory, and others are judged unsuitable by the estate managers because of the nature of their activities or because their financial references are below standard. Concentrating just on the demand for newly completed units is also misleading because, as Green, Foley and Burford (1985) showed in Leeds, estate agents market these properties more heavily than older cheaper units. This is perhaps not surprising since their commission is usually 10 per cent of the first year's rent. Vacancy rates are also difficult to interpret. Whatever the market conditions, there is always a turnover of occupants — typically 10 or 20 per cent of small units fall vacant each year — and how quickly the premises are reoccupied depends partly on legal arrangements and the extent to which the property needs to be adapted.

Studies that rely on broad indicators of market supply and demand must therefore be interpreted with caution. Nor is it possible to quantify the latent demand for small premises — to identify those potential entrepreneurs whose ambitions to start a business have been thwarted by the shortage of suitable premises. Studies of the location of new firms do, however, shed some light on the issue.

One of these studies, in the East Midlands, found that the rate of formation of new manufacturing firms varies markedly from place to place, largely according to the extent to which manufacturing employment is concentrated in large plants (Fothergill and Gudgin, 1982, ch. 6). Local economies dominated by large plants have formation rates only a third or a quarter of those where small plants predominate. It was argued that existing small firms provide the best training ground for potential founders of new small firms, so areas with few existing small firms generate few new firms. Data from the Northern region confirmed this relationship between large plant domination and rates of formation of new firms (Gudgin and Fothergill, 1984). An alternative view, based on data for East Anglia, is that local rates of formation of new firms are strongly influenced by the socio-economic composition of the local workforce: the higher the proportion of white-collar jobs, the greater the rate of formation of new firms (Gould and Keeble, 1984).

The important point is that both views emphasize the supply of entrepreneurial skills rather than the supply of space for new firms. The implication is that new firms' modest property demands can normally be met in most areas, so that the availability of property is not an important explanation for spatial variations in the formation of new firms.

Given that new firms' property needs are minimal, it might be argued that established small firms experience greater difficulty. After a few years, a new firm typically requires more spacious accommodation offering greater security of tenure. But again there is little evidence that property constraints hold back these firms. Research in Manchester and Merseyside, for example, argued that the transformation from a youthful small enterprise to an established business is primarily a managerial problem (Lloyd and Dicken, 1982). The initial development of new businesses, it was suggested, is cushioned by the use of internal funds and labour (from the proprietor and his or her family) that is not fully costed. But as the firms mature they become increasingly subject to the exigencies of the external commercial world. At this stage the weaker collapse or fail to grow further, while a few stronger firms and those with new markets make the transition. In this model, the difficulties of market penetration, access to capital, and genuine shortages of entrepreneurship are the key determinants of firms' growth. Property is not so crucial.

Recent research, therefore, plays down the significance of property in the formation and growth of small firms. It remains possible that in some areas shortages of small property have been acute, to the extent that growth has been stultified, but it is perhaps more characteristic of small firms that they continue to operate from a myriad of converted and second-hand premises rather than go out of business because a suitable property cannot be found.

Thus in a comparison of small firms in Manchester and Merseyside with those in rural Hampshire, Lloyd and Mason (1984) found that more firms in Hampshire experienced problems in obtaining premises. This was explained by the lack of an inheritance of old industrial buildings, by restrictive planning policies and by the absence of public development activity. Nevertheless, differences in the availability of premises did not cause Hampshire's small-business economy to be any less prosperous.

What can be stated with some certainty, however, is that if in recent years there had not been an explosion in the provision of new, small factory units the expansion of the small-firm sector would have been frustrated. Table 7.4 presents evidence on this point. The first column shows the increase in the number of small industrial companies in England and Wales between 1980 and 1984. These figures are estimates derived from data presented by Gallagher (1984) and Ganguly (1985). They show that the number of small industrial companies (less than 15 employees) rose by around 8,000 — an increase of 10 to 15 per cent. This mainly reflects a rate of formation of new firms that was exceptionally high by historical standards. Over the same period the increase in the number of factory units of less than 500 m², shown in the second column, was roughly 6,500 — an increase of 12 per cent.

Because of the way that each set of figures is estimated it would be wrong to infer anything from the small difference between the increase in the number of firms and the increase in the number of premises. The important point is that in the country as a whole and in individual regions there is a broad correspondence between changes in the numbers of firms and premises. So although by the mid 1980s vacancies were widespread in some new, small factory developments, especially in the assisted areas, it is questionable whether a significantly smaller increase in the stock of small premises would have been adequate to cope with the up-surge in the formation of new firms. If the property had not been forthcoming, it is difficult to see how so many new firms would have found somewhere to go.

	Increase in no. of small industrial companies	*Increase in no. of small factory units*
South East	1,750	1,280
South West	1,150	740
East Midlands	1,100	1,190
West Midlands	1,100	990
North West	750	520
Wales	650	560
East Anglia	600	330
Yorkshire and Humberside	550	270
North	450	630
ENGLAND AND WALES	8,100	6,510

Table 7.4   *Growth of the small firm sector, England and Wales, 1980–4*

Sources: Commercial and Industrial Floorspace Statistics
          Authors' estimates

As we showed, the public sector, and especially local authorities, has been the main supplier of this extra space. Indeed, in some areas it has been the only supplier. Provision was never coordinated to achieve such a fortunate balance between expansion in the number of firms and premises, but the out-turn is something with which the public sector can be justifiably pleased. However, it is perhaps ironic that local councils, and in particular Labour councils, so often criticized by government and the business lobby for their expensive forays into economic policy, should have acted as the midwife to a resurgence of small business enterprise.

8 A strategy for industrial buildings

The problem

It is frequently argued that Britain's infrastructure is crumbling. The state of repair of the housing stock is deteriorating and few new houses are being built; investment in roads and the railways has fallen to the lowest level for decades; few new schools and hospitals are being built and the rest get older; and Victorian sewers are in a state of collapse. In a sense the nation is living off its assets: the physical infrastructure that underpins everyday life and economic activity is not being renewed at the rate it is wearing out. An immediate crisis is avoided because Britain, unlike Third World countries, has such a large stock of infrastructure as a result of successive waves of investment, but the long-term problem is very real and very serious.

What is clear is that the factory stock, an important component of Britain's infrastructure, is no exception to the general rule. It may not yet be falling down, like many 1960s tower blocks, but it is getting older and is being renewed only painfully slowly. This is worrying because factory buildings are perhaps the most directly productive of all infrastructure assets. They house the industrial activity that employs a quarter of the workforce, generates a third of national income, and provides half the country's export earnings. And in many cases they do not house it very well. The preceding chapters identified a number of serious problems.

The first is the low rate of new investment. At the average rate of investment in factory buildings between 1974 and 1984 it would take nearly 75 years to replace the existing stock. At the average rate of investment between 1981 and 1984 it would take 110 years. And these estimates make no allowance for the need to provide an increase in the factory stock to accommodate any increase in industrial production. Low investment perpetuates a stock that is ageing, increasingly expensive to maintain, and often poorly suited to modern products and production methods.

Some 40 per cent of factory floorspace dates from before 1945; nearly 20 per cent dates from before 1919. It is doubtful whether any other industrial country has such an old factory stock. Associated with old buildings are other characteristics which modern manufacturing industry often finds problematic: multistorey layouts that disrupt production flows and require additional labour and machinery to move items around; and high site densities that frustrate on-site expansion and cause difficulties for car parking and the loading and unloading of lorries. There is evidence — from statistical analyses and from discussions with firms themselves — that these characteristics impede efficiency and the expansion of output and employment.

The second serious problem is the extensive mismatch between firms' property requirements and the sites and buildings they occupy. Through time, the property needs of manufacturing firms are modified by external economic conditions and technical change and by changes within the firms themselves. Sites and buildings chosen in one era can become inappropriate in another. Of course, many firms respond to this mismatch by moving to new premises, adapting their existing premises or changing the nature of their activities. But many fail to respond, usually because there are constraints on the options open to them — e.g. shortage of finance. The result is that some mismatches are perpetuated over long periods, with detrimental effects on firms' efficiency and growth. The recession in the national economy has not helped either, because it has sapped firms' confidence in bold but expensive long-term schemes to renew their factory buildings.

The third problem is the adverse locational impact of difficulties with sites and buildings. There is a political consensus that the problems of Britain's biggest cities, and their inner areas in particular, require urgent attention. During the last two decades or more, all these cities lost manufacturing jobs more quickly than the country as a whole, whereas such growth as occurred was disproportionately concentrated in small towns and rural areas. This 'urban–rural' contrast in manufacturing employment trends has a great deal to do with the supply of land and buildings for industry. The cities have, on average, the oldest factory buildings and the sites with the least room for expansion. They have less land available for new factory building, and it is usually more expensive than in surrounding areas and frequently requires expenditure on reclamation as a prelude to development. Moreover, the cities also suffer because the rising capital intensity of production and its associated reduction in 'employment density' reduces the number of workers in their existing factories.

Fourth, the supply of industrial property is uncoordinated and, negative planning controls apart, unregulated. No single ministry or agency is charged with assessing what investment in factory floorspace the country needs in order to meet reasonable targets of economic growth and in order to promote economic efficiency. In the property world, larger manufacturing firms generally go about meeting their own needs according to their own criteria. The private sector developers of speculative space are guided by market forces, which is only partially satisfactory given the notorious instability of property markets. The public sector is on the whole unresponsive to the guidance of the market except when it accumulates such a surplus of vacant space that further building is untenable; instead, each of the public agencies operates its own investment criteria. In the chapter on small firms we saw how the growth in the number of businesses has been matched by an expansion in the number of premises for them, but this was more by good luck than good management. Nobody planned it that way. Indeed, the extensive provision of small factory units by local authorities, which has been the cornerstone of the additional supply, is something that the Conservative Government of the 1980s never viewed with much enthusiasm.

These problems should not be tolerated. Factory buildings are a major input into the production process. They account for a third of all manufacturing industry's fixed assets and up to a fifth of its annual investment. Britain is a trading nation, highly integrated with the rest of the world economy and dependent to an alarming extent on the competitiveness of its manufacturing sector in order to sustain its living standards. Therefore, if there are problems with the buildings in which manufacturing industry operates, they affect more than just the firms themselves and ought to be a legitimate concern of public policy.

Reindustrialization and the role of property

A strategy for industrial land and buildings must start from the need to reindustrialize the British economy. Policies towards industrial property should be subservient to, and supportive of, that wider aim.

Over the last few years manufacturing industry has had a poor record. Its employment has fallen from over 8m in the 1960s to little more than 5m in the mid 1980s. A large part of the fall — more than 1m — occurred during the recession at the start of the 1980s. Manufacturing output has stopped growing: despite some recovery from the recession, production remains below its previous peaks. In contrast, the service sector has experienced a growth in employment, interrupted only by the recession, and some expansion in output, so that national income as a whole has risen, though only very slowly.

The contrast between the performances of the manufacturing and service sectors has fuelled the view, especially in the more prosperous parts of Southern England, that except for a few high technology sectors manufacturing industry's slide should be allowed to continue and we should concentrate instead on building the service economy of the future. Indeed, few people expect the manufacturing sector to be a major source of new jobs even if there were a significant upturn in the growth of the economy.

But to take the view that manufacturing is finished, and that reindustrialization is unnecessary and undesirable, is to fundamentally misunderstand the way the economy works. The decline of British industry has created serious problems: unemployment, in particular, is much higher than it would have been if industry had been more competitive against imports and in overseas markets. If the economy is not in as bad a shape as the erosion of its manufacturing base would suggest, this is more to do with North Sea oil than with the service sector. Since the late 1970s, oil has sustained a high and (on average) growing standard of living, as the government's substantial oil revenues curbed the need for higher taxes. The North Sea has also reduced the need for oil imports and allowed large-scale oil exports, easing the incipient imbalance in Britain's foreign trade and financing a growing flow of imported consumer goods.

The problem is that North Sea oil is running out. All projections show that production will fall sharply from its peak in the mid 1980s. What this means for the national economy is that the growth of other sectors must be increased if national income is not to fall. In particular, an alternative source of export earnings must be found. Failure to generate new exports will lead to a 'balance of payments' crisis similar to that facing many Third World 'debtor' nations, to deflation of the UK economy, rising unemployment and falling living standards.

Most services are not traded over long distances, so that although the service sector accounts for two-thirds of UK employment it provides only a quarter of export earnings. An increase in service exports is still achievable. However, the increase in export earnings required to offset the decline in oil production and any additional imports is so large that an increase in service exports of the magnitude that is feasible would by itself be insufficient. There is no alternative, if a deepening economic crisis is to be avoided, to an expansion of UK exports of manufactured goods or to the displacement of imported manufactures by UK produced goods.

In other words, reindustrialization is not so much a step back to an earlier era of development as an economic necessity for the 1990s. It need not mean that vastly more people will be employed in the manufacturing sector. Because of the inexorable rise in labour productivity, it must be accepted that manufacturing will never again employ the numbers it did in the 1960s. In practice, reindustrialization would entail a sustained expansion in manufacturing production, especially production for export, and the growth in this sector would provide the basis for an expansion in public and private services, which would be the main sources of new jobs.

Where, then, does the supply of industrial property fit into a broader strategy of reindustrialization? Three goals ought to be defined for the industrial property market.

First, no manufacturing firm should ever find its expansion delayed or frustrated by difficulties with the supply of space. The survey reported in chapter 4 found a surprising number of firms whose growth was obstructed by lack of space on their site or in their buildings. Moreover, this survey was conducted in the context of an economy in which manufacturing production was well down on previous peaks, and in the event of a sustained upturn in growth the pressure on productive capacity can be expected to increase considerably. In a country that is seriously intent on rebuilding its manufacturing capability, it is unacceptable that potential growth should be frustrated by buildings that are too small or sites that lack room for expansion. Every firm that wishes to expand should be able to do so either by extending its premises on-site or, where on-site expansion is impossible or unacceptable, by swiftly and easily moving to new, more spacious premises where the growth can be accommodated. In addition, no new firm or new branch of an existing firm should have its start delayed by a shortage of suitable premises.

Second, the efficiency of manufacturing industry should be promoted by securing the transfer of firms from old, unsuitable buildings to premises better matched to modern products and methods. Too many firms are locked into buildings that year after year add to their operating costs and sap their competitiveness. If it is commonly accepted that the government has a responsibility for ensuring a plentiful supply of trained labour to meet industry's needs, it should also be accepted that the government should ensure a plentiful supply of good quality premises.

Third, the industrial property market should operate so as to promote a more equitable distribution of job opportunities. In the past this has not happened. In the context of reindustrialization a greater share of new investment and new jobs should be diverted to depressed areas — North East England, Clydeside, Merseyside, South Wales and Northern Ireland, for example. The rate of manufacturing job loss in inner city areas should also be slowed by creating the conditions in which a higher proportion of investment in new factory floorspace can occur in these places.

It should be stressed that in the absence of appropriate economic and industrial policies the achievement of these property market goals would not by itself lead to reindustrialization. Nevertheless, we would argue that attaining these goals is an essential complement to other policies and necessary to improve the performance of British industry. Exactly what property market policies are necessary is discussed later. First, however, it is worth looking at the scale of investment needed in industrial buildings.

Floorspace requirements

Let us assume that the reindustrialization of the British economy involves a sustained growth of manufacturing output of 3.5 per cent a year. This is not so ambitious. Although much higher than the growth achieved since the mid 1970s, it is only a little more than the rate of growth during the 1950s and 1960s, and less than some of the UK's competitors have consistently achieved. The national policies that might be necessary to achieve this target include reflation, a reasonably successful industrial policy and probably some restriction on the growth of manufactured imports. Much depends on the growth of the world economy: the faster the growth in world demand the more the growth of UK exports, and the less the need for import controls.

In Britain, the long-term relationship between manufacturing output and productivity indicates that when output grows by 3.5 per cent a year, productivity increases by roughly 3 per cent a year, giving an increase of 0.5 per cent in manufacturing employment. If this annual growth in output were sustained from 1985 up to the year 2000 the resulting increase in manufacturing employment would be modest, probably less than half a million, and certainly not enough by itself to reduce unemployment to acceptable levels.

Chapter 2 showed that in the long run the ratio between manufacturing output and floorspace has remained roughly constant, so that a given increase in output has required a proportional increase in floorspace. A sustained 3.5 per cent a year growth in output could therefore be expected to require a 3.5 per cent a year increase in floorspace. In fact, floorspace requirements would be unlikely to grow so quickly. One reason is that by historical standards an above average proportion of the factory stock is vacant in the mid 1980s, and also the output/floorspace ratio remains a little depressed in the wake of the recession at the start of the decade. Also, a sustained expansion of output could be expected to increase the pressures to use factory floorspace to maximum effect, and a modest rise in the output/floorspace ratio could thus be expected. If manufacturing production grew by 3.5 per cent a year between 1985 and 2000, the cumulative increase in output would be 67 per cent; this might reasonably be expected to require a 45 per cent increase in the stock of factory space. In the UK as a whole, this is equivalent to an increase of around 115m m², or 7.5m m² a year.

This is just the net increase required to accommodate additional production. The actual addition to the stock would have to be greater to compensate for continuing losses due to demolitions and changes of use. In the late 1970s and early 1980s, these reduced the stock of industrial floorspace by an average of 2 per cent a year. In a period of reindustrialization, less industrial space would be lost in this way because fewer factories would be vacated by closures, though the competition from other uses (notably warehousing) for the space coming onto the market would increase as the economy picked up. If demolitions and changes of use together led to a reduction in the factory stock of 1.5 per cent a year — 0.5 per cent less than previously — 22.5 per cent of the stock of factory space would be lost between 1985 and 2000. This is equal to roughly 60m m².

Finally, there is the need to accelerate the movement of firms out of old inefficient buildings into premises that are better suited to their requirements. How this might be done is discussed later, but as an integral part of a strategy to reindustrialize the economy, policy should aim to dispose of perhaps 1m m² a year of industrial space more than would otherwise be the case. Over the period 1985–2000, 15m m² of floorspace might be shed in this way. To put this into perspective, the total stock of industrial floorspace dating from before 1945 is probably 100m m², so policies designed to accelerate the replacement of unsuitable buildings would address only the most inefficient portion of the older stock.

Putting all this together gives a measure of the total amount of new industrial space that would need to be built. Over the period 1985–2000, some 190m m² would be needed (115m to accommodate increased output, plus 60m to offset normal losses from the stock, plus 15m to allow for accelerated replacement). This is equivalent to 12.5m m² of new floorspace each year. These annual floorspace requirements, and the calculations from which they are derived, are shown in the first column of Table 8.1.

	UK	London and conurbations	Main assisted areas
Stock of floorspace, 1985 (approx.)	260.0	90.0	60.0
Increase to accommodate growth of output	7.5	1.5	2.8
PLUS normal losses from stock	4.0	1.5	0.9
PLUS accelerated replacement	1.0	0.6	0.3
TOTAL NEW FLOORSPACE REQUIRED	12.5	3.6	4.0

Table 8.1 *Reindustrialization: annual floorspace requirements, 1985–2000 (million m²)*

Source: Authors' estimates

All these estimates are approximate, of course. Nevertheless, they give an indication of the investment that would be required in order to permit reindustrialization. The striking feature is the scale of this investment: 12.5m m² a year contrasts with an average of 5m m² a year built in England and Wales between 1974 and 1985. Even in the mid 1970s, a prosperous period by the standards of the 1980s, only between 6m and 7m m² of new industrial floorspace was being completed each year. Translated into financial terms, the investment in new buildings and works by manufacturing industry, which averaged just under £1bn a year (at 1980 prices) in the late 1970s and early 1980s, would need to rise to around £2.5bn a year. The depths to which investment in factory space has sunk is emphasized by these figures.

Similar calculations can be made for specific areas within the UK. Two groups of areas are of special interest: the major conurbations, where so much of the manufacturing job loss has been concentrated in the past, and the areas assisted by government regional policy.

It is probably not possible to bring a permanent end to the loss of manufacturing jobs in the conurbations because the economic forces stacked against the continuation of large-scale manufacturing in urban areas are so powerful and deeply rooted. It is also not clear that a complete end to the decentralization of economic activity is entirely desirable, since the move from cities appears to correspond to a widespread preference for life in smaller towns and rural areas. However, in the context of reindustrialization one of the aims of policy should probably be to slow down the loss of industrial jobs in the cities, and their inner areas in particular. A continuing decline in manufacturing employment of 0.5 per cent a year for example — significantly less than the average during the 1960s and 1970s — might be a reasonable target. In an economy in which labour productivity in manufacturing grows by 3 per cent a year (an assumption made earlier), this implies a growth of manufacturing output in London and the conurbations of 2.5 per cent a year.

As before, this target growth in output can be translated into floorspace. The figures are shown in the second column of Table 8.1. Allowing for a modest increase in the output/floorspace ratio, an increase of 1.5m m² a year of factory space would be needed to accommodate the additional output. A further 1.5m m² would be needed to offset 'normal' losses from the stock of factory space, and a policy of accelerated replacement of old unsuitable space (which is disproportionately concentrated in Britain's cities) might require a further 0.6m m² a year to be built. Adding this all together, London and the conurbations would require 3.6m m² of new factory space to be built each year. Again, the contrast with recent trends is striking: between 1974 and 1985, extensions and new units accounted for only 1.2m m² a year of new space in these areas.

The main assisted areas comprise parts of Northern England, Wales, Central Scotland and Northern Ireland, and include just under a quarter of the UK's population. A reasonable target might be to increase their manufacturing employment by 1 per cent a year faster than in the economy as a whole. This is comparable to the relative improvement these areas experienced during the heyday of regional policy in the second half of the 1960s, and might be achieved again if the national economy grew fast enough and if regional policy were pursued with the same vigour as in that earlier period. In a national economy in which manufacturing output grew by 3.5 per cent a year, output growth of 4.5 per cent a year would be needed in the assisted areas to achieve this employment target.

The resulting floorspace requirements in the assisted areas are shown in the final column of Table 8.1. The growth in output would require an additional 2.8m m² a year. Allowing for 'normal' losses from the factory stock and for a programme of accelerated replacement, the total need for new floorspace in the main assisted areas would be 4m m² a year. This is an annual rate of increase of between 6 and 7 per cent, and once more substantially exceeds the rate of investment in new factory space that has occurred in the recent past.

Land for new factories

The calculations above are intended to be illustrative rather than accurate estimates of what is actually likely to happen, but they are worth taking a stage further.

On past form, roughly half of any newly built factory space will be in extensions to existing factories and half in entirely new factories. We estimated that between 1985 and 2000 roughly 190m m² of new factory space would be needed to permit reindustrialization of the UK economy. Half of this, 95m m², might be needed in new units.

The amount of land required for this new development can be estimated. At an initial site density of 30 per cent — typical of modern single storey developments — a 10,000 m² factory requires a site of 3.33 ha. Consequently, 1m m² requires 333 ha. To accommodate the 95m m² of floorspace in new units, 31,600 ha would therefore be required. Table 8.2 allocates this overall requirement between conurbations and other areas and between assisted areas and the rest of the country, on the basis of the employment targets and floorspace requirements discussed in the last section. A comparison between this table and figures on the supply of land for new industrial development, presented in chapter 5, is particularly interesting.

The total amount of industrial land available in Great Britain in 1982, approximately 33,500 ha, exceeds the amount required for new factory development up to the year 2000, even on these moderately optimistic assumptions about the reindustrialization of the UK economy. At first sight, therefore, there appears to be no serious problem. But complacency would be inappropriate.

First, a great deal of the available industrial land must meet the needs of

		Average annual requirements		Cumulative requirements, 1985–2000	
		New units (millions m²)	Land (ha)	New units (millions m²)	Land (ha)
Main assisted areas	Conurbations	0.5	170	8.0	2,700
	Other areas	1.5	500	23.0	7,600
Rest of country	Conurbations	1.3	430	20.0	6,700
	Other areas	2.9	970	44.0	14,600
UNITED KINGDOM		6.2	2,070	95.0	31,600

Table 8.2 *Reindustrialization: land needed for new factories*

Source: Authors' estimates

warehousing as well as those of manufacturing industry. It is difficult to assess exactly how much might go for warehousing. Between 1974 and 1984, an average of 3.3m m² a year was built in new warehousing units — more, in fact, than in new factory units — and if the growth of the economy increases this total might be expected to rise. On the other hand, it is unclear just how much of the additional warehousing space would be built on 'industrial' land. A prudent assumption might be that new warehousing would take 1,000 ha of industrial land a year, about half as much as manufacturing industry, and a total of 15,000 ha over the period 1985–2000. Immediately, then, the claims on the stock of available land appear much greater.

Second, the figure for available industrial land — 33,500 ha — includes some land available only in the long term and requiring considerable expenditure to make it usable.

Third, although additional land would become available in the normal course of events, e.g. as local authorities revise their structure plans, the demolition of older industrial buildings cannot be expected to provide much space for new industrial development. This is partly because only some sites are unsuitable for re-use by industry and partly because older factory sites tend to be densely developed, so that the demolition of a large multistorey building usually frees land for only a small single storey development. Since this source of additional land for development will be limited, the majority of any new industrial land becoming available will be 'greenfield' sites, and the release of this land is often hotly contested.

Fourth, and most importantly, although the demand for and supply of land for new factories may be in balance in the country as a whole, in the absence of appropriate policies disparities would be certain to arise at the local and regional scale. Where demand outstripped supply, some frustration of industrial growth might be expected, obstructing the goal of reindustrialization. Table 8.2, showing the amounts of land needed for reindustrialization, helps identify where the pressure on land supply is likely to arise. For example, some 9,400 ha of land would be needed for industry in London and the conurbations by the year 2000 (and this excludes warehousing's needs) whereas in 1982 only 5,400 ha were available in these places. A further 14,600 ha are estimated to be needed in non-conurbation areas outside the assisted areas — broadly the towns and rural areas of Southern England — yet these areas include many places where the supply of land for industry continues to be squeezed by restrictive planning policies.

The role of the public sector

The increases in floorspace necessary to permit reindustrialization would involve major changes in the scale of activity in the industrial property market. Inevitably, this raises the question of the extent to which market forces and existing institutional arrangements would allow these ambitious targets to be attained. Would factory space be available in sufficient quantities, in appropriate places and at the right times to ensure that no potential industrial expansion is frustrated?

In a period of sustained economic growth there is little doubt that, left to its own devices, the private sector would increase the scale of its activity in the property market. Many manufacturers would have the confidence to invest in new buildings for their own use, while private sector speculative development would be enhanced by the greater ease of letting and selling and, since industrial rents might be bid up, by the greater profitability of property investment.

Nevertheless, it is unlikely that market forces alone would be sufficient. One very important reason is that in some instances the market simply does not operate. Chapter 5, for example, noted that many urban land uses are not allocated by market forces, and once established it becomes virtually impossible for manufacturers to buy them out. One result is that it is often exceptionally difficult for firms in urban areas to acquire the land necessary to permit the expansion of their existing factories. Another reason is that in order for private sector developers to provide factory space on a speculative basis an indicator of scarcity is needed to induce them to become involved. However, a scarcity of space is the very thing which should be avoided if the aim is to remove potential obstacles to the expansion of manufacturing firms.

Furthermore, when the private sector does become involved in the provision of factory space on a speculative basis it does so in only a few segments of the market, as we saw in chapter 3. It prefers to build standard units rather than a range of designs suited to industry's diverse needs. It avoids large units because there are fewer potential tenants, and very small units because they involve a disproportionate amount of management. Its property management procedures (discussed in chapter 7) also make it difficult for some types of firms — notably very young firms — to secure a place in its developments. Most of all, the private sector steers clear of industrial investment in many parts of the country away from the South East of England.

What these failures point to is the need for public involvement in the industrial property market. There is nothing new in this, but at present the role of the public sector is strictly limited. Its factory building activities are seen as an arm of regional policy, not national industrial policy, and even in the assisted areas it becomes involved in only certain segments of the market, mainly the provision of small and medium sized units for rent, built in advance of need. What is required is a redefinition of the proper role of the public sector.

First, the public sector should take overall responsibility for ensuring an adequate supply of good quality premises to facilitate the expansion and efficiency of manufacturing industry. Land and buildings are too important to the production process to be left to the vagaries of the market; if by itself the market cannot ensure that firms obtain the buildings they need when they need them, the public sector should take steps to make sure this happens. Otherwise growth is liable to be frustrated and inefficiency is perpetuated. Public responsibility need not imply the displacement of the private sector. For the most part it would mean monitoring the supply of industrial land and buildings, guiding private sector activity to the appropriate locations, and removing unnecessary obstacles to investment. Only occasionally, where the market has failed, would it mean the active involvement of the public sector as 'pump primer' or developer.

Second, public sector responsibility for the supply of industrial property should no longer be reserved for the most depressed parts of the country — the areas assisted by regional policy, for example. In a sense, all of Britain is now a depressed area. The slump in manufacturing production and employment has been so deep and protracted that few areas have escaped, and most now have rates of unemployment exceeding those in the 'depressed' areas of the 1970s. If an existing policy towards industrial property can be shown to be effective in unlocking development potential in a traditional assisted area, there is a strong case for extending it to cover the whole country. Property market intervention, in other words, should be an arm of national industrial policy, with the ultimate aim of facilitating national economic growth, rather than merely an appendage of regional policy.

That still leaves the question of what specific policies the public sector ought to pursue. Let us look first at what might be done to facilitate industrial expansion, and then at measures to improve the efficiency of factory buildings.

Planning for expansion

Significant increases in production and employment in existing factories are normally possible only if the premises are extended, and this cannot occur on highly developed sites that have no room for expansion. A priority for public policy ought therefore to be to remove, wherever possible, the physical constraints on the expansion of existing factories. One way in which this might be achieved is by local authorities regularly consulting each of the main manufacturing employers in their areas to determine their possible requirements for additional land and premises. In some cases this would reveal that employers are unable to accommodate expansion within their existing sites, and in these circumstances the authority should use its powers to make appropriate land available, especially land adjacent to the existing sites. This might be achieved by allowing a change of use for vacant or derelict land, some of which is already in public ownership, or by the use of compulsory purchase powers.

The importance of this proposal must be stressed because the supply of land for the expansion of existing factories is often forgotten by planning authorities who concern themselves only with the supply of land for new factories. Many firms prefer to extend an existing site rather than open a new branch elsewhere since it is usually technically and administratively easier to keep production together in one factory. Relocation is often an unattractive option.

However, in some cases firms will be unable to extend their existing premises, even with assistance from the local authority, because of the nature of surrounding land uses. Many factories are hemmed in by roads, railways, houses and public buildings, and it would be impossible or unpopular for an authority to acquire and make available land for the expansion of such factories. Complete relocation, or the diversion of growth into new branch plants, is thus necessary to ensure that potential growth is not frustrated.

Relocation, the opening of a new branch or, indeed, the opening of an entirely new small business can be facilitated by ensuring that there is an adequate stock of vacant industrial premises into which firms can move. As chapter 2 showed, vacant premises comprise only a modest proportion of the stock of floorspace even in the depths of recession, and much of the vacant space is in large old buildings that are unsuitable for most firms. In a period of sustained economic growth, the stock of vacant space would be reduced. To prevent a shortage of vacant space becoming an obstacle to expansion, local authorities should monitor the stock of vacant premises within their areas and where appropriate intervene to ensure that 'market gaps' are filled.

The monitoring of vacant property ought to be easily achieved. Many local authorities already compile monthly registers of vacant premises as part of the service they offer companies, and the official floorspace statistics provide a detailed breakdown of the number and size of factory units in each area. Organizing this information to provide an up-to-date assessment of local property trends would not be difficult. Where the local authority sought to fill market gaps this might be achieved by mobilizing the private sector, e.g. by releasing land to developers, or by involving public agencies such as English Estates, or by the authority itself undertaking factory building.

To complement policies to ensure an adequate supply of premises, local authorities should make certain that there is an adequate quantity and range of sites available for new factory building in their areas. This is particularly relevant for larger firms that prefer to build to their own specification, and for private sector developers looking for appropriate sites. As with vacant premises, some authorities already monitor the supply of industrial land, but there is variation in the thoroughness and frequency with which this is done. All local authorities should be encouraged to maintain a register, regularly revised, of land available for industrial development as a basis for monitoring supply and take-up. Usually it will be possible to achieve an adequate supply by designating sufficient land for industry in structure and local plans and by ensuring its release to the private sector, though in some cases industry might have to be given precedence over other potential land uses. Occasionally, it may be necessary for local authorities to intervene directly by assembling sites of sufficient size and by undertaking reclamation and preparatory investment, for subsequent development by themselves or the private sector.

These proposed policies have locational implications. In particular, they can be expected to favour development in Britain's cities, where the physical obstacles to industrial growth have previously been greatest. This is consistent with the aim, discussed earlier, of reducing the rate of manufacturing job loss in these places.

But against this, it must be acknowledged that a widespread improvement in the supply of land and buildings for industry would work against a narrowing of the gap between Britain's depressed northern and western regions and the rest of the country. At present, one of the advantages that the assisted northern and western regions have over the rest of Britain is a more plentiful and cheap supply of land and buildings. As chapter 6 explained, this has helped attract mobile investment projects and created a more favourable environment for the establishment and growth of indigenous firms. We are arguing that in order to promote national economic growth the same favourable environment should be extended to cover the rest of the country. This would enable expansion to occur that might otherwise have been frustrated but would also reduce the relative attraction of assisted area locations. In order to ensure a fair distribution of new jobs between the 'depressed' and 'prosperous' halves of the country it would therefore be necessary to complement property market policies with a strengthening of other regional policy tools. This might involve enhanced rates of financial assistance in the assisted areas, or the selective reintroduction of locational controls (like the old Industrial Development Certificate) on potentially mobile investment projects.

The role of green belts deserves a special mention. In the 1980s they have come under increasing pressure from developers, especially in the South East of England. A policy of improving the supply of land for industry might be interpreted as a go-ahead for widespread incursions into green belt land, since that is where there are potential sites and plenty of willing occupants. On the other hand, the stringent application of green belt policy has so far been highly successful in curbing the sprawl of Britain's cities. This sensitive policy conflict is not easily resolved. It is essential, from a national economic point of view, that the growth of firms already located in and around green belts is not frustrated. It is also essential, in order to slow the rate of manufacturing job loss in London and the conurbations, that additional industrial land is made available, and sometimes the only appropriate large sites may be in the surrounding green belt. Against this, there is no reason why a new branch of a multinational company, for instance, should need to locate within a green belt rather than on a suitable plot either inside the city or beyond the green belt. The aim in dealing with such a company should be to ensure that there is a range of suitable alternative sites away from the green belt. The way to resolve the policy conflict is probably to treat each case on its merits: there may be grounds for incursions into green belts in some instances, but it is not clear that they should be widespread or sufficient to undermine the whole basis of green belt policy.

Reducing mismatch

Providing room for expansion is only a partial solution to the problem of 'mismatch'. In chapter 4 we defined mismatch as a disparity between firms' property needs and the sites and buildings they occupy. Mismatch has numerous origins, takes many forms, and affects a large slice of manufacturing industry, invariably leading to additional costs or losses in efficiency, if not to constraints on growth. As we saw, firms themselves are often unable to find ways round the physical and financial obstacles, so that mismatch is sometimes perpetuated year after year, even in firms that are otherwise profitable, efficient and innovative.

As part of wider policy to raise the efficiency of British industry, public policy must reduce the extent of mismatch. In essence, measures are needed to accelerate the movement of firms from unsuitable buildings to ones more closely matching their needs. The buildings that become available that are hopelessly unsuited to modern industry should then be removed from the stock of industrial floorspace and replaced by new premises. In this way the average age and suitability of the industrial building stock can gradually be improved.

The reasons why some firms become locked into unsuitable buildings are rarely technical: they do not stay put just because their machines are not transportable or would not fit into other buildings. Nor is the disruption of the move itself the critical factor, although there are exceptions. The main problem is simply financial: the cost of a new, purpose built unit is often prohibitive, and existing buildings are difficult to dispose of or even worthless, especially if they are large and have been adapted and extended in a piecemeal fashion over the years. This is where the market, developers and financial institutions fail and public intervention is needed. What firms should be offered is a package that would make the process of moving swift, easy and financially attractive.

As the first part of the package, the public sector should consider buying a firm's old premises (or buying out the lease) if this facilitates a move to more suitable premises. The premises would be bought at market value or, in the case of property fit only for demolition, at a minimum value per square metre to compensate the firm for the fact that the buildings have value in use to them but no value to anyone else. From the point of view of the firm this removes uncertainty and eases the cash flow problems associated with financing a move. In the case of a firm in ramshackle property it narrows the gap between what it needs to find to finance a new building and what it can get for its old one.

The old vacated premises would then be disposed of as appropriate. This may mean selling or letting them to other firms or developers, subdividing them into more marketable units, changing their use, or completely demolishing the buildings and redeveloping the site. The appropriate action would depend on the building and the development opportunities. An expanded version of English Estates (and the Scottish Development Agency and the Welsh Development Agency) would be ideal to perform this function of property purchase, development and disposal because it would have greater access to resources and specialist expertise than many local authorities.

Second, the package should include a complete information and advice service for firms, focused in one body, probably the local authority. The local registers of land and property availability, discussed earlier, would be a key component of this service. It is perhaps worth noting that during the survey reported in chapter 4 one manager who had been involved in several factory moves was very complimentary about the comprehensive relocation service offered by the Scottish Development Agency, but was currently experiencing great difficulty in organizing a relocation in the Midlands where no similar service was available.

Third, the package should include financial assistance towards the cost of the move, including the costs of moving machinery and the disruption to production. Relocation grants are already available on a discretionary basis in some inner city areas; these should be extended to cover all parts of the country.

Finally, long-term loans should be available for the construction or purchase of the buildings into which firms move. Firms should have the same opportunities as households: they should be able to obtain mortgages for 25 or 30 years, secured against the value of the property. This sort of finance would satisfy a demand that at present is not met either by short-term bank loans or by share capital. It would also enable firms to spread the cost of paying for a more suitable property over a long period, to match the benefits and savings of moving. The private sector financial institutions have more than enough money to provide this sort of long-term finance but have generally been reluctant to do so because of the risk involved. What is probably required to make more money available is a scheme whereby part of the loan is underwritten by the public sector.

The gains from a reduction in mismatch are wider than at first appears, because if factory moves are made easier there is likely to be an acceleration in the overall rate of replacement of the factory stock. More unsuitable buildings would be abandoned and demolished; more new ones would be built to replace them. Over a long period, as firms move and then move again as their needs evolve, the effect would be to upgrade the quality of buildings available to all firms looking for somewhere to start, relocate or expand. There are parallels in this respect with home improvement grants: because houses have such long lives the benefits of improvement are felt not just by the occupant making the improvements but also by subsequent occupiers. In the same way, if policy can encourage a minority of firms to invest more in property, because of the long life of factory buildings the benefits will eventually filter down to benefit other firms. The overall quality and suitability of the industrial building stock will be improved.

The importance of property

Reindustrialization would require a new wave of investment in industrial property and, as we have explained, effective policies to enable that investment to occur swiftly and smoothly. But what if the future were not so bright, and the manufacturing economy remained essentially stagnant — at least in output terms — as during the last decade or so?

In this context an active policy to improve the supply of industrial property and raise the quality of the industrial building stock would not solve the main problems facing the manufacturing sector. These problems are not, nor have they ever been, ones concerning land and buildings. The main obstacles to industrial growth are ones of demand management — the extent of reflation or deflation in the UK and world economies — and imbalances in foreign trade which mean that rapid growth in the UK, in isolation from other countries, creates an unsustainable deficit in the balance of payments. Even among supply-side constraints, it is not clear that land and property are the most important. The skills and training of management and workforce (or the all too frequent lack of them) and the reluctance of financial institutions to provide long-term industrial funding are possibly more worrying. Moreover, at least some potential difficulties with the stock of industrial land and floorspace would remain dormant if the economy continued to stagnate. Fewer firms would need to expand; lack of space for expansion would therefore be less of a problem. Less new industrial land would be needed, and the potential shortfall in Britain's cities would not be so acute.

In other respects, a stagnant economy would exacerbate the problem of industrial accommodation, as it has done in the recent past. A low rate of new investment would mean a painfully slow renewal of industrial building stock: the average age of industrial buildings would get older, in a country which probably already has the oldest industrial buildings in the world. The lack of confidence in market growth that pervades a stagnant economy would also perpetuate mismatch because firms would be unwilling to take the bold step of moving into more suitable premises. This inertia in industrial location would make it virtually impossible to pursue a successful urban and regional policy, because there would be so little new industrial investment and building to divert to the areas of greatest need.

In a stagnant economy, effective policies towards industrial property therefore continue to have a role. The emphasis changes. The need would be less to keep up the supply of land and buildings to match industry's growing demand; instead, policies to enhance mobility, to reduce the mismatch between firms' buildings and needs, probably have more value and could make a useful contribution to raising manufacturing efficiency.

Most of all, however, the strategy for industrial buildings that we have outlined is necessary to prepare the ground for an eventual recovery in British industry. When national economic policies finally create the basis for sustained growth, it would be a tragedy if industrial expansion were hindered and frustrated by problems with land and buildings.

References

Architects' Journal (1977) 'AJ Handbook of factory design', *Architects' Journal*, 1977–8.

Association of District Councils (1983) *Economic development by district councils: Paper one; Financing economic development and aid to industry*, Association of District Councils, London.

Barrett, S., Stewart, M., and Underwood, J. (1978) *The land market and development process: a review of research and policy*. Occasional paper no. 2, School of Advanced Urban Studies, University of Bristol.

Bernard Thorpe & Partners (1982) *Industrial floorspace: a major survey of vacant buildings in Greater London*, BTP, London.

Bolton, J. E. (1972) *Small firms*, Report of the committee of inquiry on small firms, HMSO, London.

Building Research Team (1982) *The small advance factories in rural areas: final report*, Department of Architecture, Oxford Polytechnic.

Cadman, D. (1984) 'Property finance in the UK in the post-war period', *Land Development Studies*, **1**, pp. 61–82.

CALUS (1979) *Buildings for industry*, College of Estate Management, University of Reading.

Cambridge Economic Consultants (1985) 'An inquiry into the benefits of the government advance factory building programme', unpublished report to the Department of Industry, CEC, Cambridge.

Cameron, S. J., Dabinett, G. E., Gillard, A. A., Whisker, P. M., Williams, R. H., and Willis, K. (1982) *Land authority aid to industry: an evaluation in Tyne and Wear*, Inner Cities Research Programme report no. 7, Department of the Environment, London.

Camina, M. (1974) 'Local authorities and the attraction of industry', *Progress in Planning*, **3**, pp. 83–182.

Central Statistical Office, *United Kingdom National Accounts*, HMSO, London, annual.

Chalkley, B. S. (1978) 'The relocation decisions of small displaced firms', unpublished Ph.D. thesis, University of Southampton.

Chandler, J. A., and Templeton, J. M. (1980) *Local authorities and employment creation*, Department of Political Studies, Sheffield City Polytechnic.

Commercial and Industrial Floorspace Statistics, HMSO, London, annual.

Coopers & Lybrand Associates (1980) *Provision of small industrial premises*, Department of Industry, London.

Coopers & Lybrand Associates (1984) *Impact of English Estates and the Welsh Development Agency on private sector provision of industrial property*, report to the Department of Trade and Industry, Coopers & Lybrand, London.

Coopers & Lybrand Associates (1986) 'The accommodation needs of modern industry', report to the Department of the Environment, Coopers & Lybrand, London.

Crum, R. E., and Gudgin, G. (1978) *Non-production activities in UK manufacturing industry*, Regional Policy Series 3, Commission of European Communities, Brussels.

Debenham, Tewson & Chinnocks (1983) *Money into property*, DTC, London.

Dennis, R. (1978) 'The decline of manufacturing employment in Greater London 1966–74', *Urban Studies*, **15**, pp. 63–73.

Department of Industry and Shell UK (1982) *Helping small firms start up and grow: common services and technological support*, HMSO, London.

Department of the Environment (1975) *Commercial property development*, Property Advisory Group, HMSO, London.

Department of Trade and Industry (1973) *Memorandum on the inquiry into location attitudes and experience, Minutes of evidence*, Trade and Industry Subcommittee of the House of Commons Expenditure Committee, session 1972–3, pp. 525–668, HMSO, London.

Department of Trade and Industry (1985) *The Small Workshop Scheme*, HMSO, London.

Falk, N. (1978) 'Growing new firms: the role of the social entrepreneur', *Built Environment*, **4**, pp. 204–12.

Fothergill, S. (1976) 'Towards a sub-regional employment strategy for North East England', unpublished B.Phil. study, Department of Town and Country Planning, University of Newcastle upon Tyne.

Fothergill, S., and Gudgin, G. (1982) *Unequal growth: urban and regional employment change in the UK*, Heinemann, London.

Fothergill, S., Kitson, M., and Monk, S. (1983) *The industrial building stock and its influence on the location of employment change*, Industrial Location Research Group working paper 5, Department of Land Economy, University of Cambridge.

Fothergill, S., Kitson, M., and Monk, S. (1985) *Urban industrial change*, Inner Cities Research Programme report no. 11, HMSO, London.

Gallagher, C. (1984) 'Major share of job generation is by small firms', *British Business*, July, pp. 388–91.

Ganguly, P. (1985) *UK small business statistics and international comparisons*, Harper & Row, London.

Goodrun, A. (1980) 'Small firms and mini-factories: do they create jobs and encourage new business?' *Planner*, September, pp. 122–3.

Gould, A., and Keeble, D. (1984) 'New firms and rural industrialisation in East Anglia', *Regional Studies*, **18**, pp. 189–202.

Green, D. H., and Foley, P. (1982) 'Small industrial units: is conversion a viable alternative?' *Estates Gazette*, August, pp. 574–5.

Green, D. H., Foley, P., and Burford, I. (1985) *Putting spare space to work*, Small Business Research Trust, London.

Gudgin, G., and Fothergill, S. (1984) 'Geographical variation in the rate of formation of new manufacturing firms', *Regional Studies*, **18**, pp. 203–6.

Hardy, B. (1979) *Finance for industrial buildings and development: a survey of sources in Birmingham*, Research Note 13, Joint Unit for Research on the Urban Environment, University of Aston.

Henneberry, J. M. (1984) 'Property for high-technology industry', *Land Development Studies*, **1**, pp. 145–68.

Herring, Son & Daw (1982) *Property and technology: the need of modern industry*, Herring, Son & Daw, London.

Hillier Parker (1982) *Industrial rent contours*, Hillier Parker, London.

Hillier Parker, (1986) *Survey of Industrial Voids*, Hillier Parker, London.

Hodge, I. D., and Whitby, M. C. (1979) *New jobs in the Eastern Borders: an economic evaluation of the Development Commission factory programme*, Agricultural Adjustment Unit monograph 8, University of Newcastle upon Tyne.

IFF Research Ltd (1980) *Industry and employment in the inner city*, Inner Cities Research Programme report no. 1, Department of the Environment, London.

Investors Chronicle/Hillier Parker (1983 onwards) *Average yields*, ICHP, London.

JURUE (1980) *Industrial renewal in the inner city: an assessment of potential and problems*, Inner Cities Research Programme report no. 2, Department of the Environment, London.

Keeble, D. (1986) 'Industrial decentralisation and the metropolis: the North West London case', *Transactions of the Institute of British Geographers*, **44**, pp. 1–54.

Keeble, D. (1980) 'Industrial decline, regional policy and the urban–rural manufacturing shift in the United Kingdom'. *Environment and Planning A*, **12**, pp. 945–62.

King & Co. (1975 onwards) *Industrial Floorspace Survey*, King & Co., London.

Leigh, D., and North, R. (1983) 'Monitoring manufacturing employment change in London 1976–81: the implications for local economic policy', unpublished report for the Department of the Environment.

Lloyd, P., and Dicken, P. (1982) *Industrial change: local manufacturing firms in Manchester and Merseyside*, Inner Cities Research Programme report no. 6, Department of the Environment, London.

Lloyd, P., and Mason, C. (1984) 'Spatial variations in new firm formation in the United Kingdom: comparative evidence from Merseyside, Greater Manchester and South Hampshire', *Regional Studies*, **18**, pp. 207–20.

Luttrell, W. F. (1962) *Factory location and industrial movement: a study of recent experience in Great Britain*, National Institute of Economic and Social Research, London.

McKean, R. (1975) *The impact of comprehensive development area policies on industry in Glasgow*, Urban and Regional discussion paper no. 15, University of Glasgow.

Marriott, O. (1967) *The property boom*, Hamish Hamilton, London.

Moore, B., Rhodes, J., and Tyler, P. (1986) *The effects of regional economic policy*, HMSO, London.

NEDO (1978) *Construction for industrial recovery*, HMSO, London.

NEDO (1983) *Faster building for industry*, HMSO, London.

Perry, M. (1985) 'The provision of small industrial premises: a geographical perspective', unpublished Ph.D. thesis, Plymouth Polytechnic.

Perry, M. (1986) *Small factories and economic development*, Gower, Aldershot.

Ratcliffe, J. (1978) *An introduction to urban land administration*, Estates Gazette, London.

Scarrett, D. (1983) *Property management*, Spon, London.

Slowe, P. M. (1981) *The advance factory in regional development*, Gower, Aldershot.

Spooner, D. J. (1972) 'Industrial movement and the rural periphery: the case of Devon and Cornwall', *Regional Studies*, **6**, pp. 197–215.

Statistics for Town and Country Planning, HMSO, London, discontinued.

Townroe, P. M. (1971) *Industrial location decisions*, Centre for Urban and Regional Studies occasional paper 15, University of Birmingham.

Urbed (1979) *Local authorities and industrial development*, Urbed Research Trust, London.

West Midlands County Council (1984) *Vacant industrial property in the Black Country*, WMCC Planning Department, Birmingham.

Willis, K. (1983) 'New jobs in urban areas: an evaluation of advance factory building', *Local Government Studies*, March/April, pp. 73–85.

Willis, K. (1985) 'Estimating the benefits of job creation from local investment subsidies', *Urban Studies*, **22**, pp. 163–77.

Wilson Committee (1980) *Report of the committee to review the functioning of financial institutions*, HMSO, London.

Index

agricultural land, 98
Alonso
    location theory of, 11
Architects Journal, 58, 59
areas, types of
    see regions; urban–rural contrast
assisted areas, 130, 133, 136, 137, 138,
        150, 157, 167, 172
    future of industry in, 165–6
Association of District Councils, 129
Avon Hosiery, Derbyshire, 65–6

balance of payments, 162, 175
Beehive Workshops Ltd, 122, 150
Blackwell Electronics,
        Nottinghamshire, 73
Board of Trade, 121
Bolton Report, 127
Brand Foods, Lincolnshire, 64
Brown, J. & Sons, Leicester, 84
building
    see construction phase; finance for
        new building; new factories
building regulations, 52
Building Research Team, 57
buildings
    'life cycle' of, 33
    role of, in industrial development,
        161, 175–6
    unsuitability of, *see* 'mismatch'
    see also factory buildings; new
        investment; old buildings

Cadman, 48
CALUS, 48, 57
Cambridge Economic Consultants, 122,
        134, 135
Cameron, 132

Camina, 127
capital, 81
case studies
    English Estates, 120–7
    local authority development, 127–31
    'mismatch', 62–6, 73–4, 75–7, 82–4
    small firms (Cornwall), 151–5
Chalkley, 140, 155
Chandler and Templeton, 128
CIN Properties Ltd, 151
cities
    see conurbations; urban land; urban
        land values; urban–rural contrast
*Commercial and Industrial Floorspace
        Statistics*, 18, 19, 32
Commission for the New Towns, 116,
        117, 119
'components of change', 31, 32
construction phase, 51–3
conurbations
    future of industry in, 165–6, 167,
        168, 172
    see also urban–rural contrast; vacant
        factories
Coopers & Lybrand Associates, 41, 61,
        135, 136, 148, 155
Cornwall
    case study, 151–5
County Ales, Leicestershire, 83
Crum and Gudgin, 29

Debenham, Tewson and Chinnocks, 48
'demand management', 9, 175
demolition, 31–3
Dennis, 102
Department of Trade and Industry,
        101, 108, 115, 121, 122, 133, 134,
        147, 155

depressed areas, 114, 137, 163, 170
Derelict Land Grants, 106, 133
design factors
    changes in, 74–5
    mechanical handling, 59
    production plant, 58–9
    services, 59
    use of space, 60
design problems, 72–3
detached and semi-detached factories,
    143
developer, types of
    see speculative development by
        private sector; new factories
development
    types of, 39–40
Development Agencies
    Scottish, 115, 118, 120, 134, 174
    Welsh, 115, 117, 118, 119, 134, 135,
        137, 174
Development Areas, 40, 136, 151
Development Boards
    Highlands and Islands, 116, 118, 120
    Rural Wales, 116, 117, 119
Development Commission, 115, 117,
    119, 121, 122, 123, 146, 150, 153,
    154
development control procedures, 52
development industry, 13–14
development process
    Pilcher Report on, 41

economic outlook, 161–2, 175–6
economic policies
    see Keynesian policies; government
        policies; 'supply-side'
Electrodynamics, Leicestershire, 65
electronics industry, 57, 60, 63
    see also case studies ('mismatch')
employment change, 100, 101, 110,
    160
    see also location of employment
employment density, 28–30, 34, 86, 88,
    91, 93–4, 95–6, 110
employment growth, 78, 113, 154
    see also job creation
employment, location of,
    see location of employment

employment trends
    manufacturing and service sectors,
        161–3
    see also floorspace and employment;
        recession
engineering industry, 57, 63, 75
    see also case studies ('mismatch')
English Estates
    case study, 120–7
    development by, 94, 115, 117, 118,
        119, 120, 133–4, 135, 136–7, 146,
        149, 151, 153, 154, 171, 174
    factories completed by, 123
    floorspace provided by, 125, 126
English Industrial Estates Corporation
    see English Estates
establishment growth, 100
expansion and extension, 21–2, 77
    economic necessity of, 162–3
    employment growth from, 78
    factors governing, 78, 86
    future need for, 167
    planning for, 170–3
    planning permission for, 78–9
    see also on-site expansion
exports, 162

factory accommodation
    types of, 141–4
factory buildings
    financial value of, 16–17
    nature of, 12
    obsolescence of, 17, 26, 81
    see also industrial property;
        'mismatch'; new factories; vacant
        factories
factory stock
    ageing of, 159
    characteristics of, 21–2
    diversity of, 15, 17
    economy and, 13
    in 1985, 18
    legacy of, 15
    long-term changes in, 26–34
    quality of, 19–20, 113
    shorter-term fluctuations in, 34–7
    surveys of, 15, 37, 97–8
    see also new factories

Falk, 141
Fancy Fabrics, Nottinghamshire, 75–6
finance for new building
  access to capital for, 81
  from financial institutions, 46–8,
    137–8
  from pension funds, 40
  local authority, 131
  see also grants and loans
financial institutions
  see finance for new building;
    institutional investment
fire regulations, 52
flatted factories, 143
Fleming Property Unit Trust, 49, 50
floorspace and employment, 35, 86, 88,
  89–91, 93–4, 95–6, 170
floorspace (industrial)
  age of, 20, 159
  case studies, 120–31
  'components of change', 31–2
  distribution of, 18, 19, 90
  from public sector, 117–20, 135
  future requirements for, 163–6
  inefficient use of, 22
  loss of, 164
  relation between output and, 26–8,
    164, 165
  shortage of, 68–71
  stock of, 30–1, 86, 88, 95–6, 117
  surplus, 71–2
  see also employment density; site
    area; small premises; urban–rural
    contrast; vacant floorspace
floorspace (warehousing)
  provision of, 120
  trends in, 31
food and drink processing, 21, 57, 63–4,
  75
  see also case studies ('mismatch')
Fothergill and Gudgin, 91, 156
Fothergill, Kitson and Monk, 20, 73,
  78, 92, 94, 97, 99, 104, 106, 133

Gallagher, 157
Gangully, 157
Goodrun, 128, 142
Gould and Keeble, 156

government policies, 9, 170
grants and loans, 40, 106, 129, 133,
  151, 174–5
Green and Foley, 142
green belts, 109, 272–3
'greenfield' sites, 168

heavy industry, 91
Herring, Son & Daw, 61
high technology sector, 61, 161
Hillier Parker, 24, 41, 44, 45
Hi-Tech Controls, Leicestershire, 64
Hodge and Whitby, 132
hosiery industry, 57, 62–3, 66, 75
  see also case studies ('mismatch')
housing market, 12–13

IFF Research Ltd, 102
import controls, 163
imports, growth of, 9
industrial constraints, 11
Industrial Development Certificate, 172
industrial geography, 11
Industrial Improvement Areas, 127
industrial land
  employment capacity of, 107
  monitoring of, 171–2
  quality and price of, 106–7
  supply of, 106–9, 167–8, 170–1
  see also new factories; vacant land
industrial location theory, 11
industrial property
  age of, 20–1
  classification of, 18
  developers' attitudes towards, 10
  primary and secondary, 44
  strategy for, 14, 159–76
  supply of, 10, 160–1
  see also public sector; tenure;
    warehousing
industrial units
  'life cycle' of, 33
  size of, 18–19, 33
  see also factory buildings;
    factory stock; new factories
infrastructure, 159
Inner Urban Areas Act, 127

institutional investment, 46–8, 137–8, 169
Intermediate Area, 137
investment criteria, 136–7
investment in property
    financial value of, 16–17, 80–1
    future importance of, 175–6
    low rate of, 159
    scale required of, 163–6
    see also finance for new building;
        institutional investment; new
        investment; output

job creation, 131–4
JURUE, 20, 97, 140

Keeble, 92, 102
Keynesian policies, 9
King & Co., 22, 23, 24, 124

labour problems, 102
land
    see industrial land; new factories;
        reindustrialization; urban land;
        urban land values; urban–rural
        contrast; vacant land
land use, 103
layout and efficiency, 72–4, 82, 159–60
    see also 'mismatch'
'leaseback', 130
leases, 40, 140, 148–9
Legal & General Group, 49, 50–1
Leigh and North, 102
Lion Breweries, Leicestershire, 83
listed buildings, 79
Lloyd and Dicken, 156
Lloyd and Mason, 157
loans
    see grants and loans
local authorities
    case study, 127–31
    development by, 116–17, 119, 147,
        151, 152, 154
    factory building by, 129
    planning for expansion by, 170–1
location
    see industrial location theory; new
        firms

location decisions, 13, 110
location of employment, 14
    property's role in 86–9, 113–14, 163
    regional influences on, 89–91
    urban–rural contrast of, 91–6
location theory, 11
locational controls, 172
Luttrell, 108

McKean, 155
managerial strategies, 82
Maritime Technology,
    Northamptonshire, 76–7
market forces, 10, 87, 155–6, 169
market influences
    see speculative development by
        private sector
'mismatch'
    case studies of, 62–6, 73–4, 75–7,
        82–4
    definition of, 14, 57, 61
    economic effects of, 84–5, 160
    influences on, 65–7
    origins of, 62–4
    problems arising from, 67–77
    reduction of, 173–5
    response to, 77–84
    scale of, 84
'modern' industry, 61
Moore, Rhodes and Tyler, 90
multiple regression analysis of
    establishment growth, 100
multistorey buildings, 21, 22, 33–4,
    143, 159, 168

National Coal Board Pension Fund, 131
NEDO, 40, 51, 52, 53, 54, 59, 60, 80,
    81
neo-classical theory, 11, 12, 86–7, 110
new factories
    availability of land for
        by region, 104, 106–8
        by type of area, 104, 105, 108–9
        future requirements, 167–8
        price and quality of, 106–7
    builders of, 102–3
    provision by public sector:
        benefits of, 112–14

evaluation of, 131–4
  its impact on private sector, 135–8
  political context of, 111, 114
  regional policies for, 11, 114, 121,
    133
  public developers of:
    agencies, 114–16
    case studies of, 120–31
    regional distribution of, 129–30
  purpose-built, 39–40
  site suitability for, 107–9
  vacant, 157
new firms
  location of, 156–7
new investment
  in buildings, 35–7, 80–1, 94
  in plant and machinery, 37
  see also development; new factories;
    recession
new machinery, 75
New or Expanded Towns, 102, 109
  see also Commission for the New
    Towns
New Town development corporations,
  116, 117, 118, 119, 120, 127, 146,
  151
new units
  see new factories
North Sea oil, 161–2
Northbrook Bodies, Leicestershire, 76
nursery units, 142

oil
  see North Sea oil
old buildings
  design problems of, 72–3
  removal from, 164
  see also layout and efficiency
on-site expansion
  reasons for, 96
  survey of:
    analysis of results, 99–102
    land, 97–8
    tenure, 98, 99
    type of stock, by area, 97–8
output
  related to floorspace, 26–8, 164, 165
  related to investment, 36

related to productivity, 163–4
  related to vacant floorspace, 34
owner-occupied accommodation
  see tenure

partnership schemes, 130, 131
pension funds, 40, 46–8, 131
Perry, 128, 129, 146, 150, 151, 153
Pilcher Report, 41
planning approvals, 52
planning authorities, 171
planning controls, 17, 78–9, 87, 160
plant and machinery, 37, 75
PLC Foods, Leicestershire, 73–4
political policies, 111, 114, 163
  see also government policies
'premises ladder', 141
private sector
  see new factories; speculative
    development by private sector
production
  see output
production process
  role of land and buildings in, 56
property cycle, 34–7
property development
  see buildings, development; industrial
    property; investment in property;
    reindustrialization
property investment markets, 46–8
property management and allocation,
  147–51, 169
property market intervention, 170
property requirements, 58–61
  see also small firms
public sector
  in property market, 14, 160
  in reindustrialization, 168–70
  see also floorspace; new factories

recession
  influence of, on employment, 88, 91,
    170
  influence of, on floorspace, 35, 91
  influence of, on new investment, 37,
    136
reflation, 9, 163
refurbished accommodation, 77, 141–2

Regional Development Grants, 133, 151
regional growth and decline, 89–91
regional policies, 111, 114, 166
regions, 18, 19, 20, 23, 24, 25, 26, 48,
    52–5, 97–8, 104, 172
    see also Cornwall; new factories;
        small premises; urban–rural
        contrast
registers of land and property, 171–2,
    174
rehabilitation, 141–2
reindustrialization
    economic aspects of, 175–6
    floorspace needed for, 163–6
    land for, 167–8
    need for, 161–2
    planning for, 170–3
    role of property in, 161–3
    role of public sector in, 168–70
relocation, 77–8, 79, 171
    financial package for, 173–5
    motives for, 80–1, 101–2
rent concessions, 151
rents, industrial
    levels of, 42–4, 112, 130–1, 150–1
    long-term growth of, 130
rural areas
    see urban–rural contrast

science parks, 143–4
service sector
    see employment trends
shared-service accommodation, 142–3
single-storey building, 33–4
site area, 33
site densities, 163
site layout, 159–60
site selection, 107
sites
    see urban–rural contrast
Slough Estates, 49–50
small firms
    Bolton Report on, 127
    case study, 151–5
    growth of, 155–8, 160–1
    position of, 139
    property needs of, 13, 14, 139–44,
        147–51

small premises
    case study, 151–5
    increase in, 157–8
    loss of, 155
    management and allocation of,
        147–51
    supply of:
        floorspace, 144–5
        fluctuations, 155–8
        private sector, 147
        public sector, 146–7
        regional distribution, 145–6, 156–8
Small Workshop Scheme, 147
Special Areas Act, 120, 121
Special Development Area, 151, 153
Special Investment Area, 153
speculative development by private
        sector
    examples of, 49–51
    market influences on, 40–6, 169–70
    types of developer, 48–51
    types of development, 39–40, 130–1
Spooner, 133
St Andrew, Leicestershire, 83
'supply-side' economic policies, 9, 10,
    175
surplus space, 71
Survey of Industrial Voids, 24, 41

technical changes, 27, 28
tenants, 135–6
tenant-selection, 147–8, 149–50, 154–5
tenure
    by area, 21, 22, 98–9
    owner-occupied, 80
    rented, 79–80
    see also leases, rents
terraced factories, 143
Thorpe, Bernard, & Partners, 24
Townroe, 108
towns
    see urban land; urban land values;
        urban–rural contrast
trading estates, 17
Tudor & Stuart, Leicestershire, 83–4

unemployment, 9, 110, 131–2, 161,
    162, 170

United Engineering, Lincolnshire, 66
United Kingdom National Accounts, 16
Universal Radiators, Leicestershire, 64
urban land, 11, 98–9
urban land values, 12, 87, 106
Urban Programme, 129, 150
urban–rural contrast
  availability of land, 103–9, 167–8
  manufacturing employment
    cities and conurbations, 92, 94, 95,
      96, 97–8
    employment change, 100, 101, 160
    employment density, 93–4, 95–6
    floorspace, 93–4, 95–6
    manufacturing growth, 99
    rural areas, 94–8
    towns, 92–8
  sites and premises, 20, 101–2
Urbed, 129

vacant factories
  monitoring of, 171
  nature of, 24–6
  new premises, 157
  statistics on, by region, 22–6
  'vacancy chains', 112–13
vacant floorspace
  fluctuations in, 34–5, 36
  regional distribution of, 23
vacant land, 22, 170–1

Walker & Jones, Derbyshire, 66
warehousing, 17, 18, 136, 164, 167–8
  see also floorspace (warehousing)
Willis, 132
Wilson Committee, 48
workforce, 29, 77, 79, 175

yields, industrial, 44–6